ARCHITECTURE DEVELOPMENT MADE SIMPLE

Charles Babers

Architecture Development Made Simple
Author: Charles Babers

CJC Publishing Co.
1208 Sumac Dr.
El Paso, TX 79925

Copyright © 2003 CJC Publishing Company
ISBN: 1-930388-90-x
Library of Congress Catalog Number: 2002116893

Editorial Assistance for CJC Publishing Company by Gary Sparkman

Cover Designed by: Scott Whittle

All rights reserved, including the right to reproduce this book or portions thereof in any form or by any means, electronic or mechanical, including photocopying, recording, or by any information storage or retrieval system, without written permission from the publisher. All inquiries should be submitted to the address above.

TABLE OF CONTENTS

Section	Page
Section One: Introduction	5
Chapter One: Introduction	7
Section Two: Product Development Guides	11
Chapter Two: The Operational Concept Description	13
Chapter Three: The Activity Model	33
Chapter Four: The Node Connectivity Description	65
Chapter Five: The Operational Information Exchange Matrix	77
Chapter Six: The Organizational Relationships Chart	93
Chapter Seven: The Logical Data Model	103
Chapter Eight: The Operational Activity Sequence & Timing Description	121
Chapter Nine: The System Interface Description	135
Chapter Ten: The System Communications Description	145
Chapter Eleven: The System^2 Matrix	155
Chapter Twelve: The System Functionality Description	165
Chapter Thirteen: The Operational Activity to System Function Traceability Matrix	175
Chapter Fourteen: The System Data Exchange Matrix	185
Chapter Fifteen: The System Performance Parameters Matrix	205
Chapter Sixteen: The System Evolution Description	213
Chapter Seventeen: The System Function Sequence & Timing Description	221
Chapter Eighteen: The System Technology Forecast	235
Chapter Nineteen: The Physical Data Model	245
Chapter Twenty: The Technical Architecture Profile	263
Chapter Twenty One: The Standards Technology Forecast	273
Chapter Twenty Two: The Overview & Summary Information	283

Chapter Twenty Three: The Integrated Dictionary	**291**
Section Three: Army Unique Products	**301**
Chapter Twenty Four: The OPFAC Equipment Description	**303**
Chapter Twenty Five: The Core Systems & Quantities Inventory	**311**
Chapter Twenty Six: The Horseblanket	**317**
Chapter Twenty Seven: Non-Standard Products	**325**
Section Four: Product Relationships	**331**
Chapter Twenty Eight: Product Relationships	**333**
Chapter Twenty Nine: Recommended Architecture Development Process	**352**
Section Five: Product Users & Uses	**355**
Chapter Thirty: Product Users & Uses	**357**
Bibliography	**364**
Glossary	**365**
Appendix: Data Requirements Worksheet Format	**384**

Section One: INTRODUCTION

CHAPTER ONE

INTRODUCTION: An **ARCHITECTURE** is a detailed depiction of an enterprise (e.g., a subject area, functional area, or organization). It uses both textual and graphical elements to describe characteristics of the enterprise. The architecture description addresses organizational elements, relationships among and between organizations, systems, personnel, tasks, information requirements, information exchanges, technology, and operational environments. It may also address rules, assumptions, limitations, and constraints. An architecture is documented through the creation of a number of architecture **products**, each of which describes some subset of the enterprise characteristics listed above. The products can be grouped into three different categories based on the types of information. The three categories correspond to three architecture "views", or types of architectures. Products that describe the tasks, processes, organizational relationships, and information/data exchanges associated with the conduct of an operation or mission comprise the operational architecture or operational view. Products that describe the characteristics and capabilities of the systems that are used to perform enterprise tasks comprise the system architecture or system view. Products that document technical standards and mandates that govern the performance of enterprise systems, or the construction of architecture products comprise the technical architecture or technical view. An architecture may contain products from one, two, or all three views.

The operational architecture (or operational view) is the core of any enterprise architecture. It defines **what** must be done, **who** does it, **when** it's done, **how** it's done, **why** it's done, and under what **conditions** it's done. For an existing enterprise, the operational architecture is descriptive in nature. However, for proposed or future enterprises and for enterprises that are being updated or modified, the operational architecture defines enterprise requirements.

The system architecture (or system view) overlays material solutions (i.e., systems) on the requirements defined in the operational architecture. For existing enterprises, it describes the **types** and **quantities** of systems and equipment used to perform operational architecture tasks, the **locations** where those systems are fielded and used, the system **capabilities**, and the **connections** between systems. For proposed or future enterprises, or for enterprises that are being updated or modified, the system architecture defines the types, quantities, and capabilities required of new or modified systems. It also delineates the required, projected, or expected schedule for fielding new systems or capabilities.

The technical architecture (or technical view) lists the mandated or acceptable performance standards for enterprise systems. Additionally, the technical architecture attempts to project those enterprise performance standards that will be acceptable or mandated in the future, to include predicting how current performance standards will evolve over time. Finally, the technical architecture prescribes standards to be followed in the development of selected architecture products.

PURPOSE: This handbook serves as a companion to the Department of Defense (DoD) Command, Control, Communications, Computers, Intelligence, Surveillance, and Reconnaissance (C4ISR) Architecture Framework document. The Architecture Framework[1] document identifies and describes each of the architecture views and their associated products and provides general guidance on how to develop and use architectures. This handbook provides detailed information on how to implement the general development guidance from the Architecture Framework document. The primary purpose of this handbook is to provide a simple, easy to follow set of instructions for the development of architectures and architecture products. While it is targeted primarily at the US Army, the majority of the techniques, processes, and products described in this handbook are equally usable by other branches of the armed forces as well as non-military organizations and entities.

SCOPE: This handbook addresses all products described in the DoD C4ISR Architecture Framework document, and three US Army unique architecture products (the OPFAC Equipment Description, the Core Systems & Quantities Inventory, and the Horseblanket) that support Army institutional processes. It is recognized that architecture development is but a part of an overall enterprise architecture strategy that also includes architecture planning, integration, validation, usage, and management. While this handbook does not address these other areas in detail, the development methodologies and techniques described here are meant to support such a comprehensive strategy.

HOW TO USE THIS HANDBOOK: The majority of this handbook consists of sections devoted to a discussion of individual architecture products. Each product discussion is organized as described below, and includes information on the product, its users and uses, its relationships to other architecture products, and instructions for its development. The following is a brief overview of the information contained in each product discussion:

PRODUCT NAME: The standard product name. This is usually the name used in the DoD C4ISR Architecture Framework document.

---

[1] Command, Control, Communications, Computers, Intelligence, Surveillance and, Reconnaissance (C4ISR) Architecture Framework Version 2.0, US Department of Defense C4ISR Architecture Working Group, Washington, DC. 1997.

OTHER ALIASES: Other names that may be used to refer to the product. This may include: alternative names for the same product; names for equivalent products from Structured Analysis and Design or Object Oriented modeling techniques; or names for legacy products that contain the same information as the referenced architecture product.

PRODUCT DESIGNATION: The standard designation for the product from the DoD C4ISR Architecture Framework document. The designation is in the form of a two-letter code that specifies the architecture view (i.e., OV for the ORGANIZATIONAL view, SV for the SYSTEM view, TV for the TECHNICAL view, and AV for ALL views), followed by a number that specifies the individual product.

ARCHITECTURE VIEW:
The "view" of which the product is a part. The three standard architecture views are the OPERATIONAL, the SYSTEM, and the TECHNICAL. Additionally, some products are to be included in ALL architecture views, and are designated accordingly. Finally, this document addresses three products that are not included in the DoD Architecture Framework, but which support ARMY INSTITUTIONAL processes.

PRODUCT DEFINITION: A brief definition of the product.

PRODUCT DESCRIPTION:
A general description of the product, to include the reasons why it is developed, the type of information it contains, and a sample product template.

PRODUCT FORMAT:
Indicates whether the product is primarily graphical or textual, or is a combination of both.

USERS & USES:
A listing of the likely users and potential uses of the architecture product. This is not limited to past or current users and uses, but includes recommendations of additional new product users and uses.

TYPICAL INFORMATION SOURCES:
A listing of documents, individuals, or other sources from which information may be received or extracted for inclusion in the architecture product.

TOOLS:
A listing of the types of tools that may be used to develop and document the architecture product.

PARTICIPANTS: A listing of individuals, organizations, or communities that should participate in the development of the product,

PRODUCT DEVELOPMENT: A recommended methodology for developing the architecture product. This section may also describe alternative development methodologies.

RECOMMENDED DEVELOPMENT SEQUENCE: The recommended relative order in which the product should be developed

KEY RELATIONSHIPS: A listing of other related architecture products.

CRITICAL SUCCESS FACTORS: A description of critical "do's" and "don'ts" associated with the development of the architecture product.

CHECKLIST: A reiteration of the product development methodology in a checklist format. The checklist is designed to be removed from the handbook and used separately.

Section Two: PRODUCT DEVELOPMENT GUIDES

CHAPTER TWO

PRODUCT NAME: OPERATIONAL CONCEPT DESCRIPTION

OTHER ALIASES: Operational Concept, Concept of Operations, Concept, Operations Concept, Concept Description, OPCON, CONOPS

PRODUCT DESIGNATION: OV-1

ARCHITECTURE VIEW: OPERATIONAL

PRODUCT DEFINITION: The OPERATIONAL CONCEPT DESCRIPTION defines, using text and pictures, how available resources and assets will be employed and deployed to accomplish a mission.

PRODUCT DESCRIPTION: The Operational Concept (OPCON) Description includes both a high-level operational concept diagram and an accompanying textual description of the operational concept. Together, these two define, using text and pictures, how the organization plans to deploy and employ available resources, forces and assets to accomplish and support strategic, operational, tactical, corporate, civic, or national goals and missions. The Operational Concept Description should be the first architecture product developed, as it provides the operational foundation upon which all other products are developed and it introduces the operational elements, missions/tasks, interfaces, and information exchanges that are further defined in the other architecture products. While the initial OPCON Description is created early in the architecture development process, it should be revised and refined throughout the process to reflect knowledge gained in the development of other architecture products.

The textual Operational Concept does more than simply provide a caption for the picture presented on the OPCON Graphic—it abstracts and summarizes all the information contained in the whole architecture and its separate products. In this respect, the Operational Concept may be viewed as an executive summary of the architecture. It provides brief descriptions of the operational elements, nodes, and organizations that comprise the enterprise, functional area, or Family of Systems (FoS). These elements, nodes, and organizations may reflect real entities or notional types or classes of entities. The Operational Concept also defines the tasks performed by the operational elements, nodes, and organizations to a sufficient level of detail to allow the reader to understand the interactions of the elements with each other and with the external environment, and to provide a foundation for the development of other architecture products such as the Activity Model and the Operational Activity Sequence and Timing Description. It describes the connectivity among the elements, nodes, and organizations that comprise the enterprise, functional area, or FoS, and between architecture elements and the external environment. This connectivity description provides the basis for the development of the Organizational Relationships Description, the Node Connectivity Description, and the Operational Information Exchange Matrix.

In addition to the information listed above, the Operational Concept may also include information that is not truly architectural information. For example, it should describe why the concept, itself, is needed. It should define the major contribution(s) of the enterprise, functional area, or FoS to the accomplishment of overarching operational and strategic missions. This might also include a description of the shortcomings that would exist without the enterprise, functional area, or FoS.

The concept should describe the operational environment in which all architecture missions and tasks are performed. For military related architectures, this includes an indication of those strategic theaters within which tasks are, or are expected to be, performed. It also includes an indication of those levels of conflict [e.g., peace, stability and sustainment operations (SASO), small scale contingency operations (SSCO), and major theater war (MTW)] that are supported by the enterprise, functional area, or FoS. For non-military architectures it addresses the areas, nations, and regions where operational tasks take place. The description of the operational environment may also identify the physical conditions that promote or are required for the performance of tasks, as well as those that constrain or prevent task performance. Other aspects of the operational environment that may be captured in the Operational Concept are the socio-political considerations--requirements, limitations, and constraints—that influence the performance of architecture missions and tasks. Finally, the description of the operational environment includes a description of key external elements, nodes, and organizations that support or are the objects of architecture tasks and actions. Among those external elements, nodes, and organizations are the threats that are countered by elements of a military architecture.

The Operational Concept should also describe its relationship to other operational concepts.

The OPCON Graphic is the architecture "picture that's worth a thousand words". The product contains both graphical and textual elements. It includes a two- or three-dimensional background representing the operational environment within which the architecture elements are employed and architecture tasks are performed. This environmental background graphic may depict key geographic, socio-political, or military control features (e.g., key terrain such as mountain ranges and bridges; population centers; and organization boundaries) that limit, constrain, or control architecture tasks, and should include an indication of the physical dimensions of the area within which operational elements, nodes, and organizations normally operate.

The OPCON graphic includes representations of the primary operational elements, nodes, and organizations that comprise the enterprise, functional area, or FoS. These representations may be either generic geometric figures (boxes, circles, ovals, etc.), standard military symbols, representative icons (e.g., miniature depictions of equipment, vehicles, buildings, and people), or a combination. Line segments, arrows, arcs, lightning bolts, or other connectors are drawn between icons to show command and control (C2), coordination, or communications connectivity among and between operational elements, nodes, and organizations. The connectors may be color coded or otherwise altered to indicate different types of relationships between nodes.

The OPCON Graphic incorporates three different textual elements: labels, lists, and legends. Every icon should be labeled to indicate the element, node, or organization represented. Connectors may also be labeled to specify the type of relationship being depicted and/or the nature of the information being exchanged. Critical geographic, socio-political, or military control features may also be labeled. Lists are added to specify the high level missions and tasks associated with the enterprise, functional area, or FoS as a whole, or those associated with the individual elements, nodes, and organizations. Other lists such as lists of critical assumptions and constraints applicable to the architecture may also be added. The diagram legend defines the terms, acronyms, and symbols shown on the diagram.

OPERATIONAL CONCEPT TITLE

PRODUCT FORMAT: Text and graphics.

USERS & USES:

USERS:

Corporate/Non-Military

- Strategic Planner
- Operations Manager
- Human Resource Manager
- Resource Manager
- Information Manager
- Quality Assurance Manager
- Facilities Manager
- Security Manager
- Supervisors
- Workers
- Software Developers
- Trainers
- Research and Development
- Policy Writers
- Public Relations Department
- Sales Department

Military

- Combat Developer
- Concept Developer
- Trainer
- Training Developer
- Force Developer
- Program/Project/Product Developer
- Resource Manager
- Operational Architect
- Systems Architect
- Technical Architect
- Systems Engineer
- Software Developer
- Manufacturer
- Test & Evaluation Community

- Modeling & Simulation Community
- Warfighter

USES:

Corporate/Non-Military

- Strategic Business Planning
- Development of Procedures Guides and User's Manuals
- Organizational Design
- Identification of Personnel Requirements
- Business Process Reengineering
- Development/validation of SOPs
- Development of Capital Investment Strategies
- Quality Control/Quality Management
- Description of Required System Capabilities
- Baselining of Functionality
- Functional Allocation
- Database Design
- Development/Modification of Operational Concepts
- Identification of Operational Issues
- Allocation Of Communication Assets
- Communications Network Burden Assessment
- Wargaming Alternatives
- Design of Human-Computer Interface
- Performance of Cost/Benefits Analysis
- Development of Training Materials

Military

- Development/Modification of Operational Concepts
- Identification of Operational Issues
- Identification/Validation of Operational Needs/Requirements
- Standardization of Processes, Activities and Tasks
- Development/Validation Of Tactics, Techniques & Procedures (TTPs)
- Development/Validation Of SOPs
- Identification Of Functional Information Requirements

- Identification of IERs
- Development/Validation Of Models & Simulations
- Allocation Of Communication Assets
- Development/Validation Of Mission Training Plans
- Planning For Organization Exercises
- Planning For System Tests
- Network Burden Assessment
- Identification of OPFAC Hardware Requirements
- Data Modeling
- Standardization of Data Elements
- Development/Modification Of Standard Messages
- Development Of System Software
- Comparing User's Vision To Developer's Implementation
- Baselining Of Functionality
- Wargaming Alternatives
- Prioritizing Activities For Implementation
- Providing Roadmap For System Improvement
- Battlefield/Business Process Reengineering
- Development of Procedures Guides and User's Manuals
- Design of Human-Computer Interface
- Performance of Cost/Benefits Analysis
- Development of Training Materials

TYPICAL INFORMATION SOURCES:

Corporate/Non-Military

- Function/Task Lists
- Long Range Plans
- Organization Descriptions
- Operational Concepts
- Policy and Procedures Guides
- Standing Operating Procedures (SOPs)
- Strategic Plans
- Subject Matter Experts
- System Descriptions
- Task Descriptions
- Vision Statements
- Business Plans

- Corporate Brochures
- Annual Reports

Military

- Subject Matter Experts
- Policy and Procedures Guides
- Doctrinal Publications
- Operational Concepts
- Operational and Organizational Plans
- Vision Statements
- Future Operational Capabilities (FOCs)
- Long Range Plans
- Strategic Plans
- Modernization Plans
- Master Plans
- Organization Descriptions (including TOEs, MTOEs, TDAs)
- Function/Task Lists (including METLs, UJTL, Service Task Lists)
- Task Descriptions
- Standing Operating Procedures (SOPs)
- Interface Descriptions
- System Descriptions

TOOLS:

- Text Editor
- Drawing/Graphics Tool
- Database

PARTICIPANTS:

Corporate/Non-Military

- Strategic Planner
- Operations Manager
- Human Resource Manager
- Resource Manager
- Information Manager

- Quality Assurance Manager
- Facilities Manager
- Security Manager
- Supervisors
- Workers
- Software Developers
- Trainers
- Policy Writers
- Operational Architect/Facilitator
- Subject Matter Expert

Military

- Combat Developer
- Concept & Doctrine Developer
- Training Developer
- Force Developer
- Operational Architect/Facilitator
- Subject Matter Expert
- Warfighter
- Program/Project/Product Developer
- Systems Architect
- Technical Architect
- Systems Engineer

PRODUCT DEVELOPMENT:

A key consideration in the development of the OPCON Description is that it should capture the essential nature of the enterprise or functional area in as few words and pictures as possible. Detailed information should be addressed in other products. Other considerations in the development of the Operational Concept description include the variability of the concept, the concept development mode, and the methodology to be used. A discussion of these considerations follows.

Concept Variability

Not every operational concept is unitary; that is, not every operation can be conducted in the same way under all foreseeable conditions. The functions that are performed and the manner in which those functions are performed may vary based on a multitude of factors.

One of these factors is the presence or absence of particular organizations, systems, or operational elements. The functions that can be performed by each organization, system or element are dependent upon the unique capabilities of each. The absence of an organization, system or element means that the functions and information unique to that organization, system, or element will not be available to the enterprise, functional area, or FoS. These differences should be accounted for in the operational concept description.

A second factor is the operational environment in which operations are conducted. Different operational regions (e.g., military theaters of operations) present different operational and physical requirements and constraints that may have to be accounted for in the description of the operational concept. Regional considerations that impact operational requirements may include such factors as the Middle Eastern reluctance to do business with women, or Jewish kosher dietary laws. Examples of theater specific military operational requirements and constraints include the requirement to coordinate actions with allied and coalition forces and local governmental agencies, and socio-political restrictions on the tactics that may be employed, sites that may be occupied by military forces, and facilities and areas that may be targeted for attack. Physical requirements and constraints include all those associated with operations in extreme environmental conditions, such as the requirement for increased airborne reconnaissance and surveillance in mountainous terrain.

A third factor is time. It may be possible to project how operations will change over time as new organizations, systems, and capabilities are fielded or new tactics are adopted.

Operational concept variability and conditionality may be reflected in the development of multiple OPCON graphics. When all the operational, physical, and temporal changes in the concept of operations cannot be illustrated on a single diagram, it may be advantageous to produce additional diagrams.

Development Modes

The specific process used in producing the Operational Concept description depends, in part, on the development mode. The four primary development modes are based on whether or not an operational concept already exists and whether or not that existing concept can be used, with or without modification, to address the operational/functional area being architected. The development modes are described briefly below.

1. <u>Creation of a wholly new operational concept where none existed before.</u>
2. <u>Update of all or part of an existing concept for the same operational/functional area.</u> The update may encompass changes to the existing concept to incorporate:

- Different (e.g., more, fewer, newer) elements or nodes.
- Different tasks.
- Different connections or interfaces.
- Different environmental conditions.

3. <u>Adaptation or modification of an existing concept from a related operational/ functional area.</u>
4. <u>Creation of a more specific, more narrowly focused operational/functional area concept from an existing high level, overarching concept.</u>

Development Methods

1. <u>Document search/review</u>: This method presupposes the existence and availability of documentation containing information that may be extracted for inclusion in the operational concept. The available document, or documents, may include all the information required to develop the concept, and the architect will need only to compile the information in the appropriate format. This will usually not be the case, however. Usually, the available documentation will contain only a portion of the required information and will require the development of additional information to fill in the holes. Sometimes, the information available in different documents may be inconsistent or conflicting and that the architect take steps to resolve the inconsistencies. This is the least manpower intensive of the methodologies.
2. <u>SME surveys</u>: In this method, surveys and questionnaires are developed and distributed to SMEs whose expertise and experience is in the operational or functional area being architected. The information provided by the SMEs in response to the surveys is then compiled to produce the concept. The keys to success in using this methodology are choosing the right questions for inclusion on the survey questionnaire and selecting the right SMEs as respondents.
3. <u>Individual SME interviews</u>: This method replaces the SME surveys with one-on-one interviews. As with the use of the surveys, the keys to success in using this methodology are choosing the right questions for the survey interview and selecting the right SMEs as respondents. An advantage of individual interviews over surveys is that the interviewer can tailor the questions asked to the unique knowledge and experience of the interviewee and can make dynamic adjustments during the conduct of the interview to pursue promising leads or abandon unpromising lines of questioning. A major disadvantage of conducting individual interviews is that the method limits the number of SMEs from whom information can be solicited.
4. <u>Facilitated workshops</u>: The foundation of this methodology is the conduct of a series of workshops in which two categories of individuals participate: facilitators and SMEs. Facilitators are experts in the architecture development process who assist the SMEs in expressing their knowledge and experience with the enterprise in a manner consistent with the format of an operational concept. Facilitators do not decide what to include in the concept,

but determine how best to capture and document the information provided by SMEs. SMEs draw upon their personal knowledge and experience to identify the appropriate activities/functions to be included in the concept; the information required to be exchanged to support, control or constrain those functions and the individuals, organizations or systems required to perform the functions. In addition to their own knowledge and experience, SMEs also should have access to information contained in appropriate descriptive, doctrinal, technical and regulatory documentation. An advantage of this methodology is that it allows the input from a relatively large number of individuals to be collected in a relatively short amount of time. The main disadvantages of this method are the cost and amount of planning and coordination required to assemble such a large number of individuals in one place at one time[2].
5. <u>Combination(s)</u>: This is simply the execution of two or more of the methods mentioned above. For example, a document search may be used to develop an initial concept draft that is refined in a facilitated workshop.

Process For Determining the Mode and Method to Be Used

The next two sections provide step-by-step instructions for creating the textual operational concept and the OPCON Graphic. These instructions are applicable to all development modes and methodologies. In applying these instructions, however, consideration must be given to the mode and methodology selected. For each part of the textual operational concept or OPCON graphic, information and data should be extracted from available source documents (to include existing operational concepts) or developed with the assistance of SMEs. If an existing concept is being modified to create the new operational concept, then the information contained in the pre-existing concept must be modified and augmented as necessary to describe adequately and accurately the target enterprise. Information and data extracted from source documents should be reviewed by SMEs to assure its validity and applicability. Likewise, information developed with the assistance of SMEs should be validated against available source documents.

The following questions must be answered in order to determine the appropriate development mode and methodology to be used:

1. Does an OPCON exist already for the operational/functional area, enterprise, or FoS?
2. Does it need to be changed/updated?
3. What portion(s) need to be updated?
4. How do they need to be updated?
5. What is the best source of information needed to execute the update?

---

[2] A Discussion of the Activity Model and Its Role As A Part of the Operational Architecture, Version 1.0, Quantum Research, International, El Paso, TX, 1999.

6. Are those information sources available/accessible? If not, are there alternatives?
7. If no OPCON for target operational/functional area, enterprise, or FoS exists, is there an existing OPCON for a related area that can be modified?
8. What portion(s) need to be modified?
9. How do they need to be modified?
10. What is the best source of information needed to execute the modification(s)?
11. Are those information sources available/accessible? If not, are there alternatives?

Developing the (Textual) Operational Concept

Developing the textual description of the operational concept entails ensuring that all the essential elements of information addressed below are included. Additional, non-essential elements of information may be added as desired, and as time and resources permit. A listing of the information that should be included in the textual concept description follows.

1. Determine the appropriate level of detail to be included in the operational concept description. The level of detail to which each element of information is addressed is contingent upon the uses to which the concept will be put, the availability of required information, the knowledge and experience of the architecture development team and the contributing SMEs, the amount of time available to develop the concept, and the relative familiarity or novelty of the concept being described. Some intended uses require a more detailed description of the operational concept than do other uses. Despite the intended use, however, the availability of information and/or the lack of knowledge and experience on the part of the individuals involved in the creation and documentation of the concept may limit the level of detail that can be captured. Operational concepts that are already familiar to architecture developers and intended users need not be described in excruciating detail to be understandable and useful. Novel concepts, on the other hand, should be described in sufficient detail to ensure that all users can truly comprehend them.

2. Identify and describe the enterprise, functional area, or FoS for which the concept is being developed. As a minimum, the name of the enterprise, functional area, or FoS must be provided. Additionally, describe the key characteristics and features that define the enterprise. Describe what makes it unique and distinguishes it from other enterprises. Next, define the scope of the enterprise—what is and is not included as a part of it. [NOTE: If the architecture and operational concept description only addresses a portion of the enterprise, it may be necessary to establish separate scoping statements for the enterprise and for the operational concept.] Establishing scope is important because it sets boundaries that guide the development of not just the operational concept but all the products of the architecture. The scope lets you know when you've gone as far as you need to go in developing a particular product and don't need to go any further. It also lets you know when you haven't gone far enough and need to keep working. Finally, describe how the enterprise relates to other enterprises, functional areas and FoS.

3. *Describe why the concept is needed.* List and describe the known and projected uses to which the operational concept will be put. Projected uses are those for which the concept was not specifically designed, but for which the developer has a reasonable expectation that it might be utilized. For a wholly new operational concept, describe why it must be developed; i.e., why an existing concept cannot be used as-is or modified to be made usable. If an existing concept is being updated or modified, describe both the nature of the updates or modifications and the reasons that they must be made.

4. *Define the timeframe addressed by the concept.* The timeframe may be addressed in general (e.g., as-is or to-be), relative (e.g., current, interim, or objective), or specific terms (e.g., 2010 or 2020). The temporal focus of the concept may also be described in operational terms (e.g., prior to reorganization, during reorganization, after reorganization, pre-deployment or post-deployment). For concepts that vary over time, you should describe all timeframes addressed in concept.

5. *List and describe the operational elements, nodes, and organizations that comprise the enterprise, functional area, or FoS.* Elements, nodes, and organizations may be described by name/designation, by type, or by echelon. They may also be identified by one or more characteristics that they share in common (for example, all foreign branch offices and subsidiaries, all organizations assigned or attached to the Third US Corps). There may even be instances when it makes more sense to identify the elements, nodes, and organizations that are not included than to attempt to specify those that are.

6. *Describe the missions and tasks performed by the operational elements, nodes, and organizations.* The operational concept need not address every function, mission, or task performed by every element, node or organization, but it should address every functional or mission area. The level of detail to which the functions, tasks, and missions are described should be established in consideration of the fact that greater detail may be provided in other architecture products such as the Activity Model and Operational Activity Sequence and Timing Description.

As a minimum, provide the name of each high level function, mission, task, or functional/mission area. Where useful, also describe how and why the functions, tasks, and missions are performed. If doing so is necessary for a full understanding of the function, missions, or tasks, and if the information to do so is available, list the resources (information, data, time, and other raw materials) needed to perform each. Associate the functions, missions, and tasks with the elements, nodes, and organizations that perform them.

7. *Describe the connectivity among elements, nodes, and organizations, and between architecture elements and the external environment.* Just as every function, mission, or task need not be described in the operational concept, neither does the connectivity between every two operational elements, nodes, and organizations—only those connections critical to a full understanding of the enterprise and the concept. For those connectivities that are described, the descriptions should include the identities of the two connected elements, the nature of the connection and, perhaps, the conditions under which the connection is activated. Types of connectivity between elements include, but are not limited to, command, control, coordination, communication, and support. Connectivities may also be characterized as either one-way, two-way, broadcast, or multi-cast. For each connectivity described, there could be some utility in stating the type of information exchanged.

8. Describe the environment within which architecture missions and tasks are or will be performed. The description of the environment should focus on defining those characteristics of the environment that facilitate an understanding of the physical and operational bounds of, and constraints imposed on, the enterprise. It should also address the manner in which the enterprise interfaces with key external elements and activities. In addressing the physical environment, it may describe the locations, areas, and regions in which enterprise elements can or cannot operate, as well as those in which they must operate. Other physical environmental factors that may be addressed include natural (e.g., terrain, weather, and climatic) and induced (nuclear, biological, chemical, and electromagnetic) effects.

The description of the operational environment may address a number of factors including: socio-political requirements, limitations, and constraints; key external elements, nodes, and organizations; external interfaces and threats to be countered.

9. Describe the relationship of the Operational Concept to other existing operational concepts. The operational concept being described may be subordinate to another higher level concept, or it may be "parent" to one or more subordinate concepts. The concept may also be one of a family of related and co-equal concepts. Finally, the concept may be derived from, or serve as the basis for, other concept(s). List other existing or developmental concepts to which the operational concept being produced is related. For each related concept, define the nature of the relationship.

10. Develop a glossary of key terms, abbreviations, and acronyms used in the concept. Include all elements, nodes, organizations, systems, missions, mission areas, functions, tasks, and other labeled components covered in the concept description.

11. List the individuals, organizations, and agencies involved in the development of the concept.

12. Submit the Textual Operational Concept Description to SMEs for review and comment. Include information on the portions of the Textual Operational Concept Description to be reviewed, the types of comments to be provided, the desired comment format, the individual(s) or organization(s) to whom/which comments are to be submitted, and the suspense for comment submission.

13. Update Textual Operational Concept Description based on comments received. Modify the Textual Operational Concept Description as necessary to incorporate approved change recommendations resulting from the SME review.

Developing the OPCON Graphic

The OPCON Graphic is the graphical companion to the textual operational concept description. As was stated earlier, multiple OPCON Graphics may be developed to depict different views of a single operational concept.

Outlined below is a sequential process for developing an OPCON Graphic. Following this process will help to ensure that the Graphic contains all the required elements. The two basic steps that are iterated to create the graphic are to add a graphical element, and label the element to indicate its role or nature.

1. Outline the operational area. The outline serves as a background for other graphical elements and as a frame for the whole diagram. As appropriate, include key physical features such as national or regional boundaries, urban areas, vegetation, hydrologic features, and key terrain. Indicate the physical dimensions of the area covered in the diagram.

2. Add graphics to represent internal and external operational elements, nodes, and organizations. They may be depicted as generic geometric shapes (e.g., circles, squares, and ovals), standard symbols (military, civil, or commercial), representative icons, or a combination of two or more of these different types.

3. Label the elements, nodes, and organizations. Indicate the name/designation of the element, node, or organization. Alternately, indicate the element, node, or organization type and/or echelon.

4. Connect internal and external elements, nodes, and organizations to show C2, coordination, or communications connectivity. Connectivity will normally be depicted by lines joining the elements, nodes, and organizations. A single line style may be used for all connectivities, or different line styles may be used to depict different types of connections.

5. Label connectors to define the type of connection/relationship or the types of information exchanged.

6. Add list(s) of high level missions and tasks performed by the enterprise, functional area, or FoS as a whole, or by each individual element, node, or organization. If the functions, missions, and tasks are associated with a particular element, node, or organization then show them as labels or lists on or in close proximity to the graphical symbol that represents the associated element/organization. Show functions/missions/tasks common to multiple elements, nodes, and organizations, or applicable to the enterprise as a whole within diagram "empty" space or outside the boundaries of the diagram.

7. Add lists of critical requirements, assumptions, and constraints associated with the architecture. If the requirements, assumptions, and constraints are associated with a particular element, node, or organization then show them as labels or lists on or in close proximity to the graphical symbol that represents the associated element/organization. Show requirements, assumptions, and constraints common to multiple elements, nodes, and organizations, or applicable to the enterprise as a whole within diagram "empty" space or outside the boundaries of the diagram.

8. Add a legend to define acronyms, terms, and symbols shown on the diagram.

9. Submit the Operational Concept Graphic to SMEs for review and comment. Include information on the portions of the Operational Concept Graphic to be reviewed, the types of comments to be provided, the desired comment format, the individual(s) or organization(s) to whom/which comments are to be submitted, and the suspense for comment submission.

10. Update Operational Concept Graphic based on comments received. Modify the Operational Concept Graphic as necessary to incorporate approved change recommendations resulting from the SME review.

RECOMMENDED DEVELOPMENT SEQUENCE: First

KEY RELATIONSHIPS:

- Node Connectivity Description: The nodes depicted on the Node Connectivity Description should be the same as, or at least directly traceable to the operational elements, nodes, and organizations described in the textual operational concept and the OPCON graphic.
- Organizational Relationships Chart: The nodes and the command and control relationships depicted on the Organizational Relationships Chart should be the same as or directly traceable to those described in the textual operational concept and the OPCON graphic.
- Operational Information Exchange Matrix: The sending and receiving nodes, connectivities, and exchanged information elements captured in the Operational Information Exchange Matrix should be the same as or directly traceable to those described in the textual operational concept and the OPCON graphic.
- Activity Model: The activities contained in the Activity Model should be directly traceable to the functions, missions, and tasks described in the textual operational concept and the OPCON graphic. The information exchanges defined in the Activity model should be the same as or directly traceable to those described in the textual operational concept and the OPCON graphic. If the Activity Model defines the elements, nodes, and organizations that perform

the activities, they should be the same as or directly traceable to those described in the textual operational concept or shown on the OPCON graphic.
- Operational Activity Sequence & Timing Description: The activities contained in the Operational Activity Sequence & Timing Description should be directly traceable to the functions, missions, and tasks described in the textual operational concept and the OPCON graphic.
- Logical Data Model: The data elements contained in the Logical Data Model should be traceable to the nodes, elements, organizations, interfaces, information exchanges, functions, missions, and tasks described in the textual operational concept or depicted on the OPCON graphic.
- OPFAC Equipment Description: The operational element depicted in an OPFAC Equipment Description should be the same as or directly traceable to an element, node, or organization described in the textual operational concept or shown on the OPCON graphic.

CRITICAL SUCCESS FACTORS:

DO'S:
- Check for the existence of a usable operational concept before beginning to develop a new one.
- Whenever possible, validate information extracted from source documents through SME reviews, interviews, or workshops.
- Ensure that the textual operational concept description is consistent with the OPCON graphic.

DON'TS:
- Don't try to capture too much information in the operational concept or the OPCON graphic. Capture detailed information in other architecture products.
- Don't venture outside the boundaries established by the architecture scoping statement.

CHECKLIST: The Operational Concept Description

Developing the Textual Operational Concept

Process Steps	Complete
1. Determine the appropriate level of detail to be included in the operational concept description.	
2. Identify and describe the enterprise, functional area, or FoS for which the concept is being developed.	
3. Describe why the concept is needed.	
4. Define the timeframe addressed by the concept.	
5. List and describe the operational elements, nodes, and organizations that comprise the enterprise, functional area, or FoS.	
6. Describe the functions, missions, and tasks performed by the operational elements, nodes, and organizations.	
• How the tasks are performed.	
• Why the tasks are performed.	
• By whom the tasks are performed.	
• What resources are needed to perform or support the tasks.	
— Information and data	
— Time	
— Raw materials	
7. Describe the connectivity among elements, nodes, and organizations, and between architecture elements and the external environment.	
8. Describe the operational environment within which architecture missions and tasks are or will be performed:	
• Physical conditions	
• Socio-political requirements, limitations, and constraints	
• Key external elements, nodes, and organizations	
• Threats to be countered	
9. Describe the relationship of the Operational Concept to other existing operational concepts.	
10. Develop a glossary of key terms, abbreviations, and acronyms used in the concept.	
11. List the individuals, organizations, and agencies involved in the development of the concept.	
12. Submit the Textual Operational Concept Description to SMEs for review and comment.	
13. Update Textual Operational Concept Description based on comments received.	

Developing the OPCON Graphic

Process Steps	Complete
1. Lay out the physical/operational environment as a background.	
• Dimensions	
• Key features	
• Requirements/limitations/constraints	
2. Add graphical symbols to represent operational elements, nodes, and organizations (generic, military standard, or representative icons).	
3. Label elements, nodes, and organizations.	
4. Connect internal and external elements, nodes, and organizations to show C2, coordination, or communications connectivity (Generic, or use different connectors to depict different relationship types).	
5. Label connectors to define the type of connection/relationship or the types of information exchanged.	
6. Add list of high level functions, missions, and tasks performed by the enterprise, functional area, or FoS as a whole, or by each individual element, node, or organization.	
7. Add lists of critical requirements, assumptions, and constraints associated with the architecture.	
8. Add a legend to define acronyms, terms, and symbols shown on the diagram.	
9. Submit the Operational Concept Graphic to SMEs for review and comment.	
10. Update Operational Concept Graphic based on comments received.	

CHAPTER THREE

PRODUCT NAME: ACTIVITY MODEL

OTHER ALIASES: Functional Model, Process Model, Task Model, Functional Flow Model, Use Case, Use Case Model

PRODUCT DESIGNATION: OV-5

ARCHITECTURE VIEW: OPERATIONAL

PRODUCT DEFINITION: The ACTIVITY MODEL is a graphical and textual description of the activities (functions or processes) performed by/within an organization or system, and the information exchanges associated with the performance of those activities.

PRODUCT DESCRIPTION: The Activity Model describes the applicable activities associated with the architecture, the data and/or information exchanged between activities, and the data and/or information exchanged with other activities that are outside the scope of the model (i.e., external exchanges). The models are hierarchical in nature; that is, they begin with a single box that represents the overall activity and proceed successively to decompose the activity to the level required by the purpose of the architecture.

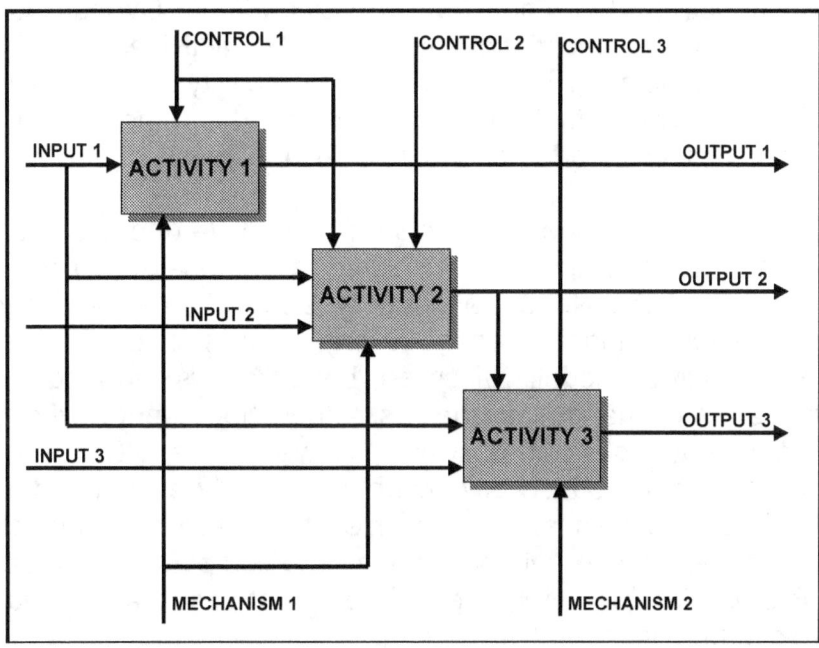

Activity Modeling And Its Contribution To The OA

In order to appreciate fully the contribution of the Activity Model to the OA, one need only look at the definition of the OA listed above. According to that definition, the OA is meant to describe:

- operational elements
- assigned tasks
- information flows required to accomplish or support a warfighting function
- type of information to be exchanged
- frequency of exchange
- tasks supported by the information exchanges.

Of these six elements of information, four (i.e., operational elements, assigned tasks, type of information exchanged and tasks supported by the information exchanges) can be described totally within an Activity Model. A fifth, the information flows, is partially supported by the Activity Model; it can show the information to be exchanged with external elements and the internal elements that produce or consume the information, but it cannot show the external elements that produce the external input or consume the external output. The only OA element of information not supported by the Activity Model is the frequency of information exchange. One of the Activity Model's primary contributions to the OA, therefore, is that it is a single product that contains most of the information required to be included in the OA.

A second area wherein the Activity Model contributes constructively to the OA is in providing a means to translate the abstract operational concepts and generalized connectivity depictions from the Operational Concept Graphic and the Node Connectivity Description into specific activities and information exchanges. Without the specifics provided by the Activity Model, users of the OA would be left to fall back on their own experience and judgment to interpret what the operational architect intended to show in these relatively high level products.

The Activity Model also provides the OA's only complete documentation of tasks and activities and the elements to which they are allocated. The Operational Concept Graphic and the Node Connectivity Description should each include listings of general tasks and activities, but they do not provide the level of detail contained in the Activity Model. Likewise, because it is required to relate the external information exchanges to the tasks that they support, the OIEM also contains references to tasks and activities. However, the OIEM lists only those tasks and activities that produce or consume externally exchanged information. It does not address those tasks or activities that have no connection to the external environment--those whose inputs and outputs are produced and consumed internal to the enterprise. These "internal" tasks and activities, however, are captured in the Activity Model.

Activity Modeling can provide a structured approach for identifying information to be included in the operational information exchange matrix (OIEM). There are several advantages to developing the OIEM from an Activity Model. First, it ensures that every external information exchange captured in the OIEM is associated with a validated warfighter task or activity. Secondly, extracting inputs, controls and outputs (ICO) from the Activity Model increases the likelihood that all required information exchanges are captured in the OIEM-- there is less of a chance that an element of information exchange will be missed because it is new, rare or not obvious. Thirdly, the Activity Model depicts the information exchanges in context. This reduces the potential for misinterpreting the true nature of the information exchange in those cases where an information element name can be interpreted in more than one way or where an element of information can have more than one definition, depending on its use. Finally, the Activity Models developed for two different systems or organizations can be crosswalked at the ICO level to identify information correspondences and disconnects and rapidly develop an OIEM between the two systems or organizations. This is especially helpful when the operational architect for either system/organization is not familiar with the other system/organization. The Activity Models serve as detailed descriptions of the capabilities and needs of each interfacing system/organization. The capabilities and needs of one system/organization can then be compared to the capabilities and needs of the other in order to reach agreement on the information to be exchanged between them.

The inputs, controls, outputs and mechanisms (ICOMs) contained in the Activity Model can provide a start point for developing the Logical Data Model. In some cases, an individual ICOM may describe a single, basic element of data. In most cases, however, an ICOM will be a "bundle" of information that includes multiple elements of basic data. Using the Activity Model ICOMs to identify the data will require that each ICOM be "decomposed" to the point at which the data underlying the information becomes evident. These underlying data elements can then be captured in the Logical Data Model. The advantages of developing the Logical Data Model based on the Activity Model are very similar to the advantages associated with using the Activity Model to develop the OIEM. It provides traceability of each data element to a validated warfighter task or activity. It reduces the likelihood that any required data element will be missed and it provides the context within which the data are used, which increases the likelihood that the correct element of data will be identified.

The Activity Model can provide a means to standardize tactics, techniques and procedures (TTPs) and information exchanges within organizations, functional areas and enterprises. Where related organizations, systems, agencies or elements perform the same or similar functions but utilize different detailed processes, the joint development of an Activity Model can facilitate gaining consensus on a common process to be used by all.

What Happens Without Activity Modeling

Despite the advantages listed above, there are still those who argue, for several reasons, that it is not necessary to include an Activity Model in the OA. While it is true that one could develop an OA that does not contain an Activity Model, and while that OA might do a good job of capturing and conveying many of the enterprise's requirements, there are a number of key characteristics of the OA that would be missing or poorly addressed without the Activity Model.

The lack of an Activity Model provides tacit support for the continuation of non-standard processes by the elements within the enterprise. It suggests that even though separate elements of the enterprise perform the same or similar functions, it is acceptable for them to use different processes as long as they share their outputs with each other. One could argue that process standardization might be effected by some means other than the development of an Activity Model. This is true, but if process standardization is ongoing within the enterprise it ought to be captured in the OA, and the most logical way to depict it is through an Activity Model.

Without an Activity Model, new OIEMs will tend to be defined in terms of existing interfaces or interface messages. The resulting OIEM might not reflect accurately the actual information exchanges requirement to support all user tasks. The producer of the OIEM likely will identify the information to be included in the OIEM based on his own knowledge of and experience with similar interfaces or similar systems, organizations or functional areas, if no similar interfaces have been previously described. This easily could cause one to miss key information exchanges that ought to be captured in the OIEM. The three types of information exchanges most likely to be missed are:

- Information exchanges that are unique to a particular interface and, therefore, have not been reflected in any existing interface description.
- Future information exchange requirements that are not met by any existing form, message or set of messages.
- Information that was previously for internal use only, but that must now be exchanged externally.

Without an Activity Model to provide contextual information, the true nature of some information exchanges may be unclear. For example, simply stating that two systems/organizations must exchange "Status Information" probably is not sufficient to determine what specific status information must be exchanged between them. The lack of context to aid in refining the information exchanges might lead to a system/organization receiving or producing more information than is needed or less information than is required, or it may result in the wrong elements of information being exchanged.

Without an Activity Model, the Logical Data Model will be developed primarily based on the OIEM. If the OIEM contains extraneous or incorrect information, or if it is missing information, then the Data Model will contain extraneous or incorrect data elements, or will be missing required data elements.

Why Two Types Of Activity Models

Depending on the temporal focus of the information contained in them, Activity Models may be divided into two types: As-Is and To-Be. An As-Is model describes the current tasks/activities and information exchanges of an enterprise. A To-Be model describes the enterprise as it will, may or should be in the future. Depending on the goals and objectives of the OA, either or both types of Activity Models may be required. Each type adds a particular set of characteristics to the OA and is developed to address a particular set of needs.

Reasons For Developing An As-Is Activity Model

The As-Is Activity Model is essentially a "snapshot" of the enterprise as it currently exists. An As-Is model should be developed any time that it is important to capture and document what the enterprise looks like and how it functions today. Specifically, the As-Is Activity Model can be used:

- To capture and consolidate, in a single product, information about the enterprise or organization that currently resides in disparate and disconnected segments of the organization or elements of the enterprise. The different segments or elements of an organization or enterprise may have a good idea what each does individually, but there may be no depiction or appreciation of how all the parts work together. Developing an Activity Model can provide a mechanism for bringing together information from and about all the parts of the enterprise or organization.

- To achieve consensus among elements of the enterprise on the tasks that the enterprise performs; which elements, segments or components of the enterprise perform those tasks; how the tasks are performed, and what information is exchanged in the performance or support of the tasks.

- To capture "metrics" that can support analyses of the operational effectiveness of the enterprise. Metrics associated with tasks/activities and information exchanges include, but are not limited to:
    – Which element, segment or component of the enterprise does what tasks, where, why and how?
    – How often are tasks/activities or information exchanges executed?

- How long does it take to perform each task/activity or information exchange?
- How well are the tasks/activities performed?
- What is the cost associated with the execution of each task/activity (Activity Based Costing)?
- How efficient is the enterprise at converting inputs into outputs (productivity analysis)?
- What resources are required to execute each task/activity?

- To catalog tasks, activities and processes and provide detailed descriptions to support:
    - Cross training of personnel in new tasks, activities or processes.
    - Training and orientation of new personnel.
    - Presentations and briefings to groups or persons outside the enterprise

- To provide a powerful tool for managers that:
    - Lists tasks/activities to be performed along with required inputs, controls and outputs.
    - Serves as a checklist against which to evaluate individual and group compliance with established procedures.
    - Serves as a set of standards against which to evaluate individual and group performance.

- To serve as the basis for developing and/or validating executable models and simulations of systems, organizations and processes.

- To serve as the baseline for redesigning the enterprise through the identification of operational issues and improvement opportunities.

Reasons For Developing The To-Be Activity Model

The To-Be Activity Model is a depiction of the enterprise as it could, should or will be in the future. A To-Be model should be developed any time that it is more important to describe the future state of the enterprise than it is to describe the current state. Specifically, a To-Be Activity Model can be used:

- To describe and define wholly new enterprises in terms of tasks/activities and information exchanges (i.e., inputs, controls, outputs and mechanisms).

- To perform strategic planning for an existing enterprise by identifying and documenting the strategic vision or the future requirements of the enterprise in terms of:
    - Organizations/elements/segments/components
    - Capabilities

- Tasks/activities
- Processes
- Information/data exchanges
- Resources
- Outputs

- To "wargame" various options for designing or redesigning organizations by developing model "excursions" that include:
  - New or modified tasks/activities.
  - New or modified mechanisms.
  - New or modified ICOs.

- To support the conduct of Business Process Reengineering (BPR) using the operational issues and improvement opportunities identified in the As-Is Activity Model as the baseline for defining desired or required changes to the structure, functions and connectivities of the enterprise. BPR may involve any or all of the following:
  - Modifying, merging, reorganizing or deleting existing tasks/activities.
  - Adding new tasks/activities.
  - Modifying, merging, reorganizing or deleting existing information exchanges.
  - Adding new information exchanges/connectivities.
  - Incorporating new technology.
  - Allocating tasks/activities to different elements, segments or components.

- To develop and/or justify enterprise-wide investment strategies by relating projected expenditures to specific benefits to be gained through the implementation of future operational capabilities

- To serve as the basis for developing and/or validating executable models and simulations of future systems.

- To provide a common vision to guide the actions of all segments of the enterprise.

Relating As-Is And To-Be Activity Models

For some uses, it may be necessary to develop both As-Is and To-Be Activity Models of the same enterprise. For example, in conducting BPR, the As-Is Activity Model is used to identify operational issues and improvement opportunities, while the To-Be Activity Model describes how the enterprise will address the issues and take advantage of the improvement opportunities. If the As-Is Activity Model is being developed to support only BPR, then it need be defined only to a level of detail such that it addresses the operational issues and improvement opportunities. If the To-Be Activity Model is being developed to support only BPR, then it should include, where possible and prudent, the same names for identical tasks/activities and ICOMs that also appear in the As-Is Activity Model. In this way, any differences between the As-Is and the To-Be models may be construed as proposed or planned changes to the structure and function of the enterprise. When both types of models are developed to support BPR, the As-Is model should be developed first.

It is possible to conduct BPR without an As-Is Activity Model. In situations where the operational issues and shortcomings are well understood and documented, these issues and shortcomings may replace the As-Is Activity Model as the basis for developing the To-Be Activity Model.

There may be situations where As-Is and To-Be Activity Models are developed of the same enterprise, but they are not developed to support BPR. In such situations, it is not necessary that the two models contain the same tasks/activities and ICOMs, nor that the As-Is model be developed first. The models may be developed independently by different modeling groups and the tasks/activities and ICOMs included in each may be tailored to the specific uses to which each model will be put. Whenever possible, however, it is suggested that the tasks/activities and ICOMs be kept as common as is prudent. This will support the comparison of the architectures over time. Should the decision be made later to conduct BPR, the models will be usable with relatively slight modifications instead of having to be recreated from scratch.

Categories Of Activity Models[3]

In additional to there being two types of Activity Models, there are also seven categories of Activity Models. The categories are:

- System models,
- Organizational models,
- Functional Area models,
- Common (or template) models,
- Family of Systems (FoS) models,
- Integration models and
- Model Views.

Model views can be further divided into three sub-categories: Extensions, Excursions and Extracts.

---

[3] The descriptions of the categories of Activity Models presented here presuppose an understanding of Integrated Definition for Functional Modeling (IDEF0) modeling standards and syntax.

The System, Organizational and Functional Area categories are considered primary categories. The other four are considered special categories in that they are really specialized versions of one of the three primary categories.

The unique characteristics of each category or sub-category of Activity Models mean that they can support a wide variety of model uses, but that certain categories are best for certain purposes and uses. The operational architect must, therefore, carefully select both the type and the category of Activity Model that best supports the uses to which the OA will be put. Developing the wrong Activity Model limits its utility and wastes resources. It may also result in the wrong type of information being captured in the model. The categories and sub-categories of Activity Models are described further below.

System Activity Model

A System Activity Model describes the internal operations of a system and its interactions with its external environment. A "system" can be defined as a single, self-contained end item that performs one or more primary functions (e.g., a vehicle or a television set), or a collection of components that normally are used together to perform a single function (e.g., a computer, that is composed of a keyboard, a monitor, a central processing unit, one or more disk drives and a printer). The focus of the System Activity Model is on the association of the activities and ICOMs to a system and/or its components. The activities depicted in the System Activity Model are the functions or tasks that are performed by the system. Inputs to a System model are the resources or information that are used by the system in the performance of each activity. Controls on a System model may be either informational (e.g., rule sets, procedure manuals or software applications), or physical/mechanical (e.g., on/off switches, valves or regulators). The outputs of a System model are the information/data or products that are created by the system. The mechanisms depicted in a System model may include the human operators of the system and the system sub-components.

Organizational Activity Model

An Organizational Activity Model describes the tasks/activities performed by an organization, allocates organization tasks/activities to individuals or subordinate elements, shows how the elements of the organization interact with each other and shows how the organization interacts with its external environment. Inputs to an Organizational model are the resources and information that are used by the organization in the performance of each task/activity. Controls on an Organizational model may be information (e.g., plans, rule sets, procedure manuals, vision statements or guidance), or they may reflect the availability or status of required resources. The outputs of an Organizational model are the information/data, products or services that are provided by the organization. Mechanisms depicted in an Organizational model may include individuals, sub-elements of the organization, or systems owned and operated by the organization.

Functional Area Activity Model

A Functional Area Activity Model focuses on describing the activities and information exchanges that occur in the performance of a particular function or related group of functions. The Functional Area Activity Model places greater emphasis on defining the activities and information exchanges than on describing the organizations and/or systems that execute those activities or information exchanges. The activities shown in a Functional Area Activity Model are the subordinate tasks that comprise the overall function or functional area. For example, the functional area "Cooking" might include the activities "Baking", "Broiling", "Barbecuing", "Frying", "Grilling" and "Roasting". The inputs, controls, and outputs of a Functional Area model are similar to those of an Organizational model. The mechanisms depicted in a Functional Area model may include the organizations and individuals that perform or support the overall function, the systems owned and operated by those organizations or individuals, and the software applications that run on those systems.

Common (Template) Activity Model

A Common Activity Model describes those tasks/activities and information exchanges that are common to a number of systems, organizations or functional areas. When it is produced prior to the development of the Activity Models for any specific system, organization or functional area, then it can serve as a template to be used to produce specific models. When it is produced after the development of specific models, then it can be used to standardize processes and information exchanges across systems, organizations and functional areas.

Common Activity Models are normally produced as complete, stand-alone models; however, another use of the Common Activity Model concept is the development of modules containing a description of a limited set of common functions that are meant to be inserted into other models. The modules provide a consistent description of the set of common functions across a number of Activity Models. They reduce the time and resources required to develop a group of models by eliminating the need for each modeler or model development team to develop independent (and potentially inconsistent) descriptions of the same set of common functions.

Family Of Systems Activity Model

A Family of Systems (FoS) Activity Model is a hybrid between a System model and a Functional Area model. It shows how multiple systems cooperate in the performance of a common function and associates particular activities and information exchanges with individual systems that comprise the FoS. For example, a System model of the Army's PATRIOT missile system would show how that system operates in the performance of it primary function of destroying hostile aircraft and missiles, but a FoS model of Theater Air and Missile Defense (TAMD) would show how PATRIOT, the Army's Theater High Altitude Area Defense (THAAD) system, the Navy's Aegis system and other Army, Navy, Air Force and Marine Corps systems work together as a FoS to perform TAMD. A key feature of a FoS model is that it shows the information exchanged among and between individual systems. The activities described in a FoS model include both common functions and tasks performed by multiple systems, and unique functions and tasks performed by individual systems. The inputs, controls and outputs of a FoS model are the inputs, controls, and outputs of the individual systems that comprise the FoS. This may include inputs, controls, or outputs that would not be needed by any system in the FoS if they were operating independently, but are necessary for them to operate efficiently together. The mechanisms for a FoS model may include the individual systems that make up the FoS, the sub-components of those systems, and the software applications that run on those systems or their sub-components. However, because it describes a family of systems, it does not associate activities and information exchanges to organization as is done in a Functional Area model.

Integration Activity Model

An Integration Activity Model is a special category of model that shows how two or more systems, organizations or functional areas may be integrated. It begins with two or more existing Activity Models, and combines them to create a new, integrated Activity Model. The context diagrams of the existing Activity Models become first level sub-activities of the integrated model. The inputs and controls from each model are connected to the equivalent outputs from the other models to show how the models are related to each other. It may be necessary to rename, decompose or "bundle" ICOs from one or more models in order to allow them to be connected to equivalent ICOs from other models. For the most part, the ICOMs depicted in an Integration model are those of the individual models that it integrates.

Activity Model Views

An Activity Model View is a special category of Activity Model that presents an alternative view of another existing Activity Model. As stated earlier, there are three sub-categories of Activity Model Views: the model Extension, the model Excursion and the model Extract. The most basic sub-category of model Views is the Extract, which shows a subset (a "slice") of the original model without changing any aspect of it. A model Extension takes all or part of the original model and extends or expands its activities and/or ICOMs to provide additional detail. A model Excursion changes one or more activities or ICOMs from the original model in order to allow the operational architect or modeler to explore and evaluate alternatives.

Selecting The Right Type And Category Of Activity Model

The matrix below shows typical uses for the different types and categories of models, and can aid in determining the correct model for the use to which the model will be put. The As-Is column indicates those uses for which only an As-Is model is required. The To-Be column identifies those uses for which a To-Be model must be developed. The "EITHER" column reflects those uses for which either an As-Is or a To-Be model may be developed. The "BOTH" column reflects those uses for which both an As-Is and a To-Be model are required normally. The table treats the three sub-categories of model views separately in order to bring out the differences in their uses.

ACTIVITY MODEL CATEGORY	ACTIVITY MODEL TYPE			
	AS-IS	TO-BE	EITHER	BOTH
SYSTEM	Capture and consolidate information about the system Capture metrics that support system operational effectiveness analysis	Describe and define requirements for new systems Explore options for system functionality and interfaces Develop or justify system investment strategies	Support presentations and briefings Develop or validate executable models and simulations of systems Describe the internal operations of a system Describe how a system interacts with its external environment	Business Process Reengineering-System Improvement
ORGANIZATIONAL	Capture and consolidate information about the organization Achieve consensus among elements of the organization Capture metrics that support organizational effectiveness analysis Support cross training of organization personnel Support training and orientation of new personnel Support evaluation of individual or group compliance with established procedures Provide a set of standards against which to evaluate individual or group performance	Describe and define requirements for new organizations Support or perform strategic planning Explore options for organizational operations, functional allocation and/or organizational interfaces Develop or justify organizational investment strategies Provide a common vision to guide the actions of all elements of the organization	Support presentations and briefings Develop and validate executable models and simulations of organizations Allocate tasks and information exchanges to organizational sub-elements Describe how the elements of an organization interact with each other Describe how an organization interacts with its external environment	Business Process Reengineering-Organizational redesign, functional reallocation, process modification

ACTIVITY MODEL CATEGORY	ACTIVITY MODEL TYPE			
	AS-IS	TO-BE	EITHER	BOTH
FUNCTIONAL AREA	Capture and consolidate information about the functional area Achieve consensus among elements of the functional area Capture metrics that support operational effectiveness analysis Support evaluation of individual or group compliance with established procedures Provide a set of standards against which to evaluate individual or group performance	Describe and define requirements for new systems and/or organizations Support or perform strategic planning Explore options for design and operations of functional area systems and/or organizations Develop or justify enterprise-wide investment strategies Provide a common vision to guide the actions of all segments of the functional area	Support presentations and briefings Develop or validate executable models of systems and/or organizations that comprise the functional area Describe the activities, organizations and systems that comprise the total functional area Describe how the elements of the functional area interact with each other Describe how the functional area interacts with its external environment	Business Process Reengineering
COMMON (TEMPLATE)	Capture and consolidate information about the enterprise Capture metrics that support operational effectiveness analysis	Describe and define requirements for new systems and/or organizations Support or perform strategic planning Explore options for design and operations of systems and/or organizations Develop or justify enterprise-wide investment strategies Provide a common vision to guide the actions of all segments of the enterprise	Support presentations and briefings Develop or validate executable models of systems and/or organizations that comprise the enterprise Describe the activities, organizations and systems that comprise the total enterprise Describe how the elements of the enterprise interact with each other Describe how the enterprise interacts with its external environment Describe common tasks/activities and information exchanges Provide a consistent description of common tasks and activities across organizations, systems and functional areas	Business Process Reengineering

ACTIVITY MODEL CATEGORY	ACTIVITY MODEL TYPE			
	AS-IS	TO-BE	EITHER	BOTH
FAMILY OF SYSTEMS	Capture and consolidate information about the enterprise Capture metrics that support operational effectiveness analysis	Describe and define requirements for new systems Support or perform strategic planning Explore options for FoS functionality and interfaces Develop or justify FoS-wide investment strategies by prioritizing acquisition of or improvements to individual systems Provide a common vision to guide the actions of all segments of the enterprise	Support presentations and briefings Develop or validate executable models of systems that comprise the FoS Describe the activities and systems that comprise the total FoS Describe how the individual systems of the FoS interact with each other Describe how the FoS interacts with its external environment	Business Process Reengineering
INTEGRATING	Capture and consolidate information about the enterprise Capture metrics that support operational effectiveness analysis		Support presentations and briefings Develop or validate executable models of systems and/or organizations that comprise the enterprise Describe how two or more system, organizational or functional area models are related Describe the activities, organizations and systems that comprise the total enterprise Describe how the elements of the enterprise interact with each other Describe how the enterprise interacts with its external environment	Business Process Reengineering

ACTIVITY MODEL CATEGORY	ACTIVITY MODEL TYPE			
	AS-IS	TO-BE	EITHER	BOTH
EXTRACT	Capture and consolidate information about the enterprise Capture metrics that support operational effectiveness analysis Support evaluation of individual or group compliance with established procedures Provide a set of standards against which to evaluate individual or group performance	Describe and define requirements for new systems and/or organizations Support or perform strategic planning Explore options for design and operations of systems and/or organizations Develop or justify enterprise-wide investment strategies Provide a common vision to guide the actions of all segments of the enterprise	Describe a specific subset of the activities associated with a particular enterprise Support presentations and briefings Develop or validate executable models of systems and/or organizations that comprise the enterprise Describe the activities, organizations and systems that comprise the enterprise Describe how the elements of the enterprise interact with each other Describe how the enterprise interacts with its external environment	Business Process Reengineering
EXTENSION	Capture and consolidate information about the enterprise Capture metrics that support operational effectiveness analysis Support evaluation of individual or group compliance with established procedures Provide a set of standards against which to evaluate individual or group performance	Describe and define requirements for new systems and/or organizations Support or perform strategic planning Explore options for design and operations of systems and/or organizations Develop or justify enterprise-wide investment strategies Provide a common vision to guide the actions of all segments of the enterprise	Further decompose all or a part of an existing model Support presentations and briefings Develop or validate executable models of systems and/or organizations that comprise the enterprise Describe the activities, organizations and systems that comprise the total enterprise Describe how the elements of the enterprise interact with each other Describe how the enterprise interacts with its external environment	Business Process Reengineering

ACTIVITY MODEL CATEGORY	ACTIVITY MODEL TYPE			
	AS-IS	TO-BE	EITHER	BOTH
EXCURSION	Capture and consolidate information about the enterprise Capture metrics that support operational effectiveness analysis Support evaluation of individual or group compliance with established procedures Provide a set of standards against which to evaluate individual or group performance	Describe and define requirements for new systems and/or organizations Support or perform strategic planning Explore options for design and operations of systems and/or organizations Develop or justify enterprise-wide investment strategies Provide a common vision to guide the actions of all segments of the enterprise	Modify one or more activities from an existing model to explore alternatives Support presentations and briefings Develop or validate executable models of systems and/or organizations that comprise the enterprise Describe the activities, organizations and systems that comprise the total enterprise Describe how the elements of the enterprise interact with each other Describe how the enterprise interacts with its external environment	Business Process Reengineering

Additional Uses Of The Activity Model

A well-developed Activity Model may support uses other than those described above. Some of these additional uses include:

- Operational Architecture Integration. This involves relating the activities and ICOMs from the Activity Model in one OA to the corresponding activities and ICOMs in another OA. Integration of architectures allows the creators and/or users of one architecture to understand how their architecture relates to another, and may result in the development of a single OA that subsumes the contents of the two previously independent OAs. There are essentially three levels of Activity Model integration. Level 1 requires only that the two models be crosswalked and a lexicon or crosswalk matrix be developed to show the related activities and ICOMs. Level 2 requires that the names and definitions of the related activities and ICOMs in one or both models be changed such that they are identical in both models. Level 3 requires the development of a single Activity Model that replaces the two related models.

- Development or Validation of Training Plans. This involves using the operational issues associated with an As-Is Organizational model as the basis for identifying the tasks on which the organization will be trained, the conditions under which the training is to take place and the standards to which the tasks must be performed.

- Development of Procedures Guides and User's Manuals. This involves expanding the activity and ICOM descriptions from a System Activity Model into appropriate system task and operator-system interface (OSI) descriptions.

- Planning for Organization Exercises or System Tests. This involves developing Activity models that depict the tasks and information exchanges to be executed, and the organizations, individuals and systems to be included in these events.

- Activity Based Cost analysis. This involves assigning an actual or estimated cost to each discrete activity. The cost of the overall process or any subset of activities can then be determined based on the costs of the individual activities, with consideration given to the fact that some activities can be performed concurrently, while others must be performed in a specific sequence. Activity based cost analysis may be used to prioritize activities or processes, assess alternative process flows or support an investment strategy.

- Process duration analysis. This involves assigning an actual or estimated duration for each discrete activity. The duration of the overall process or any subset of activities can then be determined based on the duration for each of the individual activities, with consideration given to the fact that some activities can be performed concurrently, while others must be performed in a specific sequence. Process duration analysis may be used to identify process "bottlenecks" that cause unexpected or undesirable delays in a particular process string, to identify long duration process strings for which shortcuts may need to be developed or to assess alternative process flows.

- Process frequency analysis. This involves assigning an actual or estimated frequency of occurrence for each activity. Process frequency analysis may be used to prioritize activities or processes, assess alternative process flows or support an investment strategy.

- Decision tree mapping. This involves using an Activity Model to represent a decision tree by depicting each decision point as an activity. The decisions made at each decision point are the outputs of the activities, and also serve as the inputs or controls for later decision point activities. The mechanisms for the activities are the decision-makers. An Activity Model developed in the form of a decision tree can provide perspective by presenting a graphical representation of the entire decision process. This would aid each decision-maker in understanding his or her role in the overall process.

- Developing a graphical depiction of a Work Breakdown Structure (WBS). This involves converting the individual tasks from the WBS into activities in an Activity Model. The products of each WBS task are the outputs of the respective activities. The resources required for each WBS task are the inputs and controls for the activities. The individuals or organizations to which the WBS tasks are assigned are the mechanisms for the activities.

PRODUCT FORMAT: Graphics and text

USERS & USES:

USERS:

Corporate/Non-Military

- Strategic Planner
- Operations Manager
- Human Resource Manager
- Resource Manager
- Information Manager
- Quality Assurance Manager
- Facilities Manager
- Security Manager
- Supervisors
- Workers
- Software Developers
- Trainers
- Research and Development
- Policy Writers
- Public Relations Department
- Sales Department

Military
- Combat Developer
- Concept Developer
- Trainer
- Training Developer
- Force Developer
- Program/Project/Product Developer
- Resource Manager

- Operational Architect
- Systems Architect
- Technical Architect
- Systems Engineer
- Software Developer
- Manufacturer
- Test & Evaluation Community
- Modeling & Simulation Community
- Warfighter

USES:

Corporate/Non-Military

- Strategic Business Planning
- Development of Procedures Guides and User's Manuals
- Organizational Design
- Identification of Personnel Requirements
- Business Process Reengineering
- Development/validation of SOPs
- Development of Capital Investment Strategies
- Quality Control/Quality Management
- Description of Required System Capabilities
- Baselining of Functionality
- Functional Allocation
- Database Design
- Development/Modification of Operational Concepts
- Identification of Operational Issues
- Allocation Of Communication Assets
- Communications Network Burden Assessment
- Wargaming Alternatives
- Design of Human-Computer Interface
- Performance of Cost/Benefits Analysis
- Development of Training Materials

Military

- Development/Modification of Operational Concepts

- Identification of Operational Issues
- Identification/Validation of Operational Needs/Requirements
- Standardization of Processes, Activities and Tasks
- Development/Validation Of Tactics, Techniques & Procedures (TTPs)
- Development/Validation Of SOPs
- Identification Of Functional Information Requirements
- Identification of IERs
- Development/Validation Of Models & Simulations
- Allocation Of Communication Assets
- Development/Validation Of Mission Training Plans
- Planning For Organization Exercises
- Planning For System Tests
- Network Burden Assessment
- Identification of OPFAC Hardware Requirements
- Data Modeling
- Standardization of Data Elements
- Development/Modification Of Standard Messages
- Development Of System Software
- Comparing User's Vision To Developer's Implementation
- Baselining Of Functionality
- Wargaming Alternatives
- Prioritizing Activities For Implementation
- Providing Roadmap For System Improvement
- Battlefield/Business Process Reengineering
- Development of Procedures Guides and User's Manuals
- Design of Human-Computer Interface
- Performance of Cost/Benefits Analysis
- Development of Training Materials

TYPICAL INFORMATION SOURCES:

Corporate/Non-Military

- Function/Task Lists
- Long Range Plans
- Organization Descriptions

- Operational Concepts
- Policy and Procedures Guides
- Standing Operating Procedures (SOPs)
- Strategic Plans
- Subject Matter Experts
- System Descriptions
- Task Descriptions
- Vision Statements
- Business Plans
- Corporate Brochures

Military

- Subject Matter Experts
- Policy and Procedures Guides
- Doctrinal Publications
- Operational Concepts
- Operational and Organizational Plans
- Vision Statements
- Future Operational Capabilities (FOCs)
- Long Range Plans
- Strategic Plans
- Modernization Plans
- Master Plans
- Organization Descriptions (including TOEs, MTOEs, TDAs)
- Function/Task Lists (including METLs, UJTL, Service Task Lists)
- Task Descriptions
- Standing Operating Procedures (SOPs)
- Interface Descriptions
- System Descriptions
- Existing Activity Models

TOOLS:

- Text Editor
- Drawing/Graphics Tool
- Activity/Process Modeling Tool

- Object Modeling Tool
- Flow Charting Tool

PARTICIPANTS:

Corporate/Non-Military

- Strategic Planner
- Operations Manager
- Human Resource Manager
- Resource Manager
- Information Manager
- Quality Assurance Manager
- Facilities Manager
- Security Manager
- Supervisors
- Workers
- Software Developers
- Trainers
- Policy Writers
- Operational Architect/Facilitator
- Subject Matter Expert

Military

- Combat Developer
- Concept & Doctrine Developer
- Training Developer
- Force Developer
- Operational Architect/Facilitator
- Subject Matter Expert
- Warfighter
- Program/Project/Product Developer
- Systems Architect
- Technical Architect
- Systems Engineer

PRODUCT DEVELOPMENT:

There are three primary methods of developing the Activity Model: modifying and existing model, extracting information from available source documents, and conducting facilitated modeling workshops. The method to be used for a particular model is dependent on the development time and resources available, the level to which model information is already captured in existing models or source documents, and the knowledge and experience of the modeler(s).

The following is a description of the facilitated method of developing an Activity Model. This methodology has been employed by a number of modeling activities within the DoD and the Army and has proven itself to be both easy to implement and thorough. It is the recommended methodology when development time and development cost are not primary considerations. The foundation of this methodology is the conduct of a series of facilitated modeling workshops in which three categories of individuals participate: facilitators, modelers and subject matter experts (SMEs). Facilitators are experts in the activity modeling process who assist the SMEs in expressing their knowledge and experience with the enterprise being modeled in a manner consistent with the IDEF0 modeling syntax. Facilitators do not decide what to model, but determine how best to model the information provided by SMEs. SMEs draw upon their personal knowledge and experience to identify the appropriate activities/functions to be included in the model; the information required to support, control or constrain those functions; the outputs of the functions; the individuals, organizations or systems required to perform the functions and the relationships of the functions to each other and to the external environment. In addition to their own knowledge and experience, SMEs also should have access to information contained in appropriate descriptive, doctrinal, technical and regulatory documentation. Modelers use their knowledge of the IDEF0 modeling techniques and tools to create and modify activity model diagrams that capture the information provided by the SMEs.

The specific steps in the methodology are:

1. ***Identify the need for the development of an Activity Model.*** This is primarily the job of the Operational Architect.
2. ***Identify and document the model purpose, scope and viewpoint.*** The model purpose is the reason(s) for which the model is being developed (i.e., the uses to which the finished model will be put). The model scope is the depth and breadth of the activities and ICOMs to be included in the model. Another way of describing the model scope is that it allows one to draw a box around the enterprise--everything inside the box is part of the enterprise and should be captured in the Activity Model. Everything outside the box is part of the external environment, and should not be included in the model. The model viewpoint identifies from whose point of view the activities and ICOMs in the model are described. This is important because a description of the

same activity might be quite different if presented from different points of view. For example, the reassignment of an individual from one department to another within the same organization would be a loss from the viewpoint of the department that he left, a gain from the viewpoint of the department that he was reassigned to, and a lateral transfer with no change in overall end strength to the parent organization of the two departments. Together, the purpose, scope and viewpoint serve two purposes. First and foremost, they guide and focus the developers of the model and ensure that the model is complete (i.e., includes all pertinent information) and concise (i.e., contains no extraneous information). Secondly, they provide a summary description of the model for users, reviews and other readers of the model.

3. ***Based on the purpose, scope and viewpoint, determine the appropriate type (As-Is or To-Be) and category (system, organizational, functional area, common, integration or view) of model to be developed***.
4. ***Identify and gather resources and references required to support model development.***
5. ***Identify and notify SMEs.*** Development of the model may require the participation of several groups of SMEs:
   a. Those who will participate in the modeling sessions.
   b. Those who will not participate in the modeling sessions, but will provide input via face-to-face interviews with facilitators/modelers.
   c. Those who will review and provide comment on drafts and the final model.
   d. Those whose knowledge of a specific subject area will be solicited only when needed.
6. ***Conduct face-to-face interviews with SMEs not participating in the working sessions***.
7. ***Conduct modeling session.*** During the modeling session, the facilitator will guide and direct the discussion, but the main source of information and input will be the SMEs in attendance.
   a. Develop the Context Diagram and the initial activity decomposition.
   b. Add appropriate ICOMs to the activities and the Context Diagram.
   c. Draft definitions for all activities and ICOMs.
   d. Further decompose activities one at a time:
      1.) Add lower level activities that comprise each activity being decomposed.
      2.) Decompose existing ICOMs to a level of detail consistent to the level of decomposition of the associated activities.
      3.) Add new ICOMs as necessary to capture information associated with the new activities.
      4.) Define new activities and ICOMs. Also update the definitions of existing activities and ICOMs to reflect any changes necessitated by the addition of the new activities and ICOMs.
      5.) Repeat 1-4.
   e. Review results of the modeling session. Ensure that all modeling session participants agree on what was accomplished during the session, what

actions are to be performed between sessions and what goals are to be established for the next session.
   f. Identify any outstanding issues from the modeling session.
   g. Assign outstanding issues to selected participants for resolution.
8. ***Update the model by incorporating the results of the modeling session.*** This is primarily the job of the facilitator and modeler(s) between modeling sessions. It includes making all agreed to changes to the model and "cleaning up" the model for publication/distribution.
9. ***Publish and distribute the updated model to modeling session participants and other specified reviewers for review and/or comment.*** If no comments or recommended changes are received, go to step 13 below.
10. ***Receive, review and respond to recommended changes to the draft model.***
11. ***Incorporate approved changes into an updated model draft.***
12. ***Repeat from step 9.***
13. ***Conduct additional modeling sessions as necessary.***
14. ***Finalize the model.***
15. ***Identify and document operational issues and improvement opportunities resulting from model development.*** In order to facilitate later actions to improve the enterprise, it is recommended that each issue and improvement opportunity be described in detail. Each issue description may also include a recommendation as to how it may be resolved, and each improvement opportunity description may include a recommendation as to how it may be capitalized upon. Additionally, they may be assigned to specific individuals or elements for action. For military architectures, relate the issues and improvement opportunities to the appropriate DTLOMS (doctrine, training, leader development, organizations, materiel and soldiers) or DOTMPLF (doctrine, organization, training, materiel, personnel, leader development, or facilities) domain.
16. ***Publish the final Activity Model.***

An alternative to the facilitated modeling workshop methodology is extracting model activities from source documents such as field manuals; task lists; operations manuals; standing operating procedures (SOPs) and operational concepts. This methodology can be used when Activity Model development time and funding are limited, and existing source documents contain information that describes enterprise functions and tasks in some detail. The steps in this methodology are:

1. ***If source document function/activity/task information is grouped hierarchically in the document, use it as or modify it slightly to fit the modeling syntax.*** It may be necessary to regroup functions/activities/tasks in order to be in compliance with the syntax of the modeling tool being used. For example, IDEF0 activity modeling requires that each decomposed function/activity/task be broken down into between three and nine subordinate

functions. Other modeling tools have similar requirements and constraints that must be considered when extracting the functions/activities/tasks.
2. ***If function/activity/task information is not grouped hierarchically, identify related and equivalent tasks and group them together.*** Identifying related tasks may be as simple as reviewing the task names used in the source document. However, it may be necessary to review the definition or description of the tasks contained in the document.
3. ***Develop higher-level "parent" tasks for each related group.*** The parent task should be named and defined based on the subordinate tasks grouped under it.
4. ***If function/activity/task information is extracted from multiple sources, first identify how tasks from each relate to the other(s), then resolve any conflicts.***
   a. Same task with the same name: No resolution is required. Use the function/activity/task as is.
   b. Same task, but with different name(s): Select a single name to be used in the model. This may also require selecting from among alternative definitions for the task. The definition that is used in the model need not be adopted from the same source document as the task name. Select the definition that best matches the enterprise being architected.
   c. Different tasks, but with the same name: Determine whether both/all tasks will be used in the model. If so, rename one or more of the duplicate tasks so that the Activity Model will not include multiple tasks with the same name
   d. Related tasks that are different parts of a larger whole: Group the tasks together and develop an appropriate parent task.
   e. Related tasks, one of which is subordinate to the other: Capture the tasks in the model as parent and child in accordance with the modeling syntax.
   f. Alternative processes for achieving the same result: Either adopt one process (task hierarchy) in total, or attempt to combine the alternative processes into a single, more comprehensive process hierarchy.
5. ***Once the function decomposition is developed and documented, have it reviewed by SMEs for accuracy and completeness.*** If necessary, clearly define for SMEs the aspect(s) of the model on which they are to concentrate their review. Are they to review the entire model, or only a portion? Are they to review the model structure, or only function/activity/task and ICOM naming conventions?
6. ***Incorporate SME recommendations into an updated model.***
7. ***Finalize the model.***
8. ***Identify and document operational issues and improvement opportunities resulting from model development.*** In order to facilitate later actions to improve the enterprise, it is recommended that each issue and improvement opportunity be described in detail. Each issue description may also include a recommendation as to how it may be resolved, and each improvement opportunity description may include a recommendation as to how it may be capitalized upon. Additionally, they may be assigned to specific individuals or elements for action. For military architectures, relate

the issues and improvement opportunities to the appropriate DTLOMS (doctrine, training, leader development, organizations, materiel and soldiers) or DOTMPLF (doctrine, organization, training, materiel, personnel, leader development, or facilities) domain.
9. **Publish the model**.

The final standard methodology is to develop the Activity Model from an existing model. As with extracting model information from source documents, this methodology can be used when Activity Model development time and funding are limited. The use of this methodology is also contingent on the availability of an Activity Model with activities and ICOMs that can be reused. The steps in this methodology are:

1. ***Review the existing model to identify activities and ICOMs that can be recycled.*** In some cases, the entire model can be adopted as is. In other cases, a whole section of the existing model can be adopted to reflect the entire enterprise being modeled. In most cases, however, portions of several sections of the existing model will be usable, but other portions will not.
2. ***Copy the existing model and rename the copied model to reflect the enterprise being modeled.*** At this point, the only difference between the original model and the copy is the model name. Other aspects of the copied model will be modified in later steps.
3. ***Delete from the new model unusable activities and ICOMs.*** Before deleting an activity or ICOM, be sure that it cannot be made usable through modification. Only those without any utility should be deleted from the model.
4. ***Reorganize remaining activities and ICOMs as necessary to reflect the enterprise being modeled.*** This may involve grouping together individual activities from different sections of the model, or moving ICOMs from one activity to another.
5. ***Modify reused activity and ICOM names and/or definitions to capture subtle differences between the enterprise being architected and the one from which the model was borrowed.*** Model differences may be the result of differences in the purpose, scope, or viewpoint of the two enterprises. Usually, few activity or ICOM name changes will be required. The area wherein most changes will have to be made is in the definitions of the activities and ICOMs
6. ***Add new activities and ICOMs as required.*** This will involve two separate actions. The first is the further decomposition of existing activities in order to provide the requisite level of detail. The second is the creation of new sections of the model (i.e., new high level activities with decompositions) to address functions not included at all in the original model.
7. ***Once the function decomposition is developed and documented, have it reviewed by SMEs for accuracy and completeness.*** If necessary, clearly define for SMEs the aspect(s) of the model on which they are to concentrate their review. Are they to review the entire model, or only a portion? Are they

to review the model structure, or only function/activity/task and ICOM naming conventions?
8. ***Incorporate SME recommendations into an updated model.***
9. ***Finalize the model.***
10. ***Identify and document operational issues and improvement opportunities resulting from model development***. In order to facilitate later actions to improve the enterprise, it is recommended that each issue and improvement opportunity be described in detail. Each issue description may also include a recommendation as to how it may be resolved, and each improvement opportunity description may include a recommendation as to how it may be capitalized upon. Additionally, they may be assigned to specific individuals or elements for action. For military architectures, relate the issues and improvement opportunities to the appropriate DTLOMS (doctrine, training, leader development, organizations, materiel and soldiers) or DOTMPLF (doctrine, organization, training, materiel, personnel, leader development, or facilities) domain.
11. ***Publish the model***.

Another Activity Model development method that may be used, but that is not recommended, is for a single modeler/SME to develop the model based on his own knowledge and expertise. This method should only be used when time and cost are constraints, and no source documents or Activity Models exist to describe the enterprise or related enterprises.

The model development methodologies described above may also be combined. For example, an initial model draft may be developed based on information from existing source documents and then further decomposed and refined in facilitated modeling workshops. Or source documents may be used as references during the conduct of facilitated workshops. Information from source documents may also be used to expand on the activities and ICOMs extracted from an existing model.

RECOMMENDED DEVELOPMENT SEQUENCE: Second, immediately after or in conjunction with the Operational Concept Description.

KEY RELATIONSHIPS:

- Operational Concept Description: The functions/activities/tasks captured in the Activity Model should be directly traceable to the high level missions, tasks and activities described in the Operational Concept Description. The ICOMs in the Activity Model should be traceable to the information exchanges shown in the Operational Concept Description. The Activity Model scope should be consistent with the scope of the Operational Concept. The Activity Model mechanisms (if they are included) should be the same as or directly traceable

to the operational elements, nodes, and systems described in the Operational Concept Description.
- Node Connectivity Description: The ICOMs in the Activity Model should be traceable to the information exchanges shown in the Node Connectivity Description. The Activity Model mechanisms (if they are included) should be the same as or directly traceable to the operational elements, nodes, and systems described in the Node Connectivity Description.
- Operational Information Exchange Matrix: The ICOMs in the Activity Model should be traceable to the information exchanges shown in the Operational Information Exchange Matrix. The Activity Model mechanisms (if they are included) should be the same as or directly traceable to the sending and receiving nodes in the Operational Information Exchange Matrix.
- Organizational Relationships Chart: The Activity Model mechanisms (if they are included) should be the same as or directly traceable to the operational elements, nodes, and systems shown in the Organizational Relationships Chart.
- Operational Activity Sequence & Timing Description: The Operational Activity Sequence and Timing Description tasks and information elements should be the same as the Activity Model activities and ICOMs. Ideally, the Operational Activity Sequence and Timing Description should be created using the same activities and information elements captured in the Activity Model.
- Logical Data Model: The data entities and attributes included in the Logical Data Model should be traceable to the ICOMs from the Activity Model. The ICOMs from the Activity Model should be decomposed into the basic elements of data of which they are composed. These basic elements of data then become the basis for defining data model entities and attributes.
- Physical Data Model: The data entities and attributes included in the Logical Data Model should be traceable to the ICOMs from the Activity Model.
- System Interface Description: The high level systems/nodes that are decomposed on the System Interface Description should be directly traceable to Activity Model mechanisms (if they are included).
- System Function Description: The system functions captured in the System Function Description should be directly traceable to activities and tasks in the Activity Model.
- Operational Activity to System Function Traceability Matrix: The Operational Activity to System Function Traceability Matrix includes the activities/tasks from the Activity Model.
- OPFAC Equipment Description: The high level nodes that are decomposed in the OPFAC Equipment Description should be directly traceable to Activity Model mechanisms (if they are included).

CRITICAL SUCCESS FACTORS:

DO'S:

- Clearly establish a purpose, scope and viewpoint for the Activity Model.
- Remain within the established model purpose, scope, and viewpoint.
- Document all activities and ICOMs in accordance with the syntax of the modeling tool selected.
- Define all activities and ICOMs in the model.
- Ensure that the Activity Model is consistent with the Operational Concept Description.
- Have SMEs validate information extracted from source documents.
- Use some method to indicate which ICOs are exchanged externally. This will facilitate the development of the Node Connectivity Description and the OIEM. Possible methods include ICO naming conventions, annotations in the ICO definitions, the use of User Defined Properties (UDPs), External Referents, notes, special color coding, and special line styles.
- Extract the activity and ICOM list from the Activity Model for presentation to high-level decision-makers.

DON'TS:

- Add unnecessary detail (i.e., extra activities and ICOMs) to the model.
- Use the same name for multiple activities or ICOMs.
- Repeat activities within the model.

CHECKLIST: The ACTIVITY MODEL

Facilitated Modeling Workshops

Process Steps	Complete
1. Identify the need for the development of an Activity Model	
2. Identify and document the model purpose, scope and viewpoint	
3. Based on the purpose, scope and viewpoint, determine the appropriate type (As-Is or To-Be) and category (system, organizational, functional area, common, integration or view) of model to be developed.	
4. Identify and gather resources and references required to support model development. Identify and notify SMEs.	
5. Conduct face-to-face interviews with SMEs not participating in the working sessions.	
6. Conduct modeling session	
7. Update the model by incorporating the results of the modeling session.	
8. Publish and distribute the updated model to modeling session participants and other specified reviewers for review and/or comment.	
9. Receive, review and respond to recommended changes to the draft model.	
10. Incorporate approved changes into an updated model draft.	
11. Repeat from step 9.	
12. Conduct additional modeling sessions as necessary.	
13. Finalize the model.	
14. Identify and document operational issues and improvement opportunities resulting from model development.	
15. Publish the final Activity Model.	

Extracting model activities from source documents

Process Steps	Complete
1. If source document function/activity/task information is grouped hierarchically in the document, use it as is or modify it slightly to fit the modeling syntax.	
2. If function/activity/task information is not grouped hierarchically identify related and equivalent tasks and group them together.	
3. Develop higher-level "parent" tasks for each related group.	
4. If function/activity/task information extracted from multiple sources, first identify how tasks from each relate to the other(s).	
5. Once the function decomposition is developed and documented, have it reviewed by SMEs for accuracy and completeness.	
6. Incorporate SME recommendations into an updated model.	
7. Finalize the model.	
8. Identify and document operational issues and improvement opportunities resulting from model development.	
9. Publish the model.	

Develop the Activity Model from an existing model

Process Steps	Complete
1. Review the existing model to identify activities and ICOMs that can be recycled.	
2. Copy the existing model and rename the copied model to reflect the enterprise being modeled.	
3. Delete from the new model unusable activities and ICOMs.	
4. Reorganize remaining activities and ICOMs as necessary to reflect the enterprise being modeled.	
5. Modify reused activity and ICOM names and/or definitions to capture subtle differences between the enterprise being architected and the one from which the model was borrowed.	
6. Add new activities and ICOMs as required.	
7. Once the function decomposition is developed and documented, have it reviewed by SMEs for accuracy and completeness.	
8. Incorporate SME recommendations into an updated model.	
9. Finalize the model.	
10. Identify and document operational issues and improvement opportunities resulting from model development.	
11. Publish the model.	

CHAPTER FOUR

PRODUCT NAME: NODE CONNECTIVITY DESCRIPTION

OTHER ALIASES: Connectivity Diagram

PRODUCT DESIGNATION: OV-2

ARCHITECTURE VIEW: OPERATIONAL

PRODUCT DEFINITION: The NODE CONNECTIVITY DESCRIPTION is a graphical depiction of those operational elements, organizations and units (i.e., nodes) that are required to exchange information directly with each other, and the types of information they are to exchange.

PRODUCT DESCRIPTION:
The Node Connectivity Description provides a graphical and textual description of the information exchanged among and between elements of the enterprise in the conduct or support of architecture functions, missions, and tasks.

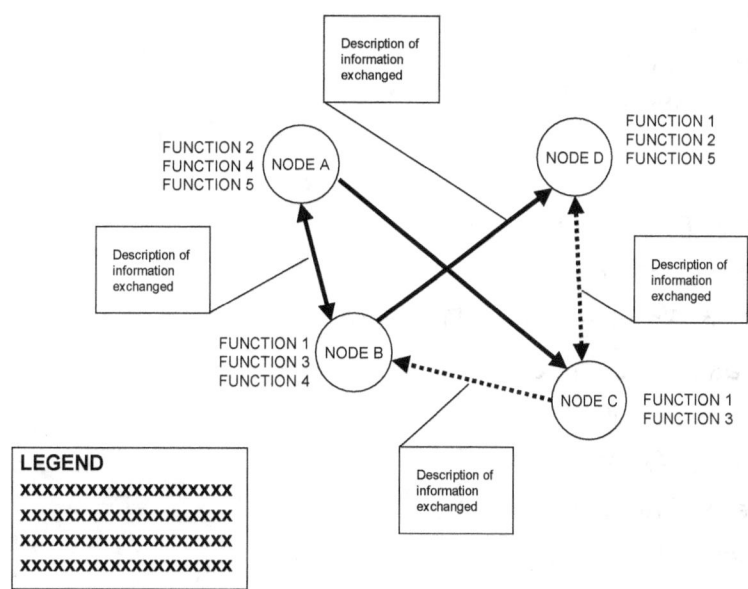

In addition to depicting connectivity among and between enterprise nodes, elements, and systems, the Node Connectivity Description also depicts connectivity between the enterprise and its external environment. It shows not simply that two nodes exchange information, but also provides information on the nature of the exchange. It may show the general types and categories of information exchanged, and the direction(s) of information flow. The Node Connectivity Description also depicts the high level functions, missions, and tasks performed by each included node.

PRODUCT FORMAT: Graphical, with textual annotations.

USERS & USES:

USERS:

Corporate/Non-Military

- Strategic Planner
- Operations Manager
- Human Resource Manager
- Information Manager
- Quality Assurance Manager
- Security Manager
- Supervisors
- Workers
- Software Developers
- Policy Writers

Military
- Combat Developer
- Concept Developer
- Program/Project/Product Developer
- Operational Architect
- Systems Architect
- Technical Architect
- Systems Engineer
- Software Developer
- Manufacturer
- Test & Evaluation Community
- Modeling & Simulation Community
- Warfighter

USES:

Corporate/Non-Military

- Strategic Business Planning
- Development of Procedures Guides and User's Manuals
- Organizational Design
- Business Process Reengineering
- Development/validation of SOPs
- Development of Capital Investment Strategies
- Quality Control/Quality Management
- Description of Required System Capabilities
- Development/Modification of Operational Concepts
- Identification of Operational Issues
- Allocation Of Communication Assets
- Communications Network Burden Assessment
- Wargaming Alternatives
- Performance of Cost/Benefits Analysis
- Development of Training Materials

Military

- Development/Modification of Operational Concepts
- Identification of Operational Issues
- Identification/Validation of Operational Needs/Requirements
- Development/Validation Of Tactics, Techniques & Procedures (TTPs)
- Development/Validation Of SOPs
- Identification Of Functional Information Requirements
- Identification of IERs
- Development/Validation Of Models & Simulations
- Allocation Of Communication Assets
- Planning For Organization Exercises
- Planning For System Tests
- Network Burden Assessment
- Identification of OPFAC Hardware Requirements
- Standardization of Processes, Activities, and Tasks

- Development/Modification Of Standard Messages
- Development/Validation of Training Plans
- Development Of System Software
- Comparing User's Vision To Developer's Implementation
- Providing Roadmap For System Improvement
- Battlefield/Business Process Reengineering
- Development of Procedures Guides and User's Manuals
- Performance of Cost/Benefits Analysis

TYPICAL INFORMATION SOURCES:

Corporate/Non-Military

- Function/Task Lists
- Organization Descriptions
- Operational Concepts
- Policy and Procedures Guides
- Standing Operating Procedures (SOPs)
- Subject Matter Experts
- Task Descriptions

Military

- Subject Matter Experts
- Policy and Procedures Guides
- Doctrinal Publications
- Operational Concepts
- Operational and Organizational Plans
- Vision Statements
- Long Range Plans
- Strategic Plans
- Modernization Plans
- Master Plans
- Organization Descriptions (including TOEs, MTOEs, TDAs)
- Function/Task Lists (including METLs, UJTL, Service Task Lists)
- Task Descriptions
- Standing Operating Procedures (SOPs)
- Interface Descriptions

TOOLS:

- Text Editor
- Drawing/Graphics Tool
- Database
- Network Design Tool

PARTICIPANTS:

Corporate/Non-Military

- Operations Manager
- Information Manager
- Security Manager
- Supervisors
- Workers
- Policy Writers
- Operational Architect/Facilitator
- Subject Matter Expert

Military

- Combat Developer
- Concept & Doctrine Developer
- Training Developer
- Operational Architect/Facilitator
- Subject Matter Expert
- Warfighter
- Program/Project/Product Developer
- Systems Architect
- Technical Architect
- Systems Engineer

PRODUCT DEVELOPMENT:

The Node Connectivity Description should be developed based on information contained in the textual Operational Concept Description, the OPCON Graphic, the Activity Model, Operational Information Exchange Matrix, SME working group sessions and/or one-on-one SME interviews, and the review of available documentation. If either the Textual Operational Concept or the OPCON Graphic has already been developed, the Node Connectivity Description should be based on the element, node, and organizational relationships described or depicted in these products. If the Activity Model already exists, and if it includes operational elements, nodes, and organizations as mechanisms (see discussion of the Activity Model), then nodes shown in the Node Connectivity Description should be based on or traceable to the Activity Model mechanisms. If the Operational Information Exchange Matrix is developed prior to the Node Connectivity Description, then the operational nodes included on the Node Connectivity Description should be directly related to the sending and receiving nodes from the Operational Information Exchange Matrix. Regardless of the origin of the information, the steps required to convert that information into a useful Node Connectivity Description is outlined below.

1. Determine the type of node connectivity diagram to be produced. The Node Connectivity Description may take on any one of three basic forms: single node centric, bi-nodal, or multi-nodal. The single node centric form shows all the interfaces associated with a single critical operational node/element. The bi-nodal form uses multiple diagrams to depict the interfaces among and between enterprise by concentrating on two nodes at a time. Each individual diagram shows the connectivity between two, and only two, operational nodes.

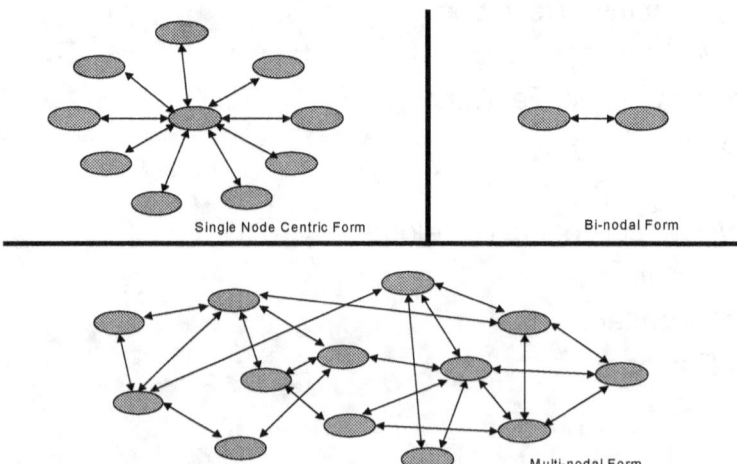

Different Forms of the Node Connectivity Description

The multi-nodal form shows on a single diagram all the operational nodes within the enterprise and the interfaces among them, as well as the external operational nodes to which enterprise nodes are connected. The most appropriate form to be used for a particular architecture is dependent, in large part, on the uses to which the Node Connectivity Description will be put.

2. Add graphical symbols to represent the appropriate operational nodes. Use either geometric shapes (e.g., circles, ovals, or rectangles), standard symbols, representative icons (e.g., small pictures of people, vehicles, computers, weapons, radios, or buildings), or a combination of these types to depict each operational node. Add a separate symbol to represent each individual node, each type of node, or each "family" of nodes.

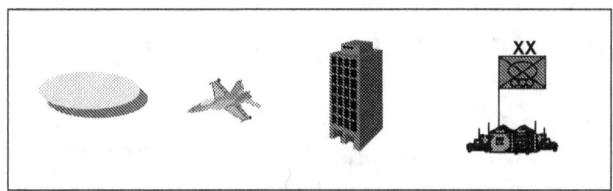

Sample Operational Node Graphical Symbols

3. Label the nodes. Place on or near each node symbol a label that indicates the name, designation, or identifier of the node; the type of node depicted; or the node's echelon of employment.

4. Connect the nodes with arrows that indicate the direction of information flow. Draw arrows to connect each pair of interfacing nodes. Connect the point of the arrow to the node(s) that is/are the recipient(s) in the information exchange—use single pointed arrows for one-way information exchanges and double pointed arrows to show two-way exchanges. If desired, use different types (e.g., bold, solid, dashed, double) or colors of arrows to provide additional information about the nature of the exchanges. For example, use solid arrows to indicate mandatory exchanges and dotted lines to reflect conditional exchanges.

5. Label the connecting arrows to indicate the information being exchanged. Place a label, box, or caption on or near each connecting arrow to indicate the information being exchanged between the interfacing nodes. The label should be a list of the actual information elements being exchanged, the general categories of information being exchanged, or a code that references a separate information list or Operational Information Exchange Matrix. Shown below are a number of ways in which connecting arrows may be labeled.

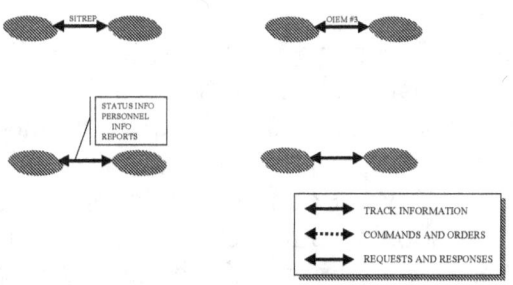

6. Add lists of high level missions and tasks performed at each node. Show the high level missions for each node in a list box placed near the symbol for the node. Only the three to five most critical functions, missions, or tasks need be shown on the Node Connectivity Description, as the missions and tasks are described in greater detail in the Activity Model and/or the Operational Activity Sequence and Timing Description. If the Textual Operational Concept Description or the OPCON Graphic has already been developed, extract the high level functions/missions/tasks from it. The functions/missions/tasks may also be extracted or derived from the Activity Model if it has been developed prior to the Node Connectivity Description.

7. Add a legend to define acronyms, terms, and symbols shown on the diagram.

8. Provide the Node Connectivity Description to SMEs for review and comment. Include information on the portions of the Node Connectivity Description to be reviewed, the types of comments to be provided, the desired comment format, the individual(s) or organization(s) to whom/which comments are to be submitted, and the suspense for comment submission.

9. Modify the Node Connectivity Description based on comments received. Update the Node Connectivity Description as necessary to incorporate accepted change recommendations resulting from the SME review.

10. Publish the final Node Connectivity Description.

RECOMMENDED DEVELOPMENT SEQUENCE: Third, following the Activity Model.

KEY RELATIONSHIPS:

- Operational Concept Description: The operational nodes, information exchanges, and high level missions and tasks shown on the Operational Node Connectivity Description should be the same as or directly traceable to those captured in the Operational Concept Description.

- Organizational Relationships Chart: Each organizational element shown on the Organizational Relationships Chart should be traceable to an operational node depicted on the Node Connectivity Description. Every command relationship on the Organizational Relationships Chart should be reflected in one or more information exchange relationships in the Node Connectivity Description.

- Operational Information Exchange Matrix: The Node Connectivity Description should graphically condense the Operational Information Exchange Matrix. The operational nodes illustrated in the Node Connectivity Description should be the same as the sending and receiving nodes described in the Operational Information Exchange Matrix. Each pair of connected nodes on the Node Connectivity Description should be reflected by a sending node-receiving node pair on the Operational Information Exchange Matrix. The elements of

information shown on the Node Connectivity Description should be directly associated with specific information exchange elements detailed in the Operational Information Exchange Matrix.
- Activity Model: The high level missions and tasks for each node shown on the Node Connectivity Description should be directly traceable to activities captured in the Activity Model. If the Activity Model includes mechanisms to represent the operational elements that perform each activity, then the operational nodes shown on the Node Connectivity Description should be directly traceable to the Activity Model mechanisms. Every information exchange element shown on the Node Connectivity Description should be traceable to one or more information elements from the Activity Model.
- System Interface Description: The operational nodes captured on the Node Connectivity Description should be decomposed on the System Interface Description to the individual systems resident at each node. The inter-nodal information exchanges shown on the System Interface Description should be directly traceable to exchanges between nodes shown on the Node Connectivity Description.
- OPFAC Equipment Description: Each OPFAC Equipment Description should describe a single node shown on the Node Connectivity Description.

CRITICAL SUCCESS FACTORS:

DO'S:
– Check for the existence of a usable Node Connectivity Description before beginning to develop a new one.
– Whenever possible, validate information extracted from source documents through SME reviews, interviews, or workshops.
– Use information contained in the Operational Concept Description or the Activity Model to identify required external information exchanges.

DON'TS:
– Don't venture outside the boundaries established by the architecture scoping statement.

CHECKLIST: The NODE CONNECTIVITY DESCRIPTION

Process Steps	Complete
1. Determine the type of node connectivity diagram to be produced—single node centric, bi-nodal, or multi-nodal.	
2. Add graphical symbols to represent the appropriate operational nodes.	
3. Label the nodes.	
4. Connect the nodes with arrows that indicate the direction of information flow.	
5. Label the connecting arrows to indicate the information being exchanged.	
6. Add lists of high level functions, missions, and tasks performed at each node.	
7. Add a legend to define acronyms, terms, and symbols shown on the diagram.	
8. Provide the Node Connectivity Description to SMEs for review and comment.	
9. Modify the Node Connectivity Description based on comments received.	
10. Publish the final Node Connectivity Description.	

CHAPTER FIVE

PRODUCT NAME: OPERATIONAL INFORMATION EXCHANGE MATRIX

OTHER ALIASES: Information Exchange Requirement, Information Exchange Matrix, IER, IER Matrix

PRODUCT DESIGNATION: OV-3

ARCHITECTURE VIEW: OPERATIONAL

PRODUCT DEFINITION: The OPERATIONAL INFORMATION EXCHANGE MATRIX provides a detailed description of the information to be exchanged between operational nodes.

PRODUCT DESCRIPTION: Operational Information Exchange Matrices identify *who* exchanges *what* information with *whom, why* the information is necessary, and in *what manner* the information is exchanged. They identify the elements of warfighter information used in support of a particular node, element, system or organization and between any two nodes, elements, systems, or organizations.

Activity Reference (Rationale)	Event/ Action	Information Chartacterization	Sending Node	Receiving Node	Critical	Format	Timeliness	Classification	Optional
Activity/Task Number	Event Name	Information Category (Specific Information Element(s))	Node Name(s)	Node Name(s)	Y/N	Information Exchange Format or Medium	Required Timeliness of Information Receipt	Security Classification Level	Additional Information
Activity/Task Number	Event Name	Information Category (Specific Information Element(s))	Node Name(s)	Node Name(s)	Y/N	Information Exchange Format or Medium	Required Timeliness of Information Receipt	Security Classification Level	Additional Information
Activity/Task Number	Event Name	Information Category (Specific Information Element(s))	Node Name(s)	Node Name(s)	Y/N	Information Exchange Format or Medium	Required Timeliness of Information Receipt	Security Classification Level	Additional Information
Activity/Task Number	Event Name	Information Category (Specific Information Element(s))	Node Name(s)	Node Name(s)	Y/N	Information Exchange Format or Medium	Required Timeliness of Information Receipt	Security Classification Level	Additional Information

There are several general types of OIEMs. One type is single node centric, and comprises all the information exchanged by or with a single node, element, system, or organization. A second type catalogs all information exchanged between two (and only two) nodes, elements, systems, and organizations. A third type addresses all information exchanges associated the members of an enterprise, functional area, or family of related systems. A fourth type describes the information exchanged between a single node and the members of an enterprise, functional area, or family of related systems. A fifth type defines the information exchanges between the members of one enterprise, functional area, or family of systems and the members of another. A sixth type covers all information exchanges associated with a particular operation, mission, event, or activity.

The OIEM includes two different categories of information. The first information category is fairly consistent across all matrices, regardless of their use. It is the description of the information element to be exchanged. Specific elements of data that fall into this category include the name of the information element and the names of the sending and receiving nodes. Other optional data elements that may be a part of this category include the producing and consuming activities; the task, mission, or event supported by the information element; and the generic information category to which the specific information exchange element belongs.

The second category of information captured in the OIEM is information about the nature of the exchange. This category includes both qualitative and quantitative data elements. Qualitative data elements include, but are not limited to: the timeframe in which the exchange is or will be implemented, the formatted message used to effect the information exchange, the exchange medium, the security classification of the information being exchanged, the precedence of the exchange, the operational impact of not conducting the exchange, the status of the exchange, and the directionality of the exchange. Quantitative data elements include, but are not limited to: the physical size of the message to be exchanged, the frequency of the exchange, the perishability of the information being exchanged, and the required speed of service.

The actual qualitative and quantitative data elements captured in a particular OIEM are dependent on the uses to which the matrix will be put. For some common uses, standard matrix formats have already been established. For other uses, the format should be defined cooperatively by the producer(s) of the matrix and the expected user(s).

PRODUCT FORMAT: Best as a Database, but may be captured as a Table or Spreadsheet.

USERS & USES:

USERS:

Corporate/Non-Military

- Strategic Planner
- Operations Manager
- Human Resource Manager
- Information Manager
- Quality Assurance Manager
- Security Manager
- Supervisors
- Workers
- Software Developers
- Policy Writers

Military
- Combat Developer
- Concept Developer
- Trainer
- Training Developer
- Program/Project/Product Developer
- Operational Architect
- Systems Architect
- Technical Architect
- Systems Engineer
- Software Developer
- Manufacturer
- Test & Evaluation Community
- Modeling & Simulation Community
- Warfighter

USES:

Corporate/Non-Military

- Strategic Business Planning
- Development of Procedures Guides and User's Manuals
- Business Process Reengineering
- Development/validation of SOPs
- Development of Capital Investment Strategies
- Quality Control/Quality Management
- Description of Required System Capabilities
- Development/Modification of Operational Concepts
- Identification of Operational Issues
- Allocation Of Communication Assets
- Communications Network Burden Assessment
- Wargaming Alternatives
- Performance of Cost/Benefits Analysis
- Development of Training Materials

Military

- Development/Modification of Operational Concepts
- Identification of Operational Issues
- Identification/Validation of Operational Needs/Requirements
- Standardization of Processes, Activities and Tasks
- Development/Validation Of Tactics, Techniques & Procedures (TTPs)
- Development/Validation Of SOPs
- Identification Of Functional Information Requirements
- Identification of IERs
- Development/Validation Of Models & Simulations
- Allocation Of Communication Assets
- Development/Validation Of Mission Training Plans
- Planning For Organization Exercises
- Planning For System Tests
- Network Burden Assessment
- Identification of OPFAC Hardware Requirements

- Data Modeling
- Standardization of Data Elements
- Development/Modification Of Standard Messages
- Development Of System Software
- Comparing User's Vision To Developer's Implementation
- Baselining Of Functionality
- Wargaming Alternatives
- Prioritizing Activities For Implementation
- Providing Roadmap For System Improvement
- Battlefield/Business Process Reengineering
- Development of Procedures Guides and User's Manuals
- Design of Human-Computer Interface
- Performance of Cost/Benefits Analysis
- Development of Training Materials

TYPICAL INFORMATION SOURCES:

Corporate/Non-Military

- Function/Task Lists
- Organization Descriptions
- Operational Concepts
- Policy and Procedures Guides
- Standing Operating Procedures (SOPs)
- Subject Matter Experts
- Task Descriptions

Military

- Subject Matter Experts
- Policy and Procedures Guides
- Doctrinal Publications
- Operational Concepts
- Operational and Organizational Plans
- Vision Statements
- Future Operational Capabilities (FOCs)
- Long Range Plans

- Strategic Plans
- Modernization Plans
- Master Plans
- Organization Descriptions (including TOEs, MTOEs, TDAs)
- Function/Task Lists (including METLs, UJTL, Service Task Lists)
- Task Descriptions
- Standing Operating Procedures (SOPs)
- Interface Descriptions
- System Descriptions

TOOLS:

- Text Editor
- Database
- Network Design Tool
- Flow Charting Tool

PARTICIPANTS:

Corporate/Non-Military

- Operations Manager
- Information Manager
- Security Manager
- Supervisors
- Workers
- Policy Writers
- Operational Architect/Facilitator
- Subject Matter Expert

Military

- Combat Developer
- Concept & Doctrine Developer
- Training Developer
- Force Developer
- Operational Architect/Facilitator
- Subject Matter Expert

- Warfighter
- Program/Project/Product Developer
- Systems Architect
- Technical Architect
- Systems Engineer

PRODUCT DEVELOPMENT:

The OIEM provides a detailed description of the information to be exchanged between two operational elements, operational facilities, nodes, organizations or systems (hereinafter referred to as nodes). As with most other architecture products, there are a number of different methods that can be used to develop the matrix. The primary distinction among the different methods is the source of the information that forms the basis of the matrix. This information may be developed through interviews and discussions with SMEs; extracted from documents such as SOPs, interface descriptions, requirements documents, or functional descriptions; or extracted from other architecture products such as the Operational Concept description, the Node Connectivity Description, or the Activity Model. The determination of the best method to use is determined by the availability and comprehensiveness of these information sources. The preferred method is to base the OIEM on the information contained in the Activity Models of the two interfacing nodes, systems, or organizations. Basing the OIEM on the information flows depicted in the Activity Models ensures that each element of information exchange can be justified as supporting a validated task and that no information needed in the performance of the tasks is omitted from the matrix.

Developing the OIEM Based on a Crosswalk of Two Activity Models

1. Extract the appropriate external inputs, controls and outputs (ICOs) from the Activity Models of the interfacing nodes. Not all Activity Model ICOs are captured in the OIEM—only those that represent information exchanged with external nodes, elements, systems, and organizations. The Activity Model may explicitly identify those ICOs that are exchanged externally either in the name(s) or definition(s) of the ICOM(s), or through the use of User Defined Properties (UDPs), External Referents, notes, special color coding, or special line styles. If the Activity Model does not explicitly indicate the ICOs that are externally exchanged, it will be necessary to identify these ICOs based on cues provided by the ICO names and definitions and the activities with which the ICOs are associated. The external ICOs are captured in the first column of the OIEM and additional detail is added as described in step five below. However, not every externally exchanged ICO will be captured directly in the OIEM. If the Activity Model ICO represents information that is normally exchanged as a single transmission or in a single message, then the ICO probably should be captured in the OIEM without change. If, however, the ICO does not represent a single information exchange transmission then it must be either aggregated (i.e., multiple ICOs combined into a new, higher level information element) or decomposed (i.e., a single ICO broken down into two or more lower level information elements) to the point where a single exchange is represented.

2. Add the names of the sending and receiving nodes to the OIEM. The sending and receiving nodes are the nodes, systems, or organizations for which each of the respective Activity Models were developed. Enter the standard name(s) or designation(s) of the sending and receiving nodes in the appropriate columns of the matrix. At least one sending node name/designator and at least one receiving node name/designator must be entered for each exchanged information element. Multiple nodes also may be entered in either or both columns.

3. Conduct a crosswalk of the ICOs from the Activity Models of the two interfacing nodes, systems, or organizations. For those external interfaces for which an Activity Model of both interfacing nodes exists, the next step of the OIEM development process is the conduct of a crosswalk of the two Activity Models. Ideally, the developers of the Activity Models for both interfacing nodes, or other individuals knowledgeable of the contents of the models and the meanings of the activities and ICOs contained in them, should participate in the crosswalks. An acceptable, though not desirable, alternative is for a single individual who is knowledgeable of at least one of the models to conduct an independent crosswalk.

In conducting the crosswalk, the external outputs from one interfacing node are compared to the external inputs and controls of the other node to identify ICO (arrow) correspondences and/or disconnects. The comparisons are made on three levels. First, arrow names are compared, and identical or similar names are tentatively associated with each other. For example, if both models contain arrows named "Reports", then those arrows are tentatively associated with each other. Also, if one model contains an input named "Weather Information" and the other contains an output named "Environmental Condition Report", those two arrows would be tentatively associated. Next, the arrow definitions are compared to further refine the tentative associations. Finally, the contexts within which the arrows are used are compared, as the level of detail contained in the definitions may vary widely, and the real intent of a definition may be ambiguous until it is examined in context. This three-level analysis should result in a good understanding of arrow correspondences and/or disconnects between the two models.

Arrow correspondences are situations in which an input or control from one model is directly related to one or more outputs from the other model, or vice versa. Arrow disconnects may be in the form of inputs/controls appearing in one model with no corresponding output arrow in the other model; arrows in both models with the same or similar names but different definitions; or arrows in both models with different names but the same or similar definitions. For both arrow correspondences and arrow disconnects, a crosswalk matrix similar to the one shown in the table below should be developed to document the relationship between model arrows. The crosswalk matrix should include at least three columns. The first column will contain a listing of all the external ICOs from one of the two models. The second column will contain the ICOs from the second model that are related to the ICOs in the first column. The third column will describe what, if any, changes to either model are required and/or agreed to in order to resolve any identified disconnects.

MODEL 1 ICO	MODEL 2 ICO	REMARKS
Information Element 1	Report A	
Information Element 2	Table B	
Information Element 3	Information Element C	Information Element C combines Information Elements 1 and 3 from Model 1.
Information Element 4	Information Element D	
Information Element 5	Report E	Same Element. Change name of Report E to Information Element 5

4. Resolve differences in the information element names and descriptions captured in the two Activity Models. Arrow correspondences and the last two categories of disconnects require no changes to either model, and can be captured in the first column of the OIEM. For the first category of arrow disconnects, changes to either or both Activity Models may be required to resolve the disconnects. In step three of the process, the proponents for both nodes must agree on the specific changes to be made to either or both models, and capture their agreement in the "Remarks" column of the crosswalk matrix. If the individuals conducting the crosswalk are not the owners of the Activity Models, then they must submit to the model owners any proposed changes to the activities and ICOs prior to incorporating them into the respective models. Resolved arrow disconnects are documented in the first column of the OIEM.

5. Complete the OIEM by adding appropriate technical/performance data. Step five of the process is the completion of the OIEM through the inclusion of technical data such as the information transmission medium, the frequency of exchange, the information precedence, the information classification, the cost of information exchange failure and the size of the message or information element to be exchanged. The specific elements of technical or performance data to be included in the OIEM are dependent on the use to which the matrix will be put. For some uses, standard matrix formats have been defined and should be used. For other uses, the format should be determined cooperatively by the matrix developer and the known user(s). After determining the elements of technical and performance data to be included in the matrix, the next step is to actually populate the selected data fields. Technical and performance information to complete the OIEMs may be contained in and extracted from appropriate databases, standing operating procedures (SOPs), message descriptions, available system interface description documents, SME input and insights from experimentation and exercises.

6. Provide the OIEM to SMEs for review and comment. Reviewers should include members or representatives of both interfacing nodes. The review

should focus on ensuring that the technical/performance parameters captured in the matrix support node, system, or organization operations.
7. Update the OIEM based on the comments received. OIEM changes should be incorporated into the Activity Models as appropriate.
8. Finalize and publish the OIEM.

Developing the OIEM from a Single Activity Model
An alternative to developing the OIEM from a crosswalk of the Activity Models of the two interfacing nodes is to develop the matrix from a single Activity Model. This may be necessary if no Activity Model exists for one of the interfacing nodes. The steps in developing the matrix using this method are:

1. Extract the appropriate external inputs, controls and outputs (ICOs) from the Activity Model. It must be assumed that the information exchange ICOs in the Activity Model accurately depict all information exchanges between the node, system, or organization depicted in the model and the external node, system, or organization for which no model is available. The external ICOs are captured in the first column of the OIEM and additional detail is added as described in step three below.
2. Enter the names of the sending and receiving nodes into the matrix. The sending and receiving nodes may be identified as mechanisms in the Activity Model. If not described as Activity Model mechanisms, the sending and receiving nodes may also be directly described in, or implied by, the definitions of the respective ICOs. They may also be indicated through the use of UDPs, External Referents, notes, special color coding, or special line styles.
3. Complete the OIEM by adding appropriate technical/performance data. The next step of the process is the completion of the OIEM through the inclusion of technical data such as the information transmission medium, the frequency of exchange, the information precedence, the information classification, the cost of information exchange failure and the size of the message or information element to be exchanged. Technical information to complete the OIEMs may be contained in and extracted from appropriate databases, standing operating procedures (SOPs), message descriptions, available system interface description documents, SME input and insights from experimentation and exercises.
4. Provide the OIEM to SMEs for review and comment. Reviewers should include members or representatives of both interfacing nodes, not just representatives of the node depicted in the available Activity Model. The review should focus on ensuring that the technical/performance parameters captured in the matrix support node, system, or organization operations.
5. Update the OIEM based on the comments received. OIEM changes should be incorporated into the Activity Models as appropriate.
6. Finalize and publish the OIEM.

Developing the OIEM from the Operational Concept Description or the Node Connectivity Description

The OIEM may also be developed without an Activity Model. If no Activity Model exists, the next best source of information is the information exchange descriptions in the Operational Concept Description and/or the Node Connectivity Description. The steps of this development methodology are essentially the same as those for developing the matrix from a single Activity Model—only the source of the information elements is different.

1. Extract the appropriate external information exchange elements from the Operational Concept Description and/or the Node Connectivity Description. It may (probably will) be necessary to further decompose the high level information exchange elements depicted in the Operational Concept Description or Nodes Connectivity Description in order to provide the level of detail required in the OIEM. The external information exchange elements are captured in the first column of the OIEM and additional detail is added as described in step three below.

2. Include the names of the sending and receiving nodes in the matrix. The sending and receiving nodes are depicted or described as the operational nodes, systems, elements and organizations in the Operational Concept Description or the Node Connectivity Description.

3. Complete the OIEM by adding appropriate technical/performance data. Step three of the process is the completion of the OIEM through the inclusion of technical data such as the information transmission medium, the frequency of exchange, the information precedence, the information classification, the cost of information exchange failure and the size of the message or information element to be exchanged. Technical information to complete the OIEMs may be contained in and extracted from appropriate databases, standing operating procedures (SOPs), message descriptions, available system interface description documents, SME input and insights from experimentation and exercises.

4. Provide the OIEM to SMEs for review and comment. Reviewers should include members or representatives of both interfacing nodes. The review should focus on ensuring that node, system, or organization operations are supported by the technical/performance parameters captured in the matrix.

5. Update the OIEM based on the comments received. Changes in the OIEM should be incorporated into the information exchange descriptions in the Operational Concept Description and/or the Node Connectivity Description as appropriate.

6. Finalize and publish the OIEM.

Other OIEM Development Methods

The OIEM may also be developed without an existing Operational Concept Description, Activity Model, or Node Connectivity Description. Information exchange elements and sending and receiving nodes must be extracted from available system or organization description documents, interface descriptions, SOPs, or other doctrinal or operational publications and manuals. Alternatively, the information exchange elements and sending and receiving nodes may be identified through interviews with SMEs or the conduct of facilitated workshops.

RECOMMENDED DEVELOPMENT SEQUENCE: Fourth, following the Node Connectivity Description.

KEY RELATIONSHIPS:

- Operational Concept Description: The information exchange elements captured in the OIEM should be the same as or directly traceable to the information exchange elements captured in the Operational Concept Description. The sending and receiving nodes in the OIEM should be the same as or directly traceable to operational elements, nodes, systems, or organizations described in the Operational Concept Description.
- Node Connectivity Description: The information exchange elements captured in the OIEM should be the same as or directly traceable to the information exchange elements captured in the Node Connectivity Description. The sending and receiving nodes in the OIEM should be the same as or directly traceable to operational elements, nodes, systems, or organizations described in the Node Connectivity Description.
- Activity Model: The information exchange elements captured in the OIEM should be the same as or directly traceable to the externally exchanged ICOs captured in the Activity Model. The sending and receiving nodes shown in the OIEM should be the same as or directly traceable to the mechanisms in the Activity Model, if those mechanisms represent nodes, systems, elements, or organizations.
- Organizational Relationships Chart: The sending and receiving nodes in the OIEM should be the same as or directly traceable to operational elements, nodes, systems, or organizations described in the Organizational Relationships Chart. The information exchange elements captured in the OIEM should be consistent with the types of relationships captured in the Organizational Relationships Chart. For example, the OIEM for a relationship shown as coordination only should not include information associated with exchange of commands and orders from a higher echelon organization to a subordinate.
- Logical Data Model: The metadata associated with attributes in the Logical Data Model should be consistent with or directly traceable to the technical and performance parameters captured in the OIEM.
- Physical Data Model: The metadata associated with attributes in the Physical Data Model should be consistent with or directly traceable to the technical and performance parameters captured in the OIEM.
- System Data Exchange Matrix: The System Data Exchange Matrix should be directly traceable to the OIEM, as it reflects the system implementation of the

operational requirements captured in the OIEM. Each data exchange element in the System Data Exchange Matrix should be directly traceable to one or more information exchange elements from the OIEM. The sending and receiving system nodes identified in the System Data Exchange Matrix should be a subordinate component of or directly traceable to one or more sending or receiving operational nodes, systems, elements, or organizations identified in the OIEM.
- Technical Architecture Profile: The technical and performance parameters captured in the OIEM should be in accordance with the technical standards specified in the Technical Architecture Profile.
- Standards Technology Forecast: The technical and performance parameters shown in the OIEM may include allowances for the implementation of future technical standards as described in the Standards Technology Forecast. If such future standards are included in the OIEM, they should be identified clearly, to include the timeframe within which they are expected to be implemented. For example, an information exchange using an exchange medium that will not be available or acquired until 2010 should be identified as a future requirement and further annotated with an indication that the exchange is expected to be effective after 2010.

CRITICAL SUCCESS FACTORS:

DO'S:
– Include in the matrix information to indicate the temporal nature of each information exchange.
– Show all information exchange media that may be used to satisfy a particular information exchange requirement.
– Include in the matrix information to indicate the primary information exchange medium for those exchanges that may be executed via multiple means.
– Ensure that the sending and receiving nodes identified in the OIEM match those shown in the Node Connectivity Description.

DON'TS:
– Don't limit the OIEM to the documentation of information exchanges that are or will be implemented through the use of formatted messages.
– Don't include in the matrix information that is only exchanged internally.

CHECKLIST: The OPERATIONAL INFORMATION EXCHANGE MATRIX

Developing the OIEM Based on a Crosswalk of Two Activity Models

Process Steps	Complete
1. Extract the appropriate external inputs, controls and outputs (ICOs) from the Activity Models of the interfacing nodes	
2. Add the names of the sending and receiving nodes to the OIEM.	
3. Conduct a crosswalk of the ICOs from the Activity Models of the two interfacing nodes, systems, or organizations	
4. Resolve differences in the information element names and descriptions captured in the two Activity Models.	
5. Complete the OIEM by adding appropriate technical/performance data.	
6. Provide the OIEM to SMEs for review and comment.	
7. Update the OIEM based on the comments received.	
8. Finalize and publish the OIEM.	

Developing the OIEM from a Single Activity Model

Process Steps	Complete
1. Extract the appropriate external inputs, controls and outputs (ICOs) from the Activity Model.	
2. Enter the names of the sending and receiving nodes to the matrix.	
3. Complete the OIEM by adding appropriate technical/performance data.	
4. Provide the OIEM to SMEs for review and comment.	
5. Update the OIEM based on the comments received.	
6. Finalize and publish the OIEM.	

Developing the OIEM from the Operational Concept Description or the Node Connectivity Description

Process Steps	Complete
1. Extract the appropriate external information exchange elements from the Operational Concept Description and/or the Node Connectivity Description.	
2. Include the names of the sending and receiving nodes in the matrix.	
3. Complete the OIEM by adding appropriate technical/performance data.	
3. Provide the OIEM to SMEs for review and comment.	
4. Update the OIEM based on the comments received.	
5. Finalize and publish the OIEM.	

CHAPTER SIX

PRODUCT NAME: ORGANIZATIONAL RELATIONSHIPS CHART

OTHER ALIASES: Command Relationship Diagram, Command Relationship Chart, Organization Chart, Wiring Diagram

PRODUCT DESIGNATION: OV-4

ARCHITECTURE VIEW: OPERATIONAL

PRODUCT DEFINITION: The ORGANIZATIONAL RELATIONSHIPS CHART is a graphical depiction of the operational elements involved in a process and the lines of command, control and coordination among those operational elements.

PRODUCT DESCRIPTION: The Organizational Relationships Chart illustrates the relationships among organizations or resources in the architecture. These relationships can include command and control, coordination relationships (which influence what connectivity is needed), and many others, depending on the purpose of the architecture. These relationships are important to show in an operational view of the architecture because they illustrate fundamental roles and management relationships. For example, command and control relationships may differ under different circumstances. Differing command relationships may mean that activities are performed differently or by different organizations. Different coordination relationships may mean that connectivity requirements are changed.

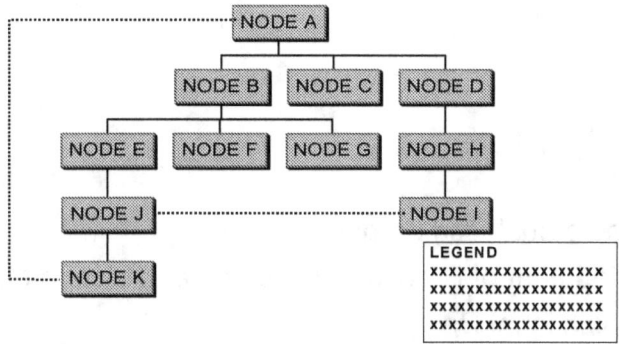

PRODUCT FORMAT: Graphical, with textual annotations

USERS & USES:

USERS:

Corporate/Non-Military

- Strategic Planner
- Operations Manager
- Human Resource Manager
- Quality Assurance Manager
- Security Manager
- Supervisors
- Workers
- Software Developers
- Policy Writers

Military
- Combat Developer
- Concept Developer
- Trainer
- Training Developer
- Force Developer
- Operational Architect
- Systems Architect
- Test & Evaluation Community
- Modeling & Simulation Community
- Warfighter

USES:

Corporate/Non-Military

- Strategic Business Planning
- Development of Procedures Guides and User's Manuals
- Organizational Design
- Identification of Personnel Requirements
- Business Process Reengineering

- Development/validation of SOPs
- Development of Capital Investment Strategies
- Quality Control/Quality Management
- Description of Required System Capabilities
- Development/Modification of Operational Concepts
- Identification of Operational Issues
- Allocation Of Communication Assets
- Communications Network Burden Assessment
- Wargaming Alternatives
- Performance of Cost/Benefits Analysis
- Development of Training Materials

Military

- Development/Modification of Operational Concepts
- Identification of Operational Issues
- Identification/Validation of Operational Needs/Requirements
- Standardization of Processes, Activities and Tasks
- Development/Validation Of Tactics, Techniques & Procedures (TTPs)
- Development/Validation Of SOPs
- Identification of IERs
- Development of System Software
- Development/Validation Of Models & Simulations
- Allocation Of Communication Assets
- Development/Validation Of Mission Training Plans
- Planning For Organization Exercises
- Planning For System Tests
- Wargaming Alternatives
- Battlefield/Business Process Reengineering
- Development of Procedures Guides and User's Manuals
- Development of Training Materials

TYPICAL INFORMATION SOURCES:

Corporate/Non-Military

- Function/Task Lists
- Organization Descriptions
- Operational Concepts
- Policy and Procedures Guides
- Standing Operating Procedures (SOPs)
- Subject Matter Experts
- Task Descriptions

Military

- Subject Matter Experts
- Policy and Procedures Guides
- Doctrinal Publications
- Operational Concepts
- Operational and Organizational Plans
- Vision Statements
- Long Range Plans
- Strategic Plans
- Master Plans
- Organization Descriptions (including TOEs, MTOEs, TDAs)
- Function/Task Lists (including METLs, UJTL, Service Task Lists)
- Task Descriptions
- Standing Operating Procedures (SOPs)
- Interface Descriptions

TOOLS:

- Text Editor
- Drawing/Graphics Tool

PARTICIPANTS:

Corporate/Non-Military

- Operations Manager
- Information Manager
- Security Manager
- Supervisors
- Workers
- Policy Writers
- Operational Architect/Facilitator
- Subject Matter Expert

Military

- Combat Developer
- Concept & Doctrine Developer
- Training Developer
- Force Developer
- Operational Architect/Facilitator
- Subject Matter Expert
- Warfighter

PRODUCT DEVELOPMENT:

The Organizational Relationships Chart should be developed based on information contained in the textual Operational Concept Description, the OPCON Graphic, the Activity model, the Node Connectivity Description, the Operational Information Exchange Matrix, SME working group sessions and/or one-on-one SME interviews, and the review of available documentation. If either the Textual Operational Concept or the OPCON Graphic has already been developed, the Organizational Relationships Chart should be based on the element, node, and organizational relationships described or depicted in these products. If the Activity Model already exists, and if it includes operational elements, nodes, and organizations as mechanisms (see discussion of the Activity Model), then nodes shown in the Organizational Relationships Chart should be based on or traceable to Activity Model mechanisms. If the Node Connectivity Description is produced prior to the Organizational Relationships Chart, then the Organizational Relationships Chart should be developed based directly on, or as a subset of, the node relationships shown in the Node Connectivity Description. If the Operational Information Exchange Matrix is developed prior to the Organizational Relationships Chart, then the operational nodes included on the Organizational Relationships Chart should be directly related to the sending and receiving nodes from the Operational Information Exchange Matrix. Regardless of the origin of the information, the steps required to convert that information into a useful Organizational Relationships Chart is outlined below.

1. Add graphical symbols to represent the appropriate organizational nodes. Use either geometric shapes (e.g., circles, ovals, or rectangles), standard military symbology such as that described in Military Standard (MIL STD) 2525, representative icons (e.g., small pictures of vehicles, weapons, radios, or buildings), or a combination of these types to depict each organizational node. Add a separate symbol to represent each individual node, each type of node, or each "family" of nodes.

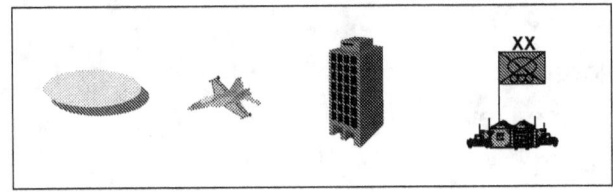

Sample Organizational Node Graphical Symbols

2. Label the nodes. Place on or near each node symbol a label that indicates the name, designation, or identifier of the node; the type of node depicted; or the node's echelon of employment.

3. Connect the nodes with arrows that indicate the existence of a command, control, or coordination relationship and to show the direction of any information flow. Draw arrows to connect the interfacing nodes. Connect the point of the arrow to the node(s) that is/are the subordinates in the relationship or that are the recipient(s) in the information exchange—use single pointed arrows for one-way information exchanges and double pointed arrows to show two-way exchanges. If desired, use different types (e.g., bold, solid, dashed, double) or colors of arrows to provide additional information about the nature of the relationship and/or the information exchanges. For example, use solid arrows to indicate command relationships and dotted lines to reflect operational control relationships.

4. Label the connecting arrows to indicate the nature of the relationship. Place a label, box, or caption on or near each connecting arrow to indicate the type of relationship that exists between the nodes. Types of relationships that may be depicted on the chart include, but are not limited to: command, control, coordination, support, augmentation, reinforcement, liaison, attachment, detachment, partnership, subsidiary, tactical control (TACON), and operational

98

control (OPCON). Relationships may also be depicted as permanent, temporary, or conditional.

5. Add a legend to define acronyms, terms, and symbols shown on the diagram.

6. Provide the Organizational Relationships Chart to SMEs for review and comment. Include information on the portions of the Organizational Relationships Chart to be reviewed, the types of comments to be provided, the desired comment format, the individual(s) or organization(s) to whom/which comments are to be submitted, and the suspense for comment submission.

7. Modify the Organizational Relationships Chart based on comments received. Update the Organizational Relationships Chart as necessary to incorporate approved change recommendations resulting from the SME review.

8. Publish the final Organizational Relationships Chart.

RECOMMENDED DEVELOPMENT SEQUENCE: Fifth, following the Operational Information Exchange Matrix. May also be developed in conjunction with the Node Connectivity Description.

KEY RELATIONSHIPS:

- Operational Concept Description: The operational nodes, relationships, and information exchanges shown on the Organizational Relationships Chart should be the same as or directly traceable to those captured in the Operational Concept Description.

- Node Connectivity Description: Each organizational element shown on the Organizational Relationships Chart should be traceable to an operational node depicted on the Node Connectivity Description. Every command relationship on the Organizational Relationships Chart should be reflected in one or more information exchange relationships in the Node Connectivity Description.

- Operational Information Exchange Matrix: The organizational nodes illustrated in the Organizational Relationships Chart should be traceable to the sending and receiving nodes described in the Operational Information Exchange Matrix.

- Activity Model: If the Activity Model includes mechanisms to represent the operational elements that perform each activity, then the organizational nodes shown on the Organizational Relationships Chart should be directly traceable to Activity Model mechanisms. Every information exchange element shown on the Organizational Relationships Chart should be traceable to one or more information elements from the Activity Model.

- System Interface Description: The organizational nodes captured on the Organizational Relationships Chart should be decomposed on the System Interface Description to the individual systems resident at each node. The inter-nodal information exchanges shown on the System Interface Description

should be directly traceable to exchanges between nodes shown on the Organizational Relationships Chart.
- OPFAC Equipment Description: Each OPFAC Equipment Description should describe a single organizational node shown on the Organizational Relationships Chart.

CRITICAL SUCCESS FACTORS:

DO'S:
- Capture both permanent and temporary relationships.
- Add text to further describe the relationships depicted on the chart.
- Develop multiple Organizational Relationship Charts to show how relationships change as a result of the tactical situation, the timeframe, or the theater of employment.
- Ensure that the nodes and relationships shown on the Organizational Relationships Chart are traceable to those captured in other architecture products such as the Operational Concept Description, the Node Connectivity Description, the Activity Model, and the Operational Information Exchange Matrix.

DON'TS:
- Do not confuse the relationships shown on the Organizational Relationships Chart with the information exchange relationships shown on the Node Connectivity Description.

CHECKLIST: The ORGANIZATIONAL RELATIONSHIPS CHART

Process Steps	Completed
1. Add graphical symbols to represent the appropriate operational nodes.	
2. Label the nodes.	
3. Connect the nodes with arrows that indicate the existence of a command, control, or coordination relationship and to show the direction of any information flow.	
4. Label the connecting arrows to indicate the nature of the relationship.	
5. Add a legend to define acronyms, terms, and symbols shown on the diagram.	
6. Provide the Organizational Relationships Chart to SMEs for review and comment.	
7. Modify the Organizational Relationships Chart based on comments received.	
8. Publish the final Organizational Relationships Chart.	

CHAPTER SEVEN

PRODUCT NAME: LOGICAL DATA MODEL

OTHER ALIASES: Data Model, Data Description, Data Element Description, Class Diagram, Entity Relationship Diagram, Entity Relationship Model

PRODUCT DESIGNATION: OV-7

ARCHITECTURE VIEW: OPERATIONAL

PRODUCT DEFINITION: The LOGICAL DATA MODEL provides a system-independent description of the data elements and data structures required to support the performance of functions described in the Activity Model.

PRODUCT DESCRIPTION: The Logical Data Model is used to document the data requirements and structural business process rules of the architecture's operational view. It describes the data and information that is associated with the information exchanges of the architecture, within the scope and to the level of detail required for the purposes of the architecture. Included are information items and/or data elements, their attributes or characteristics, and their interrelationships.

To fully appreciate the importance of the Data Model, one must first understand the relationship of "data" to "information". Data can be defined as basic facts about real world objects, concepts, or events. Information can be defined as a group of related facts to support a particular purpose or need. Essentially, data are the basic building blocks from which information is constructed. The same data elements, when combined in different ways, can generate many elements of information, just as the hundred or so naturally occurring elements of the periodic table can be combined to produce the millions of chemical compounds that make up the universe. Conversely, it is possible to distill a large number of seemingly disparate information elements down to a relatively small number of data elements with multiple interrelationships.

Currently, much interoperability among operational nodes, elements, systems, and organizations is accomplished through the exchange of highly formatted information packets commonly known as messages and reports. Often, the same element of information is included in multiple messages or reports. For example, nearly every message and report contains the name or designation of the sending organization. If it were possible to identify, document, and exchange the basic data elements that support enterprise operations and information exchange requirements, it would be possible to achieve (or even increase) interoperability while reducing the demand on the communications network used to transmit the information.

The Logical Data Model is the Operational Architecture view of the enterprise data requirements. It defines data elements, data structures, and data element relationships. The data elements identified in the Logical Data Model are directly traceable to information elements captured in the Operational Concept Description, the Activity Model, and the Operational Information Exchange Matrix.

It should be noted that a data model is not the same as an executable database. A well-defined logical data model should be independent of any node or organization that may use it, any use to which it may be put, or any database management system (DBMS) by which it may be implemented. A database, on the other hand, should be tailored specifically to the needs of the using node/organization, the intended use(s), and the selected DBMS.

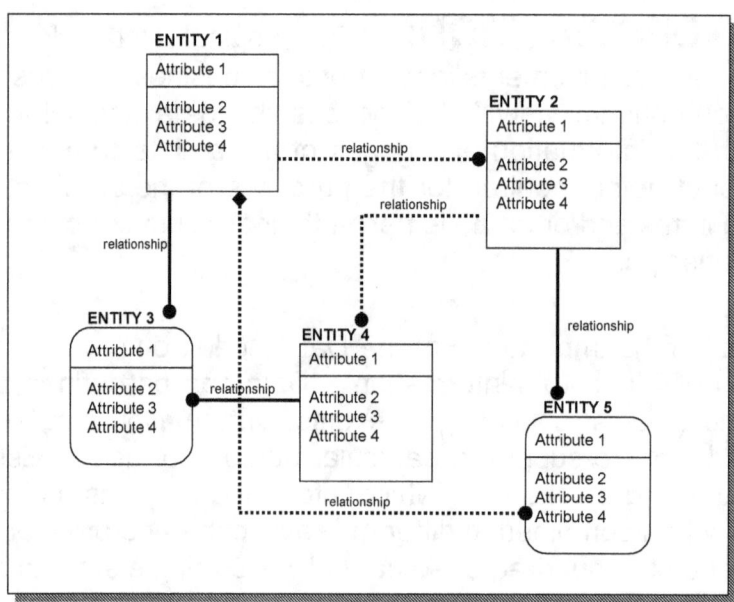

PRODUCT FORMAT: Graphics and text

USERS & USES:

USERS:

Corporate/Non-Military

- Information Manager
- Quality Assurance Manager
- Security Manager
- Workers
- Software Developers
- Research and Development

Military

- Combat Developer
- Concept Developer
- Program/Project/Product Developer
- Operational Architect
- Systems Architect
- Technical Architect
- Systems Engineer
- Software Developer
- Manufacturer
- Test & Evaluation Community
- Modeling & Simulation Community

USES:

Corporate/Non-Military

- Business Process Reengineering
- Quality Control/Quality Management
- Description of Required System Capabilities
- Database Design
- Performance of Cost/Benefits Analysis
- Development of Training Materials

Military

- Standardization of Processes, Activities and Tasks
- Identification/Validation of Operational Needs & Requirements
- Development/Validation Of Tactics, Techniques & Procedures (TTPs)
- Development/Validation Of SOPs
- Identification Of Functional Information Requirements
- Identification of IERs
- Development/Validation Of Models & Simulations
- Planning For Organization Exercises
- Planning For System Tests
- Data Modeling
- Standardization of Data Elements
- Development/Modification Of Standard Messages
- Development Of System Software
- Comparing User's Vision To Developer's Implementation
- Baselining Of Functionality
- Providing Roadmap For System Improvement
- Battlefield/Business Process Reengineering
- Development of Procedures Guides and User's Manuals
- Design of Human-Computer Interface
- Performance of Cost/Benefits Analysis

TYPICAL INFORMATION SOURCES:

Corporate/Non-Military

- Function/Task Lists
- Long Range Plans
- Organization Descriptions
- Operational Concepts
- Policy and Procedures Guides
- Standing Operating Procedures (SOPs)
- Strategic Plans
- Subject Matter Experts
- System Descriptions

- Task Descriptions
- Vision Statements
- Business Plans
- Corporate Brochures
- Annual Reports

Military

- Subject Matter Experts
- Policy and Procedures Guides
- Doctrinal Publications
- Operational Concepts
- Operational and Organizational Plans
- Vision Statements
- Future Operational Capabilities (FOCs)
- Long Range Plans
- Strategic Plans
- Master Plans
- Organization Descriptions (including TOEs, MTOEs, TDAs)
- Function/Task Lists (including METLs, UJTL, Service Task Lists)
- Task Descriptions
- Standing Operating Procedures (SOPs)
- Interface Descriptions
- System Descriptions

TOOLS:

- Text Editor
- Data Modeling Tool
- Database
- Object Modeling Tool

PARTICIPANTS:

Corporate/Non-Military

- Operations Manager

- Human Resource Manager
- Resource Manager
- Information Manager
- Facilities Manager
- Security Manager
- Supervisors
- Workers
- Software Developers
- Operational Architect/Facilitator
- Subject Matter Expert

Military

- Combat Developer
- Concept & Doctrine Developer
- Training Developer
- Force Developer
- Operational Architect/Facilitator
- Subject Matter Expert
- Warfighter
- Program/Project/Product Developer
- Systems Architect
- Technical Architect
- Systems Engineer

PRODUCT DEVELOPMENT:

The Logical Data Model is critical in the standardization of data elements, which is key to the achievement of true interoperability among systems. Certain architecture development efforts, therefore, may include the development of a Logical Data Model that would contain the standard data elements necessary to support warfighter information exchange requirements. Data model development or modification has as its basis an approved Activity Model.

There are three primary methods for Data Model development: modification of an existing Data Model, development of a new Data Model by an individual or small group of SMEs, or conduct of facilitated modeling workshops. Each of these methods starts with a determination of the enterprise data requirements and an assessment of the availability within existing Data Models or data repositories of data elements to meet those requirements. Each of these three methods is described below. The selection of the appropriate method to be used for the development of a particular data model is based on the development time available, the availability of SMEs to support modeling workshops, and the existence or absence of an enterprise Activity Model.

Modification of an Existing Data Model

1. ***Determine and document enterprise data requirements.*** The primary sources of data requirements are the Activity Model ICOMs. Review the names and definitions of the ICOMs to identify the basic elements of data of which they are comprised. Every person, place, thing, event, concept, or idea mentioned in the ICOM name or definition is a candidate data element for inclusion in the data model. If no Activity Model exists, determine the enterprise data requirements from an assessment of the information exchange elements identified in the Operational Information Exchange Matrix.
2. ***Identify available Data Models or subject area views as potential sources of data elements to meet data requirements.*** Identify all existing models that might be used, with modifications, to describe enterprise data requirements. Candidates include Data Models of closely related enterprises and higher level enterprises of which the enterprise being architected is a part. For example, in developing a Data Model of a truck, an existing Data Model of an automobile may be considered as a source.
3. ***Compare data requirements to available Data Models or subject area views.*** Compare identified enterprise data requirements to the names and definitions of data elements in the candidate Data Models. Determine which of available models best meets or matches the enterprise data requirements. Select a model (or a subordinate Data Model subject area view) to be adopted and modified to produce the enterprise Logical Data Model.
4. ***Adopt usable data elements from selected Data Model or subject area view.*** Identify individual data entities, attributes, and relationships from the selected Data Model or subject area to be retained in the enterprise Logical Data Model. Include both those that can be used as they are and those that may require relatively minor changes to accurately reflect enterprise data requirements.
5. ***Delete unneeded data elements from existing Data Model or subject area view.*** Remove from the selected Data Model or subject area view all data entities, attributes, and relationships that are not applicable to enterprise data requirements.
6. ***Modify adopted data elements as necessary to meet fully enterprise data requirements.*** Where necessary to more accurately reflect enterprise data requirements, modify data entity, attribute, and relationship names and/or definitions. Add new relationships as needed. Limit any entity, attribute, or relationship changes to the minimum needed to accommodate **unique** enterprise data requirements. In other words, do not change the names or definitions of approved, reused data elements simply because the approved name or definition is not exactly the same as that commonly used within the enterprise. This retains the greatest level of interoperability

between the enterprise being architected and that for which the original Data Model was developed, and should increase the likelihood that the modified data elements can gain approval within and outside the enterprise.

7. ***Produce a new/modified Logical Data Model.*** Change Data Model descriptive information to identify it as a new model. This includes renaming the model and updating the model purpose, scope, and viewpoint.

8. ***Provide the Logical Data Model to SMEs for review and comment.*** Review of the Logical Data Model should focus on the names and definitions of entities, attributes, and relationships as well as the level to which they fulfill known enterprise data requirements. Provide to each reviewer the data dictionary (i.e., list of entity, attribute, and relationship names and definitions) and the list of enterprise data requirements. Where possible, indicate the Data Model or subject area view that was modified, and highlight the modifications that were made. Provide to selected reviewers the actual Data Model diagram(s) for review.

9. ***Update the Logical Data Model based on SME comments.*** Review submitted comments and recommendations to determine which should be accepted and which should not. Identify and resolve any conflicts in comments and recommendations received (i.e., the change recommended in one comment is inconsistent with or counter to the change that is recommended in another). Modify the Logical Data Model in accordance with all accepted comments.

10. ***Publish the final version of the Logical Data Model.***

Individual/Small Team Development of a New Data Model

1. ***Determine and document enterprise data requirements.*** Determine the data elements necessary to fulfill enterprise data requirements as those requirements are defined, documented, or implied in enterprise Operational Concept Descriptions, Activity Models, Operational Information Exchange Matrices, or other non-architecture documents and products.

    a. ***Decompose Activity Model ICOMs to the data element level.*** If a well-developed Activity Model exists, with well-defined ICOMs, extract enterprise data elements from the ICOMs. Potential data elements may be explicitly specified in the ICOM name or definition, or they may only be implied by the ICOM definition or functional context. To decompose an ICOM into candidate data elements:

       – Record the ICOM name.

       – Record and review the ICOM definition.

       – Identify in the ICOM definition all mentions of, or references to persons, places, things, events, or concepts. Each of these represents a potential data element.

       – Determine whether each of the candidate elements represents a single piece of data (i.e., it cannot be broken down further) or a composite of multiple data elements.

- Further decompose each composite data element until it cannot be decomposed further.
- Record all identified basic data elements.
- Identify any relationships among and between identified data elements.

b. **Develop Data Requirement Worksheets (DRW) to document data needs.** If no Activity Model exists, if one exists but is relatively immature in its level of development, or if the model ICOMs are not well defined, then it will not be possible to define data requirements using the ICOM decomposition method. In these situations, data requirements may be defined through the development of data requirements worksheets. To develop a DRW:

- Identify an activity, operational concept, or functional/subject area to be analyzed.
- Define the activity, operational concept, or functional/subject area.
- Establish the activity, operational concept, or functional/subject area scope and viewpoint.
- Identify any operational rules, assumptions, or constraints associated with the activity, operational concept, or functional/subject area.
- Identify data elements associated with the selected activity, operational concept, or functional area.
- Determine business rules that define the relationships among and between identified data elements.

c. **"Mine" data from available source documents.** Data "mining" is not a single, formal process with a well-defined set of steps, but includes all techniques used to extract data elements from a wide variety of source documents. Candidates for data mining include organization and system description documents, organization SOPs, operations manuals, operational requirements documents, system specifications, interface descriptions, standardized message catalogs, and data element dictionaries. Mine data from these documents by identifying references to enterprise related persons, places, things, events, and concepts.

Document all data requirements identified through either Activity Model ICOM decomposition, development of DRWs, or data mining.

2. *Submit candidate data requirements to SMEs for review and comment.* Provide the decomposed Activity Model ICOMs, DRWs, or lists of mined data elements to reviewers with instructions on the type of review required, the format in which to provide comments and recommendations, and the suspense for providing input.

3. *Update/modify data requirements based on SME comments.* Add or delete candidate data elements, change data element names, and adjust data element relationships based on the comments and recommendations provided by SME reviewers.

4. ***Compare data requirements (candidate data elements) to existing data elements.*** Attempt to find approved data elements in existing Data Models or data repositories that match or nearly match enterprise data requirements.
5. ***Adopt appropriate data elements to meet data requirements.*** Capture the adopted data elements in an initial enterprise Logical Data Model.
6. ***Modify adopted data elements to meet enterprise data needs.*** Make changes to data element names, definitions, and relationships to more accurately reflect enterprise data requirements. Limit the changes to the minimum necessary to fully meet enterprise requirements.
7. ***Develop new data elements where none exist.***
    a. ***Create new data entities.*** Name and define new entities and identify appropriate key attributes.
    b. ***Add non-key data attributes to new entities.*** Include the attribute name, definition, and data type (e.g., character string, integer, or time).
    c. ***Add entity relationships.*** Graphically and textually depict the relationship type (e.g., identifying, non-identifying, mandatory, non-mandatory, or many-to-many), directionality, verb phrase, and cardinality.
8. ***Combine new data elements and adopted data elements to produce an enterprise Logical Data Model.***
9. ***Normalize the Logical Data Model.***
10. ***Submit the data model/data elements to SMEs for review and comment.*** Provide to most reviewers the model data dictionary (i.e., data element names and definitions) for review and comment. For those reviewers with a good working knowledge of data modeling syntax, provide the actual Logical Data Model.
11. ***Update/modify the Data Model/data elements based on SME comments.*** Add or delete data elements, change data element names, and adjust data element relationships based on the comments and recommendations provided by SME reviewers.
12. ***Publish the Data Model.***

Conduct of Data Modeling Workshops

1. Identify and gather resources and references required to support model development.
2. Identify and notify SMEs. Development of the model may require the participation of several groups of SMEs:
- Those who will participate in the modeling sessions.
- Those who will not participate in the modeling sessions, but will provide input via face-to-face interviews with facilitators/modelers.
- Those who will review and provide comment on drafts and the final model.
- Those whose knowledge of a specific subject area will be solicited only when needed.

3. Conduct face-to-face interviews with SMEs not participating in the working sessions.
4. Conduct the modeling session. During the modeling session, the facilitator will guide and direct the discussion, but the main source of information and input will be the SMEs in attendance.
- a. *Create new data entities.* Name and define new entities and identify appropriate key attributes.
- b. *Add non-key data attributes to new entities.* Include the attribute name, definition, and data type (e.g., character string, integer, or time).
- c. *Add entity relationships.* Graphically and textually depict the relationship type (e.g., identifying, non-identifying, mandatory, non-mandatory, or many-to-many), directionality, verb phrase, and cardinality.
- d. Review results of the modeling session. Ensure that all modeling session participants agree on what was accomplished during the session, what actions are to be performed between sessions and what goals are to be established for the next session.
- e. Identify any outstanding issues from the modeling session.
- f. Assign outstanding issues to selected participants for resolution.

5. Update the model by incorporating the results of the modeling session. This is primarily the job of the facilitator and modeler(s) between modeling sessions. It includes making all agreed to changes to the model and "cleaning up" the model for publication/distribution.

6. Publish and distribute the updated model to modeling session participants and other specified reviewers for review and/or comment. Include information on the portions of the Logical Data Model to be reviewed, the types of comments to be provided, the desired comment format, the individual(s) or organization(s) to whom/which comments are to be submitted, and the suspense for comment submission. If no comments or recommended changes are received, go to step 10 below.

7. Receive, review and respond to recommended changes to the draft model.
8. Incorporate approved changes into an updated model draft.
9. Repeat from step 4.
10. Conduct additional modeling sessions as necessary.
11. Finalize the model.
12. Publish the final Logical Data Model.

RECOMMENDED DEVELOPMENT SEQUENCE:
Sixth, following the Activity Model and the Operational Information Exchange Matrix.

KEY RELATIONSHIPS:

- Operational Concept Description: The data elements in the Logical Data Model should be based upon or directly traceable to the missions, tasks, activities, nodes, and organizations described in the Operational Concept Description. Any information exchanges depicted in the Operational Concept Description should be supported by data elements in the Logical Data Model.
- Operational Information Exchange Matrix: The information exchange elements and sending and receiving nodes captured in the Operational Information Exchange Matrix should be supported by data elements in the Logical Data Model. The technical and performance parameters associated with the information exchange elements in the Operational Information Exchange Matrix should be reflected in the attributes of the appropriate data elements in the Logical Data Model.
- Activity Model: The data elements in the Logical Data Model should be based upon or directly traceable to Activity Model ICOMs.
- System Data Exchange Matrix: The data exchange elements included in the System Data Exchange Matrix should be the same as those captured in the Logical Data Model.
- Physical Data Model: The Physical Data Model may be developed directly from the Logical Data Model by adding implementation-specific data characteristics. The Physical Data Model may also be developed independent of the Logical Data Model, but its physical data elements should be traceable to the logical data elements described in the Logical Data Model.
- Technical Architecture Profile: The technical standards identified in the Technical Architecture Profile may influence the structure and characteristics of the data elements captured in the Logical Data Model. For example, the adoption of a specific technical standard for reporting time may effect the way that time based data elements are captured in the Logical Data Model. Likewise, the structure and characteristics of data elements in the Logical Data Model may influence which technical standards are adopted for inclusion in the Technical Architecture Profile.
- System Technology Forecast: The technical standards identified in the System Technology Forecast may influence the structure and characteristics of the data elements captured in the Logical Data Model. For example, the adoption of a specific technical standard for reporting time may effect the way that time based data elements are captured in the Logical Data Model. Likewise, the structure and characteristics of data elements in the Logical Data Model may influence which technical standards are adopted for inclusion in the System Technology Forecast.

CRITICAL SUCCESS FACTORS:

DO'S:
- Base data elements on information elements described in the Activity Model.

- Reuse existing approved data elements whenever possible.
- Identify data element relationships two data elements at a time.
- Define all new data elements as they are developed.
- Identify the source of adopted data elements.
- Use role names to reflect enterprise unique names for adopted data elements.

DON'TS:

- Don't develop new data elements when existing data elements can be used as they are or modified slightly to meet enterprise data requirements.
- Don't capture physical implementation details in the Logical Data Model.
- Don't rename adopted data elements simply to reflect enterprise unique terminology. Use and adopt approved standard naming conventions.

CHECKLIST: The LOGICAL DATA MODEL

Modification of an Existing Data Model

Process Steps	Complete
1. Determine and document enterprise data requirements.	
2. Identify available Data Models or subject area views as potential sources of data elements to meet data requirements.	
3. Compare data requirements to available Data Models or subject area views.	
4. Adopt usable data elements from selected Data Model or subject area view.	
5. Delete unneeded data elements from existing Data Model or subject area view.	
6. Modify adopted data elements as necessary to meet fully enterprise data requirements.	
7. Produce a new/modified Logical Data Model.	
8. Provide the Logical Data Model to SMEs for review and comment.	
9. Update the Logical Data Model based on SME comments.	
10. Publish the final version of the Logical Data Model.	

Individual/Small Team Development of a New Data Model

Process Steps	Complete
1. Determine and document enterprise data requirements.	
2. Decompose Activity Model ICOMs to the data element level.	
3. Record the ICOM name.	
4. Record and review the ICOM definition.	
Identify in the ICOM definition all mentions of, or references to persons, places, things, events, or concepts.	
Determine whether each of the candidate elements represents a single piece of data (i.e., it cannot be broken down further) or a composite of multiple data elements.	
Further decompose each composite data element until it cannot be decomposed further.	
Record all identified basic data elements.	
5. Identify any relationships among and between identified data elements.	
6. Develop Data Requirement Worksheets (DRW) to document data needs.	
7. Identify an activity, operational concept, or functional/subject area to be analyzed.	
Define the activity, operational concept, or functional/subject area.	
Establish the activity, operational concept, or functional/subject area scope and viewpoint.	
Identify any operational rules, assumptions, or constraints associated with the activity, operational concept, or functional/subject area.	
Identify data elements associated with the selected activity, operational concept, or functional area.	
Determine business rules that define the relationships among and between identified data elements.	
8. "Mine" data from available source documents.	
9. Submit candidate data requirements to SMEs for review and comment.	
10. Update/modify data requirements based on SME comments.	
11. Compare data requirements (candidate data elements) to existing data elements.	
12. Adopt appropriate data elements to meet data requirements.	
13. Modify adopted data elements to meet enterprise data needs.	
14. Develop new data elements where none exist.	
Create new data entities.	
Add non-key data attributes to new entities.	
Add entity relationships.	

Process Steps	Complete
15. Combine new data elements and adopted data elements to produce an enterprise Data Model.	
16. Normalize the Data Model.	
17. Submit the data model/data elements to SMEs for review and comment.	
18. Update/modify the Data Model/data elements based on SME comments.	
19. Publish the Data Model.	

Conduct of Data Modeling Workshops

Process Steps	Complete
1. Identify and gather resources and references required to support model development.	
2. Identify and notify SMEs.	
3. Conduct face-to-face interviews with SMEs not participating in the working sessions.	
4. Conduct the modeling session.	
Create new data entities.	
Add non-key data attributes to new entities.	
Add entity relationships.	
Review results of the modeling session.	
Identify any outstanding issues from the modeling session.	
Assign outstanding issues to selected participants for resolution.	
5. Update the model by incorporating the results of the modeling session.	
6. Publish and distribute the updated model to modeling session participants and other specified reviewers for review and/or comment. If no comments or recommended changes are received, go to step 10 below.	
7. Receive, review and respond to recommended changes to the draft model.	
8. Incorporate approved changes into an updated model draft.	
9. Repeat from step 4.	
10. Conduct additional modeling sessions as necessary.	
11. Finalize the model.	
12. Publish the final Logical Data Model.	

CHAPTER EIGHT

PRODUCT NAME: OPERATIONAL ACTIVITY SEQUENCE & TIMING DESCRIPTION

OTHER ALIASES: Process Model, Operational Thread, Mission Thread, Functional Flow Diagram, State Transition Diagram

PRODUCT DESIGNATION: OV-6a, OV-6b, OV-6c

ARCHITECTURE VIEW: OPERATIONAL

PRODUCT DEFINITION: The OPERATIONAL ACTIVITY SEQUENCE & TIMING DESCRIPTION are used to describe the optimal sequencing of activities, or to assess time critical activity or information flows.

PRODUCT DESCRIPTION: The Operational Activity Sequence and Timing Description provides a means for describing or defining the time based behavior of an enterprise. It can link individual activities from the Activity Model together to describe end-to-end processes. It can show the required, preferred, or prescribed sequence of activities. It can be used to define or document the timing and duration of activities and processes. It can also be used to identify critical activities (e.g., activities that must be completed before subsequent activities may be initiated) within processes.

There are two general categories of Operational Activity Sequence and Timing Descriptions—task based and information exchange based. The difference between the two is the nature of the building blocks used to produce an individual sequence and timing description. In a task-based description, the basic building blocks are operational functions, tasks, missions, actions, or activities. In information exchange based descriptions, the basic building blocks are individual information exchange actions (e.g., transmissions, retransmissions, message deliveries, transmission acknowledgments, etc.).

Both categories of Operational Activity Sequence and Timing Description can be documented using one of three types of models. These three model types are:

- Operational Rules Model

- Operational State Transition Description

- Operational Event/Trace Description

The Operational Rules Model captures the "business rules" associated with elements of the architecture. The rules may prescribe the conditions under which actions or tasks are initiated, performed, continued, resumed, or terminated. Other rules may control or constrain the types or quantities of outputs produced by activities. These rules may take the form of algorithms, mathematical formulae, decision trees, "if/then" statements, Boolean statements, or statements and assertions in plain English.

The Operational State Transition Description describes how enterprise components (i.e., nodes/organizations, and information/data) are modified as a result of the performance of activities and processes.

The Operational Event/Trace Description is the most familiar of the three model types. It shows the sequencing of individual activities, events, and actions. An example Operational Event /Trace Description diagram is shown below.

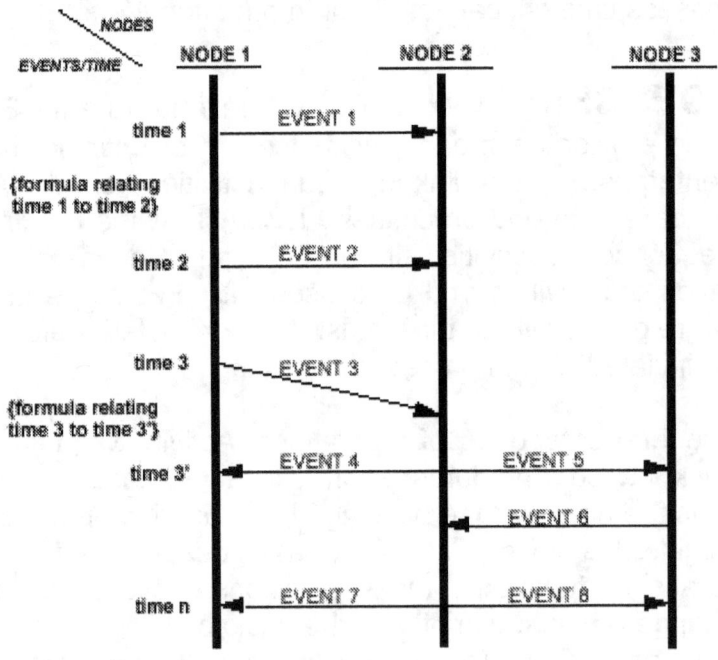

PRODUCT FORMAT: Graphical, with textual annotations

USERS & USES:

USERS:

Corporate/Non-Military

- Strategic Planner
- Operations Manager
- Information Manager
- Quality Assurance Manager
- Security Manager
- Supervisors
- Workers
- Software Developers
- Trainers
- Research and Development
- Policy Writers

Military
- Combat Developer
- Concept Developer
- Trainer
- Training Developer
- Program/Project/Product Developer
- Operational Architect
- Systems Architect
- Technical Architect
- Systems Engineer
- Software Developer
- Manufacturer
- Test & Evaluation Community
- Modeling & Simulation Community
- Warfighter

USES:

Corporate/Non-Military

- Strategic Business Planning
- Development of Procedures Guides and User's Manuals
- Business Process Reengineering
- Development/validation of SOPs
- Quality Control/Quality Management
- Description of Required System Capabilities
- Baselining of Functionality
- Functional Allocation
- Database Design
- Development/Modification of Operational Concepts
- Identification of Operational Issues
- Wargaming Alternatives
- Performance of Cost/Benefits Analysis
- Development of Training Materials

Military

- Development/Modification of Operational Concepts
- Identification of Operational Issues
- Identification of Information Exchange Requirements
- Identification/Validation of Operational Needs/Requirements
- Standardization of Processes, Activities and Tasks
- Development/Validation Of Tactics, Techniques & Procedures (TTPs)
- Development/Validation Of SOPs
- Development/Validation Of Models & Simulations
- Development/Validation Of Mission Training Plans
- Planning For Organization Exercises
- Planning For System Tests
- Development Of System Software
- Development/Modification of Standard Messages
- Baselining Of Functionality
- Wargaming Alternatives

- Battlefield/Business Process Reengineering
- Development of Procedures Guides and User's Manuals
- Design of Human-Computer Interface
- Providing Roadmap for System Improvement
- Data Modeling
- Comparing User's Vision to Developer's Implementation
- Performance of Cost/Benefits Analysis
- Development of Training Materials

TYPICAL INFORMATION SOURCES:

Corporate/Non-Military

- Function/Task Lists
- Long Range Plans
- Organization Descriptions
- Operational Concepts
- Policy and Procedures Guides
- Standing Operating Procedures (SOPs)
- Strategic Plans
- Subject Matter Experts
- System Descriptions
- Task Descriptions
- Vision Statements
- Business Plans
- Corporate Brochures

Military

- Subject Matter Experts
- Policy and Procedures Guides
- Doctrinal Publications
- Operational Concepts
- Operational and Organizational Plans
- Vision Statements
- Function/Task Lists (including METLs, UJTL, Service Task Lists)
- Task Descriptions

- Standing Operating Procedures (SOPs)
- Interface Descriptions

TOOLS:

- Text Editor
- Drawing/Graphics Tool
- Activity/Process Modeling Tool
- Object Modeling Tool
- Flow Charting Tool

PARTICIPANTS:

Corporate/Non-Military

- Strategic Planner
- Operations Manager
- Human Resource Manager
- Resource Manager
- Information Manager
- Quality Assurance Manager
- Facilities Manager
- Security Manager
- Supervisors
- Workers
- Trainers
- Policy Writers
- Operational Architect/Facilitator
- Subject Matter Expert

Military

- Combat Developer
- Concept & Doctrine Developer
- Training Developer
- Operational Architect/Facilitator
- Subject Matter Expert
- Warfighter

- Program/Project/Product Developer
- Systems Architect
- Technical Architect
- Systems Engineer

PRODUCT DEVELOPMENT:

Develop Operational Rules Model

1. *Identify critical processes for which Operational Rules Models are needed.*
2. *For each identified critical process, determine the type(s) of rules to be captured.* Determine whether the Operational Rules Model is meant to (1) describe the conditions under which actions or tasks are initiated, performed, continued, resumed, or terminated, or (2) to define the rules that control or constrain the types or quantities of outputs produced by activities.
3. *Document the operational rules in the appropriate format(s).* Define the appropriate rules in the form of algorithms, mathematical formulae, decision trees, "if/then" statements, Boolean statements, or statements and assertions in plain English.

> 1. If the value of Attribute 1 equals zero (0), then set the value of Attribute 2 to equal zero (0).
> 2. If the value of Attribute 1 is greater than or equal to one (1), then set the value of Attribute 2 equal to five (5) times the value of Attribute 1.
> 3. If the value of Attribute 2 is an even integer, then set the value of Attribute 3 to "No". Otherwise, set the value of Attribute 3 to "Yes".

4. *Provide the Operational Rules Model to SMEs for review and comment.* Include information on the portions of the event/trace description to be reviewed, the types of comments to be provided, the desired comment format, the individual(s) or organization(s) to whom/which comments are to be submitted, and the suspense for comment submission.
5. *Modify and update the Operational Rules Model based on SME comments.* Alter the model as necessary to incorporate recommended changes.
6. *Publish the Operational Rules Model.*
7. *Repeat the steps as necessary to develop additional Operational Rules Model for other critical processes.*

Develop Operational State Transition Description

1. ***Identify critical processes for which Operational State Transition Descriptions are needed.*** Select activities or processes for which it is important to understand or describe the nature of the change in state, or the conditions under which the state transition occurs.
2. ***Identify the specific activity that results in a change of state.*** Where possible, reuse an activity previously defined in the Activity Model or a mission/task defined in the Operational Concept Description. Adopt the name of the activity or mission as the title of the Operational State Transition Description.
3. ***Define the initial state.*** Determine how the architecture component (e.g., the node, organization, system, and information element) looks prior to the performance of the activity.
4. ***Define the specific conditions under which the state transition occurs.*** Determine whether the state transition is time or event driven, i.e., whether it occurs at a specified time (or time interval) or as a result of a predefined action or event. Also consider state transitions that are initiated as a result of external environmental conditions (e.g., weather, visibility, or illumination) rather than clearly defined events.
5. ***Define the final state.*** Determine the way that the architecture component is expected to look after the state transition is completed.
6. ***Identify and document interim state transitions included in the larger state transition chain.*** Define any intermediate states between the initial and end state, or any "nested" state transition processes that are a part of the larger state transition process being described.
7. ***Build Operational State Transition Description diagram.***
   - Depict the initial, interim, and end states as rounded corner boxes. Label the boxes to define/describe the state being depicted.
   - Connect the boxes with one-way arrows that reflect the events or activities that result in the transition from one state to the next.
   - Add start and stop terminators to show the beginning and end of the process. The start terminator is depicted by a single dot with an arrow pointing to the box for the beginning state. The end terminator is shown by an arrow pointing from the end state box to a circle with a dot at its center.
   - Label the end terminator arrow to indicate the final result of the state transition process being described.

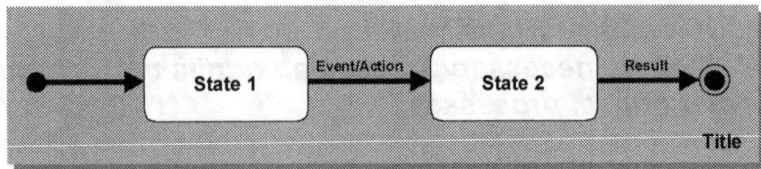

8. ***Provide the Operational State Transition Description to SMEs for review and comment.*** Include information on the portions of the Operational State Transition Description to be reviewed, the types of comments to be provided, the desired comment format, the individual(s) or organization(s) to whom/which comments are to be submitted, and the suspense for comment submission.
9. ***Modify and update the Operational State Transition Description based on SME comments.***
10. ***Publish the Operational State Transition Description.***
11. ***Repeat the steps as necessary to develop additional Operational State Transition Descriptions for other critical processes.***

Develop Operational Event/Trace Description

1. ***Identify critical processes for which Operational Event/Trace Descriptions are needed.*** Select processes for which the correct timing and sequencing of included activities and tasks is essential to mission success, those for which the sequencing and timing of activities has not been determined, or those for which a more efficient or effective sequencing and timing of activities is desired.
2. ***For each identified critical process, determine whether it should be captured as an activity based or information exchange based process.*** Consider the primary use to which the product is to be put. Identify the primary questions that the Operational Event/Trace Description is expected to answer, or the information that it is meant to illustrate.

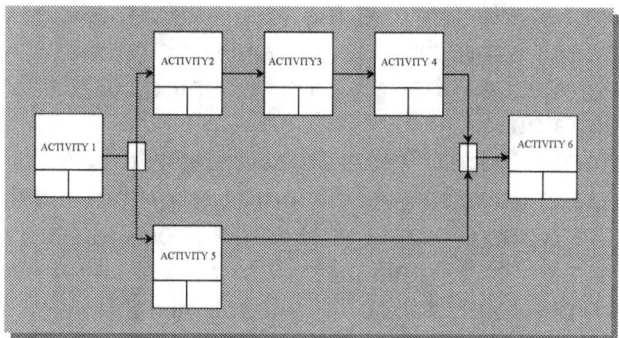

3. ***Identify activities or information exchanges included in the event/trace description.*** For activity based event/trace descriptions, identify appropriate activities from the Activity Model to be incorporated into the model(s). Identify information exchanges to be included in information exchange based even/trace descriptions by reviewing the Operational Information Exchange Matrix, the Node Connectivity Description, or the Activity Model.
4. ***Determine activity or information exchange sequencing.*** Place icons representing the selected activities or information exchange events in the

order in which the activities or information exchanges are, or should be, performed.

5. ***Identify activity or information exchange relationships.*** Determine the relationships among the activities or information exchange events included in the event/trace descriptions. Relationship types include, but are not limited to, precedence, concurrence, or alternatives. Precedence relationships are those in which one activity or information exchange must always be initiated or completed before a subsequent activity or information exchange event can take place. Concurrence relationships are those in which two or more activities or information exchanges may be performed simultaneously. Alternative relationships are those in which any one (but only one) of two or more equivalent activities or information exchanges may be activated upon the completion of a preceding activity or information exchange. Connect pairs of activities or information exchange events using connectors that indicate the types of relationships between them.

6. ***Define subordinate process threads that are included in larger event/trace descriptions.*** The process described in the event/trace description may include within it subordinate processes that encompass a smaller number of activities or information exchanges.

7. ***Define the timing of activities or information exchanges.*** Capture either activity or information exchange duration (i.e., the total time that it takes to complete an activity, information exchange, or process) or start/execution time. Activities or information exchanges may be initiated either at a specified time or at a specified interval.

8. ***Identify activity or information exchange triggers.*** Define the events, actions, or conditions that cause activities or information exchanges to be initiated.

9. ***Determine repeatability of activities, information exchanges, or subordinate process threads.*** Identify and document activities, information exchanges, and processes that may be repeated, and the conditions under which they are repeated.

10. ***Provide Operational Event/Trace Description to SMEs for review and comment.*** Include information on the portions of the event/trace description to be reviewed, the types of comments to be provided, the desired comment format, the individual(s) or organization(s) to whom/which comments are to be submitted, and the suspense for comment submission.

11. ***Modify and update Operational Event/Trace Description based on SME comments.***

12. ***Publish the Operational Event/Trace Description.***

13. ***Repeat the steps as necessary to document other critical processes.***

RECOMMENDED DEVELOPMENT SEQUENCE: As required, but following the development of the Activity Model.

KEY RELATIONSHIPS:

- Operational Concept Description: The processes, activities, tasks, and information exchanges captured in the Operational Activity Sequence and Timing Descriptions should be directly traceable to missions, tasks, activities, and information exchanges described in the Operational Concept Description.
- Activity Model: The activities and tasks included in activity based Operational Event/Trace Descriptions and the events/actions in Operational State Transition Descriptions should be reused from (or directly traceable to) the Activity Model. The information elements and exchanges depicted in information exchange based Operational Event/Trace Descriptions should be based upon or traceable to the ICOs depicted in the Activity Model.
- Operational Information Exchange Matrix: Information exchange based Operational State Transition Descriptions and Operational State Transition Descriptions should be directly traceable to information exchanges defined in the Operational Information Exchange Matrix.
- Logical Data Model: The Operational Rules Model may be developed as an IDEF1X Logical Data Model. The algorithms and formulae included in the Operational Rules Model may be incorporated into the Logical Data Model.
- Physical Data Model: The Operational Rules Model may be developed as an IDEF1X Physical Data Model. The algorithms and formulae included in the Operational Rules Model may be incorporated into the Physical Data Model.
- System Functionality Sequence & Timing Description: Each System Functionality Sequence and Timing Description may be developed as the system implementation of one or more Operational Activity Sequence and Timing Descriptions.

CRITICAL SUCCESS FACTORS:

DO'S:
– Reuse missions, activities and tasks from the Operational Concept Description and/or the Activity Model to develop Operational Activity Sequence and Timing Descriptions.
– Select the type of Operational Activity Sequence and Timing Description model based on the type of information to be described and the uses to which the finished product will be put.

DON'TS:
– Don't create new activities, tasks, events, or actions when acceptable ones already exist as a part of the Operational Concept Description, the Node Connectivity Description, or the Activity Model.

Operational Activity Sequence & Timing Description

CHECKLIST: The OPERATIONAL ACTIVITY SEQUENCE AND TIMING DESCRIPTION

Develop Operational Rules Model

Process Steps	Complete
1. Identify critical processes for which Operational Rules Models are needed.	
2. For each identified critical process, determine the type(s) of rules to be captured.	
3. Document the operational rules in the appropriate format(s).	
4. Provide the Operational Rules Model to SMEs for review and comment.	
5. Modify and update the Operational Rules Model based on SME comments.	
6. Publish the Operational Rules Model.	
7. Repeat the steps as necessary to develop additional Operational Rules Model for other critical processes.	

Develop Operational State Transition Description

Process Steps	Complete
1. Identify critical processes for which Operational State Transition Descriptions are needed.	
2. Identify the specific activity that results in a change of state.	
3. Define the initial state.	
4. Define the specific conditions under which the state transition occurs.	
5. Define the final state.	
6. Identify and document interim state transitions included in the larger state transition chain	
7. Build Operational State Transition Description diagram.	
8. Provide the Operational State Transition Description to SMEs for review and comment.	
9. Modify and update the Operational State Transition Description based on SME comments.	
10. Publish the Operational State Transition Description.	
11. Repeat the steps as necessary to develop additional Operational State Transition Descriptions for other critical processes.	

Develop Operational Event/Trace Description

Process Steps	Complete
1. Identify critical processes for which Operational Event/Trace Descriptions are needed.	
2. For each identified critical process, determine whether it should be captured as an activity based or information exchange based process.	
3. Identify activities or information exchanges included in the event/trace description.	
4. Determine activity or information exchange sequencing.	
5. Identify activity or information exchange relationships.	
6. Define subordinate process threads that are included in larger event/trace descriptions.	
7. Define the timing of activities or information exchanges.	
8. Identify activity or information exchange triggers.	
9. Determine repeatability of activities, information exchanges, or subordinate process threads.	
10. Provide Operational Event/Trace Description to SMEs for review and comment.	
11. Modify and update Operational Event/Trace Description based on SME comments.	
12. Publish the Operational Event/Trace Description.	
13. Repeat the steps as necessary to document other critical processes.	

CHAPTER NINE

PRODUCT NAME: SYSTEM INTERFACE DESCRIPTION

OTHER ALIASES: System Connectivity Diagram

PRODUCT DESIGNATION: SV-1

ARCHITECTURE VIEW: SYSTEMS

PRODUCT DEFINITION: The SYSTEM INTERFACE DESCRIPTION graphically portrays the actual or desired interfaces between enterprise systems or system nodes.

PRODUCT DESCRIPTION: The System Interface Description serves as a critical link between the Operational Architecture and the System Architecture. It graphically shows the systems that are used to execute the information exchanges between operational nodes depicted in the Node Connectivity Description. It may be considered the System Architecture version of the Node Connectivity Description.

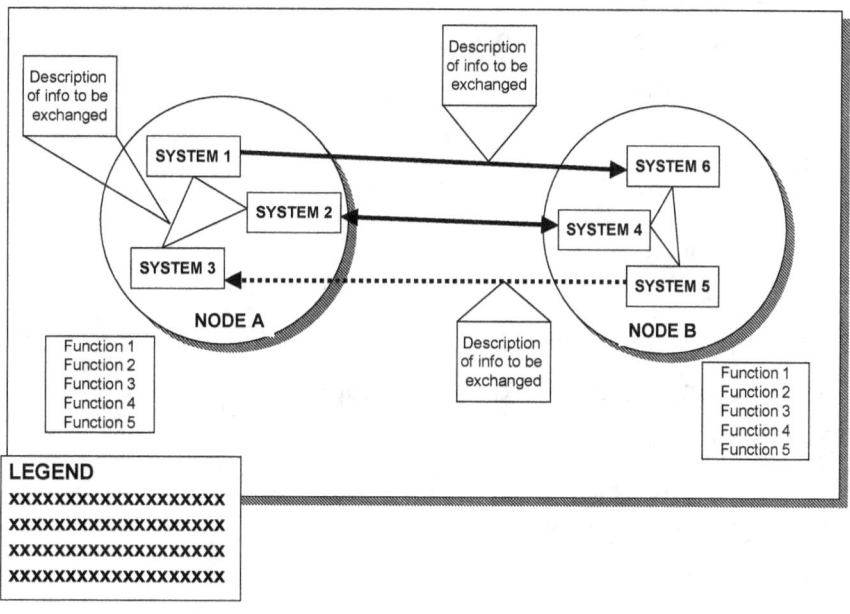

The System Interface Description can be depicted in one of two formats—intranodal and internodal. The intranodal System Interface Description shows the interfaces between systems within a single operational node (e.g., a single organization or element). It identifies the individual systems that comprise the operational node and depicts the manner in which those systems communicate with each other. The internodal System Interface Description describes the systems used to effect an interface between two or more operational nodes. It may show all the systems available within each interfacing node, or it may only show the specific communications systems that execute the interface.

PRODUCT FORMAT: Graphical, with textual annotations

USERS & USES:

USERS:

Corporate/Non-Military

- Strategic Planner
- Operations Manager
- Resource Manager
- Information Manager
- Security Manager
- Workers
- Software Developers
- Research and Development
- Policy Writers

Military

- Combat Developer
- Trainer
- Training Developer
- Program/Project/Product Developer
- Resource Manager
- Operational Architect
- Systems Architect
- Technical Architect
- Systems Engineer
- Software Developer

- Manufacturer
- Test & Evaluation Community
- Modeling & Simulation Community
- Warfighter

USES:

Corporate/Non-Military

- Organizational Design
- Business Process Reengineering
- Development of Capital Investment Strategies
- Description of Required System Capabilities
- Database Design
- Identification of Operational Issues
- Allocation Of Communication Assets
- Performance of Cost/Benefits Analysis
- Development of Training Materials
- Development of Procedures Guides and User's Manuals

Military

- Development/Validation Of Tactics, Techniques & Procedures (TTPs)
- Development/Validation Of SOPs
- Development/Validation Of Models & Simulations
- Allocation Of Communication Assets
- Planning For System Tests
- Network Burden Assessment
- Identification of OPFAC Hardware Requirements
- Development Of System Software
- Comparing User's Vision To Developer's Implementation
- Wargaming Alternatives
- Providing Roadmap For System Improvement
- Battlefield/Business Process Reengineering
- Development of Procedures Guides and User's Manuals
- Design of Human-Computer Interface
- Performance of Cost/Benefits Analysis

- Development/Validation of Training Plans
- Development of Training Materials

TYPICAL INFORMATION SOURCES:

Corporate/Non-Military

- Function/Task Lists
- Organization Descriptions
- Operational Concepts
- Policy and Procedures Guides
- Standing Operating Procedures (SOPs)
- Subject Matter Experts
- System Descriptions
- Task Descriptions

Military

- Subject Matter Experts
- Policy and Procedures Guides
- Doctrinal Publications
- Operational Concepts
- Operational and Organizational Plans
- Organization Descriptions (including TOEs, MTOEs, TDAs)
- Interface Descriptions
- System Descriptions

TOOLS:

- Text Editor
- Drawing/Graphics Tool
- Database
- Object Modeling Tool

PARTICIPANTS:

Corporate/Non-Military

- Operations Manager
- Information Manager
- Security Manager
- Supervisors
- Workers
- Policy Writers
- Operational Architect/Facilitator
- Subject Matter Expert

Military

- Subject Matter Expert
- Warfighter
- Program/Project/Product Developer
- Systems Architect
- Technical Architect
- Systems Engineer

PRODUCT DEVELOPMENT:

The System Interface Description is developed based on the information captured in the Node Connectivity Description. The node or nodes depicted in the System Interface Description should be the same as one or more operational nodes shown in the Node Connectivity Description. The recommended process for developing the product is described below.

1. ***Determine the type of System Interface Description to be developed.*** Decide whether to develop an intranodal or internodal System Interface Description.
2. ***Identify systems and nodes to be included on the System Interface Description.*** First decide the specific node or nodes to be described in the System Interface Description. Next, identify the individual systems available at each node. Finally, select which nodal systems actually are to be shown in the System Interface Description.
3. ***Determine the interfaces between pairs of systems and/or nodes.*** Identify the manner in which information and data are exchanged between nodes, interfacing systems at separate nodes, or systems within a single node.

4. ***Add graphical icons to represent systems.*** Decide on the type of graphical icon(s) to be used to represent individual systems. Icons may be geometric shapes (e.g., squares, circles, ovals, or rectangles), pictograms (i.e., small pictures of the actual system or the type of system being depicted), standard symbols, or a combination of any or all of these types. Insert an appropriate icon to represent each system included in the System Interface Description.
5. ***Label the system icons.*** Add a textual label on or near each system icon to indicate the name or designation of the depicted system.
6. ***For internodal System Interface Descriptions, group system icons by node and draw a boundary around each group to represent individual nodes.*** Place the icons for all the systems that comprise a single node near each other on the System Interface Description diagram. Draw a square, circle, or other shaped perimeter around all related systems to represent the boundary of the node of which they are a part. [NOTE: For an intranodal System Interface Description a perimeter may also be drawn around the system icons to represent the boundary of the single node being depicted.]
7. ***Label each node.*** Add a textual label on or near each node icon to indicate the name or designation of the depicted node.
8. ***For intranodal System Interface Descriptions, connect pairs of system icons to reflect the interfaces between the systems.*** Add lines or arrows to represent the fact that two systems interface (i.e., communicate) with each other. Use different line or arrow styles (e.g., solid, dotted, dashed, bold, single, double, colored, single pointed, or double pointed) to represent different types of interfaces.
9. ***For internodal System Interface Descriptions, connect related nodes at either the node or individual system level.*** Add lines or arrows to represent the fact that two systems or nodes interface (i.e., communicate) with each other. Use different line or arrow styles (e.g., solid, dotted, dashed, bold, single, double, colored, single pointed, or double pointed) to represent different types of interfaces.
10. ***Label the relationship lines.*** Add a textual label on or near each line or arrow to indicate the nature of the interface being depicted. The label may indicate the type of interface (e.g., simplex, multicast, or broadcast), the directionality of the information/data exchange (e.g., one-way or two-way), or the communications medium being used (e.g., FM voice, phone, satellite communications, etc.).
11. ***Add a legend to define terms and symbols used on the System Interface Description diagram.***
12. ***Provide the System Interface Description to SMEs for review and comment.*** Include information on the portions of the System Interface Description to be reviewed, the types of comments to be provided, the desired comment format, the individual(s) or organization(s) to whom/which comments are to be submitted, and the suspense for comment submission.
13. ***Update the System Interface Description based on SME comments and recommendations.*** Modify the System Interface Description as necessary to

incorporate approved and accepted change recommendations resulting from the SME review.

14. Publish the final System Interface Description.

RECOMMENDED DEVELOPMENT SEQUENCE: First System Architecture product, but after the development of the Operational Concept Description, the Node Connectivity Description, the Activity Model, and the Operational Information Exchange Matrix.

KEY RELATIONSHIPS:

- Node Connectivity Description: The Node Connectivity Description forms the basis for the System Interface Description. The nodes depicted on the System Interface Description should be the same as one or more operational nodes shown in the Node Connectivity Description. The interfaces shown on the internodal System Interface Description should be the same as those shown on the Node Connectivity Description.
- Operational Information Exchange Matrix: The system and node interfaces described in the System Interface Description should be directly traceable to one or more information exchanges captured in the Operational Information Exchange Matrix.
- Activity Model: The systems and operational nodes shown in the System Interface Description should be directly traceable to system based Activity Model mechanisms. The Interfaces defined in the System Interface Description may be traceable to information exchanges described in the Activity Model.
- Organizational Relationships Chart: The interfaces shown in internodal System Interface Descriptions may be traceable to command, control, or coordination relationships shown on the Organizational Relationships Chart.
- System Communication Description: The System Communication Description provides a more detailed description of the interfaces shown in the System Interface Description.
- $System^2$ Matrix: Some individual systems shown in the $System^2$ Matrix should be the same as those shown in the System Interface Description.
- System Data Exchange Matrix: The System Data Exchange Matrix should provide a detailed technical description of the nature of the data exchanges identified in the System Interface Description.
- System Performance Parameters Matrix: Selected systems shown on the System Performance Parameters Matrix should be the same as the systems shown in the System Interface Description.
- Technical Architecture Profile: The Technical Architecture Profile may identify technical standards implemented by the systems in the System Interface Description.

- OPFAC Equipment Description: The operational element identified in the OPFAC Equipment Description is the same as the operational node shown in the System Interface Description. The individual systems that comprise the operational element in the OPFAC Equipment Description are the same as the individual systems shown in the System Interface Description.
- Core Systems & Quantities Inventory: The individual systems depicted in the System Interface Description should also be included in the Core Systems and Quantities Inventory.
- Horseblanket: The individual systems depicted in the System Interface Description should also be included on the Horseblanket. The nodes shown in the System Interface Description may be captured in the Horseblanket as organizational sub-elements.

CRITICAL SUCCESS FACTORS:

DO'S:
- Label all graphical elements included in the System Interface Description diagram.
- Use approved names for systems, nodes, and interface media whenever possible.
- Include approved OPFAC Equipment Description numbers for appropriate nodes.

DON'TS:
- Don't include in the System Interface Description systems that do not exist, unless those systems are labeled or otherwise marked to indicate their notional status.
- Don't combine systems in the System Interface Description to create nonexistent nodes.
- Don't attempt to capture too much information in the System Interface Description. Use the System Communication Description to capture technical and performance details of the interface.

CHECKLIST: The SYSTEM INTERFACE DESCRIPTION

Process Steps	Complete
1. Determine the type of System Interface Description to be developed.	
2. Identify systems and nodes to be included on the System Interface Description.	
3. Determine the relations between pairs of systems and/or nodes.	
4. Add graphical icons to represent systems.	
5. Label the system icons.	
6. For internodal System Interface Descriptions, group system icons by node and draw a boundary around each group to represent nodes.	
7. Label each node.	
8. For intranodal System Interface Descriptions, connect pairs of system icons to reflect the relationships between the systems.	
9. For internodal System Interface Descriptions, connect related nodes at either the node or individual system level.	
10. Label the relationship lines.	
11. Add a legend to define terms and symbols used on the System Interface Description diagram.	
12. Provide the System Interface Description to SMEs for review and comment.	
13. Update the System Interface Description based on SME comments and recommendations.	
14. Publish the final System Interface Description.	

CHAPTER TEN

PRODUCT NAME: SYSTEMS COMMUNICATIONS DESCRIPTION

OTHER ALIASES: Component Diagram

PRODUCT DESIGNATION: SV-2

ARCHITECTURE VIEW: SYSTEMS

PRODUCT DEFINITION: The SYSTEMS COMMUNICATIONS DESCRIPTION identifies the physical characteristics of the interfaces among and between systems.

PRODUCT DESCRIPTION: The System Communications Description expands on the information presented in the System Interface Description by capturing the physical aspects of the interfaces among and between systems. It does so by identifying the communications medium/media used, or to be used, to effect information or data exchange. Physical interface/media characteristics that may be captured in the System Communications Description include the communications frequency, bandwidth, encryption and protocol; the name and type of communications network; the message or data exchange formats and standards; and the physical locations of switches, routers, repeaters, amplifiers, and other communications devices.

The System Communications Description may be developed from either an intranodal or an internodal perspective. The intranodal type depicts the connectivity among systems within a single node. The internodal type describes the nature of the connectivity among systems resident at different operational nodes.

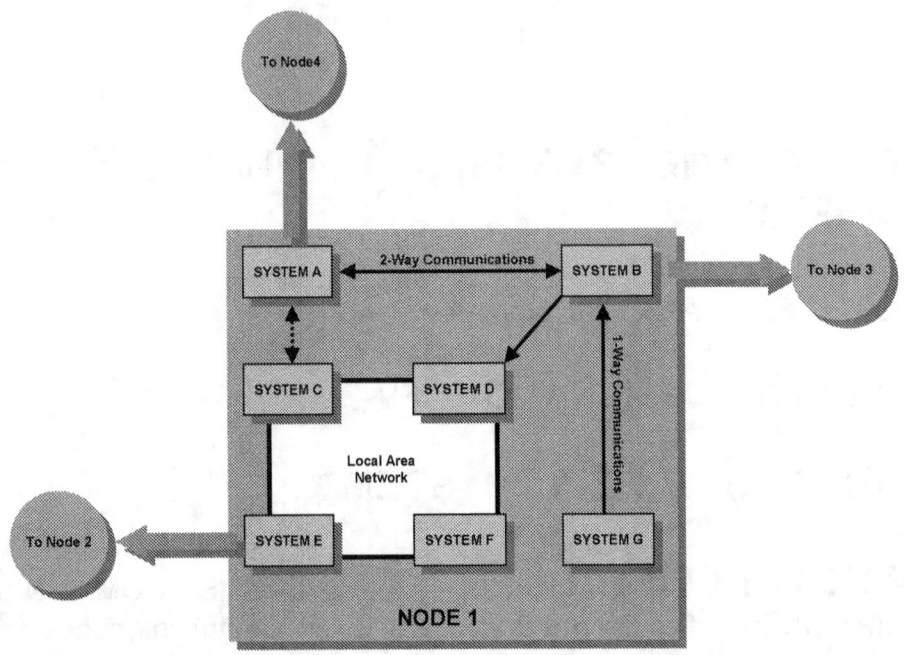

PRODUCT FORMAT: Graphical, with textual annotations

USERS & USES:

USERS:

Corporate/Non-Military

- Operations Manager
- Resource Manager
- Information Manager
- Security Manager
- Supervisors
- Workers
- Software Developers
- Research and Development
- Policy Writers

Military

- Combat Developer
- Trainer

- Training Developer
- Program/Project/Product Developer
- Resource Manager
- Operational Architect
- Systems Architect
- Technical Architect
- Systems Engineer
- Software Developer
- Manufacturer
- Test & Evaluation Community
- Modeling & Simulation Community
- Warfighter

USES:

Corporate/Non-Military

- Development of Procedures Guides and User's Manuals
- Organizational Design
- Business Process Reengineering
- Development of Capital Investment Strategies
- Development/validation of SOPs
- Description of Required System Capabilities
- Database Design
- Identification of Operational Issues
- Allocation Of Communication Assets
- Communications Network Burden Assessment
- Wargaming Alternatives
- Performance of Cost/Benefits Analysis
- Development of Training Materials

Military

- Development/Modification of Operational Concepts
- Identification of Operational Issues
- Development/Validation Of Tactics, Techniques & Procedures (TTPs)
- Development/Validation Of SOPs

- Development/Validation Of Models & Simulations
- Allocation Of Communication Assets
- Planning For System Tests
- Network Burden Assessment
- Identification of OPFAC Hardware Requirements
- Providing Roadmap for System Improvement
- Development Of System Software
- Comparing User's Vision To Developer's Implementation
- Wargaming Alternatives
- Battlefield/Business Process Reengineering
- Development of Procedures Guides and User's Manuals
- Design of Human-Computer Interface
- Performance of Cost/Benefits Analysis
- Development of Training Materials

TYPICAL INFORMATION SOURCES:

Corporate/Non-Military

- Function/Task Lists
- Organization Descriptions
- Operational Concepts
- Policy and Procedures Guides
- Standing Operating Procedures (SOPs)
- Subject Matter Experts
- System Descriptions
- Corporate Brochures

Military

- Subject Matter Experts
- Policy and Procedures Guides
- Operational Concepts
- Operational and Organizational Plans
- Organization Descriptions (including TOEs, MTOEs, TDAs)
- Standing Operating Procedures (SOPs)
- Interface Descriptions

- System Descriptions

TOOLS:

- Text Editor
- Drawing/Graphics Tool
- Database
- Network Design Tool

PARTICIPANTS:

Corporate/Non-Military

- Operations Manager
- Resource Manager
- Information Manager
- Security Manager
- Supervisors
- Workers
- Software Developers
- Policy Writers
- Operational Architect/Facilitator
- Subject Matter Expert

Military

- Combat Developer
- Subject Matter Expert
- Warfighter
- Program/Project/Product Developer
- Systems Architect
- Technical Architect
- Systems Engineer

PRODUCT DEVELOPMENT:

1. ***Determine the type of System Communications Description to be developed.*** As stated above, the System Communications Description may be developed from either an internodal or an intranodal perspective.
2. ***Determine the timeframes to be addressed in the System Communications Description.*** The timeframe(s) may be addressed in general (e.g., as-is or to-be), relative (e.g., current, interim, or objective), or specific terms (e.g., 2010 or 2020). The temporal focus of the System Communications Description may also be described in operational terms (e.g., prior to reorganization, during reorganization, after reorganization, pre-deployment or post-deployment). For system to system communications concepts that vary over time, you should describe all timeframes addressed.
3. ***Identify the systems to be included in the System Communications Description.*** The systems included in the System Communicants Description should be the same as those included in the System Interface Description. The systems may include both those that are an integral part of the enterprise being architected and external systems with which enterprise systems interface.
4. ***Select graphic icons to represent the included systems.*** Use either geometric shapes (e.g., circles, ovals, or rectangles), standard symbols, representative icons (e.g., small pictures of people, vehicles, computers, weapons, radios, or buildings), or a combination of these types to depict each system. Add a separate symbol to represent each individual system, each type of system, or each "family" of systems.
5. ***Place the icons on the diagram.*** Physically position the system icons on the diagram to facilitate connecting interfacing systems. Pairs or groups of systems that communicate with each other should be placed near each other on the diagram in order to simplify the process of illustrating system-to-system connectivity. NOTE: This step may have to be repeated during or after the performance of Step 9 below.
6. ***Label the icons to identify the systems being represented.*** Place on or near each node symbol a label that indicates the name, designation, or identifier of the system, or the type of system being depicted.
7. ***Determine the communications media among the included systems.*** Example communications media or protocols that may be depicted on the System Communications Description include database exchange, formatted message exchange, local area network (LAN), wide area network (WAN), infrared, fiber optic cable, or internet protocol.
8. ***Determine the physical characteristics of the communications media to be captured on the diagram.*** Examples include the kind of processing performed, the locations of network switches or routers, or the existence of amplifiers or repeaters in a particular communications path. The graphical presentation and/or supporting text may also describe all pertinent communications attributes (e.g., waveform, bandwidth, radio frequency, packet or waveform encryption methods).

9. ***Graphically portray both the communications media and the physical characteristics.*** Draw arrows to connect each pair of interfacing systems. Connect the point of the arrow to the system(s) that is/are the recipient(s) in the information exchange—use single pointed arrows for one-way information exchanges and double pointed arrows to show two-way exchanges. If desired, use different types (e.g., bold, solid, dashed, double) or colors of arrows to provide additional information about the nature of the exchanges. For example, use solid arrows to indicate mandatory exchanges and dotted lines to reflect conditional exchanges.
10. ***Add a legend to define terms, abbreviations, labels, symbols, icons, lines, and other graphic and textual elements included on the System Communications Description.***
11. ***Provide the draft System Communications Description to SMEs for review and comment.*** Include information on the portions of the System Communications Description to be reviewed, the types of comments to be provided, the desired comment format, the individual(s) or organization(s) to whom/which comments are to be submitted, and the suspense for comment submission.
12. ***Update and modify the System Communications Description as necessary based on SME comments and recommendations.*** Modifications to the System Communications Description may also require changes to the System Interface Description, the System^2 Matrix, or the Node Connectivity Description.
13. ***Publish final System Communications Description.***

RECOMMENDED DEVELOPMENT SEQUENCE:

Following the development of the System Interface Description.

KEY RELATIONSHIPS:

- System Interface Description: The Systems Communication Description provides a more detailed description of the interfaces shown in the System Interface Description.
- System^2 Matrix: The systems depicted on the System Communication Description should match systems shown in the System^2 Matrix. If the System^2 Matrix is developed to include communications connectivity relationships between and among systems, then the communications connectivities shown in the System^2 Matrix should match those captured on the System Communications Description.
- System Data Exchange Matrix: The system data exchange elements detailed in the System Data Exchange Matrix should be consistent with and directly traceable to one or more inter-system interfaces captured on the System Communication Description. If high-level data exchange element names

appear on the System Communications Description, they should be the same as or directly traceable to one or more system data exchange elements included in the System Data Exchange Matrix.

- Technical Architecture Profile: The communications media identified in the System Communications Description must be in accordance with the information exchange standards defined in the Technical Architecture Profile.
- OPFAC Equipment Description: The operational element reflected in the OPFAC Equipment Description should be the same as or directly traceable to an operational node (system node) shown on the System Communications Description. The individual C4ISR systems included in the OPFAC Equipment Description should match the systems included as components of the corresponding operational or system nodes on the System Communications Description.
- Core Systems & Quantities Inventory: The C4ISR systems included in the Core Systems & Quantities Inventory should match the C4ISR systems addressed in the System Communications Description.
- Horseblanket: The systems shown on the Horseblanket should match systems addressed in the System Communications Description

CRITICAL SUCCESS FACTORS:

DO'S:
- Include textual and/or graphical information to describe the nature of the interface among and between systems.
- Clearly distinguish between current and future communications media and physical communications characteristics.
- Ensure that the System Communications Description is consistent with the System Interface Description.

DON'TS:
- Don't simply show connectivity between systems.
- Don't identify system-to-system interfaces in the System Communications Description that are not captured in the System Interface Description.

CHECKLIST: The SYSTEM COMMUNICATIONS DESCRIPTION

Process Steps	Complete
1. Determine the type of System Communications Description to be developed.	
2. Determine the timeframes to be addressed in the System Communications Description.	
3. Identify the systems to be included in the System Communications Description.	
4. Select graphic icons to represent the included systems.	
5. Place the icons on the diagram.	
6. Label the icons to identify the systems being represented.	
7. Determine the communications media among the included systems.	
8. Determine the physical characteristics of the communications media to be captured on the diagram.	
9. Graphically portray both the communications media and the physical characteristics.	
10. Add a legend to define terms, abbreviations, labels, symbols, icons, lines, and other graphic and textual elements included on the System Communications Description.	
11. Provide the draft System Communications Description to SMEs for review and comment.	
12. Update and modify the System Communications Description as necessary based on SME comments and recommendations.	
13. Publish final System Communications Description.	

CHAPTER ELEVEN

PRODUCT NAME: SYSTEMS^2 MATRIX

OTHER ALIASES: None

PRODUCT DESIGNATION: SV-3

ARCHITECTURE VIEW: SYSTEMS

PRODUCT DEFINITION: The SYSTEM^2 MATRIX defines the relationship(s) between pairs of systems within and external to the enterprise.

PRODUCT DESCRIPTION: The System^2 Matrix is the most versatile of the system view/system architecture products because it can be used to show many different types of relationships between systems. The matrix is constructed by listing the names of each system along the horizontal and vertical axes.

The relationship between each pair of systems is then shown in the block where their respective row and column intersect. Different types of relationships may be shown using text or graphical elements such as icons, lines, line styles, arrows, geometric shapes, highlighting, shading, or colors. Because many different types of relationships among systems may be depicted on this product, it may be desirable to create multiple matrices, each depicting only a few types of relationships.

PRODUCT FORMAT: Table or spreadsheet

USERS & USES:

USERS:

Corporate/Non-Military

- Resource Manager
- Information Manager
- Security Manager
- Supervisors
- Workers
- Trainers
- Research and Development

Military

- Combat Developer
- Program/Project/Product Developer
- Resource Manager
- Operational Architect
- Systems Architect
- Technical Architect
- Systems Engineer
- Modeling & Simulation Community
- Manufacturer

USES:

Corporate/Non-Military

- Business Process Reengineering
- Development/validation of SOPs
- Development of Capital Investment Strategies

- Description of Required System Capabilities
- Identification of Operational Issues
- Communications Network Burden Assessment
- Allocation Of Communication Assets
- Wargaming Alternatives
- Performance of Cost/Benefits Analysis

Military

- Identification of Operational Issues
- Development/Validation Of Tactics, Techniques & Procedures (TTPs)
- Development/Validation Of SOPs
- Development/Validation Of Models & Simulations
- Allocation Of Communication Assets
- Network Burden Assessment
- Identification of OPFAC Hardware Requirements
- Development Of System Software
- Planning for System Test
- Wargaming Alternatives
- Battlefield/Business Process Reengineering
- Performance of Cost/Benefits Analysis

TYPICAL INFORMATION SOURCES:

Corporate/Non-Military

- Subject Matter Experts
- System Descriptions
- Corporate Brochures

Military

- Subject Matter Experts
- Operational and Organizational Plans
- Interface Descriptions
- System Descriptions

TOOLS:

- Text Editor
- Drawing/Graphics Tool
- Database

PARTICIPANTS:

Corporate/Non-Military

- Resource Manager
- Facilities Manager
- Security Manager
- Supervisors
- Workers
- Operational Architect/Facilitator
- Subject Matter Expert

Military

- Combat Developer
- Operational Architect/Facilitator
- Subject Matter Expert
- Warfighter
- Program/Project/Product Developer
- Systems Architect
- Technical Architect
- Systems Engineer

PRODUCT DEVELOPMENT: The System^2 Matrix is the most versatile of the System View/System Architecture products.

1. ***Determine the timeframe(s) to be addressed by the matrix.*** The timeframe(s) may be addressed in general (e.g., as-is or to-be), relative (e.g., current, interim, or objective), or specific terms (e.g., 2010 or 2020). The temporal focus of the System Communications Description may also be described in operational terms (e.g., prior to reorganization, during reorganization, after reorganization, pre-deployment or post-deployment).

2. ***Identify the systems (both internal and external tot he enterprise) to be included in the matrix.*** As a minimum, the matrix should include the systems defined in the System Interface Description or the System Communications Description Matrix.
3. ***Construct a matrix with rows and columns for each system to be included.*** The matrix may be created as a square, i.e., with the same number of rows as columns, or it may have more rows than columns or vice versa. It is probably preferable to have both a row and a column for each of the systems that is an integral part of the enterprise. However, it may be sufficient only to add additional rows or columns (but not both) for systems external to the enterprise.
4. ***Place the names and/or representative icons of each system along the matrix horizontal and vertical axes.*** The names of the systems may be supplemented with or replaced by graphical icons that represent the respective systems.
5. ***Select the types of relationships to be captured on the matrix.*** Types of relationships could include:
    a. ***Communications media/medium:*** The communications protocol or information transport means used to exchange information between systems.
    b. ***Parent system-subsystem:*** The situation in which one system—the subsystem—is a component of another system—the parent system.
    c. ***Information source-information destination:*** The situation in which one system produces information or data that is used or consumed by another system.
    d. ***Peer:*** The situation in which two systems are used by two or more different organizations or nodes to perform similar functions.
    e. ***Substitute:*** The situation in which one system can take the place of another system.
    f. ***Surrogate:*** The situation in which one system, though not a replacement for, can be used to perform similar functions as another system.
    g. ***Predecessor-Follow on:*** The situation in which one system has or will fully replace another system.
    h. ***Creator-Product:*** The situation in which one system is used to create, produce, or manufacture another system.
6. ***Graphically or textually depict or describe the relationship(s) between two systems by placing a description or an icon in the matrix cell where the respective system row and column intersect.*** The relationship between a pair of systems may be described textually or it may be indicated using arrows, lines, line styles, symbols, icons, colors, or highlighting. Multiple textual descriptions or multiple graphical indicators may be used on the same matrix to show multiple types of relationships at the same time. [NOTE: In addition to defining the relationship between systems, the matrix may also be used to document the status of the relationship (e.g., current, planned, projected, funded, or unfunded).]

7. *Add a legend to define the labels, terms, abbreviations, icons, symbols, and other textual and graphical elements included on the matrix.*
8. *Provide the draft matrix to SMEs for review and comment.* Include information on the portions of the matrix to be reviewed, the types of comments to be provided, the desired comment format, the individual(s) or organization(s) to whom/which comments are to be submitted, and the suspense for comment submission.
9. *Update and modify the matrix as necessary based on SME comments and recommendations.* Modifications of the matrix may also require changes to the System Interface Description and the System Communications Description.
10. *Publish the final matrix.*

RECOMMENDED DEVELOPMENT SEQUENCE: No recommendation.

KEY RELATIONSHIPS:

- System Interface Description: Some individual systems shown in the System^2 Matrix should be the same as those shown in the System Interface Description.
- System Communication Description: The systems depicted on the System Communication Description should match systems shown in the System^2 Matrix. If the System^2 Matrix is developed to include communications connectivity relationships between and among systems, then the communications connectivities shown in the System^2 Matrix should match those captured on the System Communications Description.
- System Data Exchange Matrix: The data exchange elements documented in the System Data Exchange Matrix should support the system to system relationships depicted in the System^2 Matrix.
- OPFAC Equipment Description: The C4ISR equipment included in the OPFAC Equipment Description should match C4ISR systems included in the System^2 Matrix.
- Core Systems & Quantities Inventory: The C4ISR equipment included in the Core Systems & Quantities Inventory should match the C4ISR equipment addressed in the System^2 Matrix.
- Horseblanket: The systems included on the Horseblanket should match systems addressed in the System^2 Matrix.

CRITICAL SUCCESS FACTORS:

DO'S:
- Consider developing multiple matrices, each showing different types and categories of system-to-system relationships.
- Include in the matrix both individual stand-alone systems and systems that are composites of multiple subsystems or components.
- If multiple versions of a particular piece or suite of hardware is used to perform different functions within the enterprise, then identify the system based on function, not hardware. For example, if one computer is used as a network file server and an identical computer is used as an e-mail server, then capture in the System^2 Matrix a Network File Server system **and** an E-mail Server system.
- On the matrix diagonals, which show the relationship of a particular system to a like system (e.g., e-mail server to e-mail server), only document unique or non-standard aspects of the relationship as they relate specifically to the enterprise being architected. Otherwise, leave the diagonal matrix cells blank.

DON'TS:
- Don't try to capture too much information in the matrix cells.
- Don't include software applications as systems.
- Don't include people or organizations as systems.

CHECKLIST: The SYSTEM² MATRIX

Process Steps	Complete
1. Determine the timeframe(s) to be addressed by the matrix.	
2. Identify the systems (both internal and external to the enterprise) to be included in the matrix.	
3. Construct a matrix with a row and a column for each system to be included.	
4. Place the names and/or representative icons of each system along the matrix horizontal and vertical axes.	
5. Select the types of relationships to be captured on the matrix	
a. Communications media/medium	
b. Parent system-subsystem	
c. Information source-destination	
d. Peer	
e. Substitute	
f. Surrogate	
g. Predecessor-Follow-on	
h. Creator-Product	
6. Graphically or textually depict or describe the relationship(s) between two systems by placing a description or an icon in the matrix cell where the respective system row and column intersect.	
a. Text	
b. Symbols	
c. Colors	
7. Add a legend to define the labels, terms, abbreviations, icons, symbols, and other textual and graphical elements included on the matrix.	
8. Provide the draft matrix to SMEs for review and comment.	
9. Update and modify the matrix as necessary based on SME comments and recommendations.	
10. Publish the final matrix.	

CHAPTER TWELVE

PRODUCT NAME: SYSTEM FUNCTIONALITY DESCRIPTION

OTHER ALIASES: System Function Model, Use Case, Collaboration Diagram

PRODUCT DESIGNATION: SV-4

ARCHITECTURE VIEW: SYSTEMS

PRODUCT DEFINITION: The SYSTEM FUNCTIONALITY DESCRIPTION is a graphical and textual depiction of the tasks performed by a system.

PRODUCT DESCRIPTION: The System Functionality Description defines how a system operates. It describes the system in terms of the functions that it performs, the information and/or resources that is uses/consumes in the performance of those functions, and the outputs that it produces as a result of the performance of those functions. The level of detail included in the System Functionality Description, and the methodology or modeling tool used to create it, is dependent on the purpose(s) for which the description is developed. For some purposes, it may be sufficient to describe the system as a "black box", focusing only on those system behaviors, inputs, and outputs that are visible to the system's external environment. For other uses, it may be necessary to describe in detail the system's internal functions, processes, and data flows.

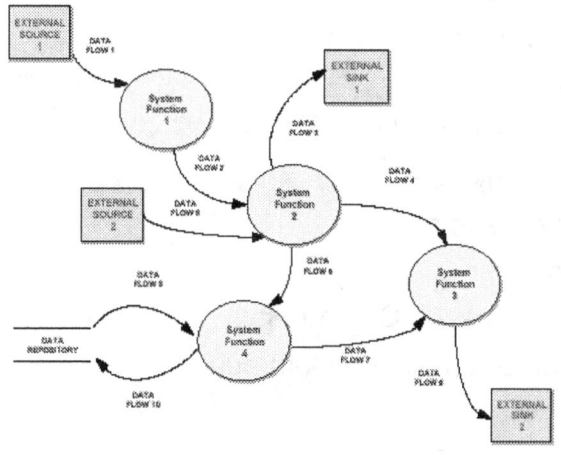

PRODUCT FORMAT: Graphics and text

USERS & USES:

USERS:

Corporate/Non-Military

- Operations Manager
- Resource Manager
- Information Manager
- Facilities Manager
- Security Manager
- Supervisors
- Workers
- Software Developers
- Trainers
- Research and Development
- Policy Writers
- Sales Department

Military

- Combat Developer
- Concept Developer
- Trainer
- Training Developer
- Program/Project/Product Developer
- Resource Manager
- Operational Architect
- Systems Architect
- Technical Architect
- Systems Engineer
- Software Developer
- Manufacturer
- Test & Evaluation Community
- Modeling & Simulation Community
- Warfighter

USES:

Corporate/Non-Military

- Development of Procedures Guides and User's Manuals
- Business Process Reengineering
- Development/validation of SOPs
- Quality Control/Quality Management
- Baselining of Functionality
- Functional Allocation
- Development/Modification of Operational Concepts
- Identification of Operational Issues
- Description of Required System Capabilities
- Allocation Of Communication Assets
- Wargaming Alternatives
- Design of Human-Computer Interface
- Performance of Cost/Benefits Analysis
- Development of Training Materials

Military

- Development/Modification of Operational Concepts
- Identification of Operational Issues
- Validation of Operational Needs/Requirements
- Standardization of Processes, Activities and Tasks
- Development/Validation Of Tactics, Techniques & Procedures (TTPs)
- Development/Validation Of SOPs
- Identification Of Functional Information Requirements
- Identification of IERs
- Development/Validation Of Models & Simulations
- Allocation Of Communication Assets
- Planning For Organization Exercises
- Planning For System Tests
- Network Burden Assessment
- Identification of OPFAC Hardware Requirements
- Comparing User's Vision To Developer's Implementation

- Baselining Of Functionality
- Wargaming Alternatives
- Providing Roadmap For System Improvement
- Battlefield/Business Process Reengineering
- Development of Procedures Guides and User's Manuals
- Design of Human-Computer Interface
- Performance of Cost/Benefits Analysis
- Development of Training Materials

TYPICAL INFORMATION SOURCES:

Corporate/Non-Military

- Function/Task Lists
- Subject Matter Experts
- System Descriptions

Military

- Subject Matter Experts
- Future Operational Capabilities (FOCs)
- Modernization Plans
- Master Plans
- Interface Descriptions
- System Descriptions

TOOLS:

- Text Editor
- Drawing/Graphics Tool
- Activity/Process Modeling Tool
- Object Modeling Tool

PARTICIPANTS:

Corporate/Non-Military

- Resource Manager

- Information Manager
- Quality Assurance Manager
- Facilities Manager
- Security Manager
- Supervisors
- Workers
- Software Developers
- Trainers
- Policy Writers
- Operational Architect/Facilitator
- Subject Matter Expert

Military

- Combat Developer
- Training Developer
- Operational Architect/Facilitator
- Subject Matter Expert
- Warfighter
- Program/Project/Product Developer
- Systems Architect
- Technical Architect
- Systems Engineer

PRODUCT DEVELOPMENT:

1. ***Identify the primary function(s) of the system.*** To identify the primary function of the system, ask the questions: "What is the main thing that this system does?" or, "What is the main thing that someone uses this system for?" The answer to either of these questions is considered to be the primary function of the system. Keep in mind, however, that a single system may have more than one primary function. For multi-functional systems, you must decide whether or not it is necessary to include all system functions.
2. ***Define and describe the primary system function(s).*** Provide a description of each of the primary system functions identified in Step 1 above. The description should include, as a minimum, a definition of the function. Where possible, the definition should be in plain, non-technical language so that it is easily understood by anyone reading it. The function description may also include a detailed discussion of the process(es) used to perform the function.

Additionally, it might define when, where, why, and under what conditions the function is performed.
3. ***Identify the input(s) to the function(s).*** The inputs are the information or other raw materials used by the system in the performance of the function(s).
4. ***Define and describe the function input(s).*** Provide a definition for each input, and discuss how each of them is used by the system in performing the function(s).
5. ***Identify the output(s) of the function(s).*** The outputs are the products of the function(s). Outputs may be in the form of information, material objects, physical actions, or changes in system's physical or operational state.
6. ***Define and describe the function output(s).*** Provide a definition for each output. Describe the conditions under which each output is produced.
7. ***Identify and document the exchange of information or data among functions.*** Internal information and data exchanges define how system functions interface with and relate to each other.
8. ***Define and describe the exchanged information and data elements.***
9. ***Identify the agent(s) that use the system to perform the function(s), or that are the users/consumers of the function output(s).*** The agents are the individuals or organizations associated with the performance of the function. They include the producers of system inputs, the users of system outputs, and the actual users and operators of the system. List all agents associated with each system function.
10. ***Define and describe the agents.*** Describe the agents by name, designation, title, position, role, or type.
11. ***Identify the conditions under which each function is performed.*** Specify the physical, operational, or temporal factors that lead to, or are required for, the performance of each function. This may include identifying functions that are precursors for other functions.
12. ***Decompose function(s) where necessary to provide additional detail.*** Identify lower level functions of which primary or high level functions are composed.
13. ***Define and describe each subordinate function.*** Describe lower level functions in the same way that primary functions were described in Step 2. The description should include, as a minimum, a definition of the function. Where possible, the definition should be in plain, non-technical language so that it is easily understood by anyone reading it. The function description may also include a detailed discussion of the process(es) used to perform the function. Additionally, it might define when, where, why, and under what conditions the function is performed.
14. ***Repeat from Step 3.*** Identify function inputs, outputs, information exchanges, and agents.
15. ***Provide the draft System Functionality Description to SMEs for review and comment.*** Include information on the portions of the System Functionality Description to be reviewed, the types of comments to be provided, the desired comment format, the individual(s) or organization(s) to

whom/which comments are to be submitted, and the suspense for comment submission.
16. *Update and modify the System Functionality Description as necessary based upon SME comments and recommendations.*
17. *Publish the final System Functionality Description.*

RECOMMENDED DEVELOPMENT SEQUENCE: Prior to the development of the System Function Sequence and Timing Matrix and the Operational Activity to System Function Traceability Matrix.

KEY RELATIONSHIPS:

- Activity Model: The system functions captured in the System Functionality Description should be directly traceable to activities, tasks, or functions included in the Activity Model.
- Operational Activity to System Function Traceability Matrix: The system functions included in the Operational Activity to System Function Traceability Matrix are exactly the same as those captured in the System Functionality Description.
- System Function Sequence & Timing Description: Each system function shown in the functionally based System Function Sequence and Timing Description should be the same as or directly traceable to one or more system functions identified in the System Functionality Description.
- System Evolution Description: The System Evolution Description may describe how the functions performed by a particular system change over time.

CRITICAL SUCCESS FACTORS:

DO'S:
— Decompose system functions to the level necessary to support the uses to which the System Functionality Description will be put.
— Describe system functions, inputs, outputs, information exchanges, and agents in operational terms whenever possible.

DON'TS:
— Don't confuse system capabilities and characteristics with system functions.

CHECKLIST: The SYSTEM FUNCTIONALITY DESCRIPTION

Process Steps	Complete
1. Identify the primary function(s) of the system.	
2. Define and describe the primary system function(s).	
3. Identify the input(s) to the function(s).	
4. Define and describe the function input(s).	
5. Identify the output(s) of the function(s).	
6. Define and describe the function output(s).	
7. Identify and document the exchange of information or data among functions.	
8. Define and describe the exchanged information and data elements.	
9. Identify the agent(s) that use the system to perform the function(s), or that are the users/consumers of the function output(s).	
10. Define and describe the agents.	
11. Identify the conditions under which each function is performed.	
12. Decompose function(s) where necessary to provide additional detail.	
13. Define and describe each subordinate function.	
14. Repeat from Step 3.	
15. Provide the draft System Functionality Description to SMEs for review and comment.	
16. Update and modify the System Functionality Description as necessary based upon SME comments and recommendations.	
17. Publish the final System Functionality Description.	

CHAPTER THIRTEEN

PRODUCT NAME: OPERATIONAL ACTIVITY TO SYSTEM FUNCTION TRACEABILITY MATRIX

OTHER ALIASES: None

PRODUCT DESIGNATION: SV-5

ARCHITECTURE VIEW: SYSTEMS

PRODUCT DEFINITION: The OPERATIONAL ACTIVITY TO SYSTEM FUNCTION TRACEABILITY MATRIX relates the activities described in the Activity Model to the system functions described in the System Functionality Description.

PRODUCT DESCRIPTION: The Operational Activity To System Function Traceability Matrix links the Operational Architecture/Operational View to the System Architecture/System View by relating operational activities to system functions. The matrix has two primary uses. First, it shows how well the functions performed by a system meet the operational requirements defined by the activities in the activity model. This allows the architecture user to assess whether or not an existing or developmental system is a viable candidate for implementing all or part of the operational architecture's activity requirements. Where multiple systems are being considered, the matrix allows a user to identify the single system, or group of systems that best meet the requirements of the operational activity model.

The second use of the Operational Activity to System Function Traceability Matrix is to document the operational activities that are associated with each system function. This allows a system's developers and/or users to understand its capabilities from an operational perspective.

	Sys Func 1	Sys Func 2	Sys Func 3	Sys Func 4	Sys Func 5	Sys Func 6	Sys Func 7	Sys Func 8	Sys Func 9	Sys Func 10	Sys Func 11	Sys Func 12	Sys Func 13	Sys Func 14	Sys Func 15	Sys Func 16	Sys Func 17	Sys Func 18
Opnl Act 1																		
Opnl Act 2																		
Opnl Act 3																		
Opnl Act 4																		
Opnl Act 5																		
Opnl Act 6																		
Opnl Act 7																		
Opnl Act 8																		
Opnl Act 9																		
Opnl Act 10																		
Opnl Act 11																		
Opnl Act 12																		

PRODUCT FORMAT:
Table or spreadsheet. May also be developed as an annotated list.

USERS & USES:

USERS:

Corporate/Non-Military

- Operations Manager
- Resource Manager
- Information Manager
- Workers
- Research and Development

Military

- Combat Developer
- Program/Project/Product Developer
- Operational Architect
- Systems Architect
- Systems Engineer
- Software Developer
- Manufacturer
- Test & Evaluation Community
- Warfighter

USES:

Corporate/Non-Military

- Business Process Reengineering
- Functional Allocation
- Identification of Operational Issues
- Allocation Of Communication Assets
- Wargaming Alternatives
- Performance of Cost/Benefits Analysis

Military

- Identification of Operational Issues
- Standardization of Processes, Activities and Tasks
- Development/Validation Of Models & Simulations
- Planning For System Tests
- Development Of System Software
- Wargaming Alternatives
- Prioritizing Activities For Implementation
- Providing Roadmap For System Improvement
- Battlefield/Business Process Reengineering
- Performance of Cost/Benefits Analysis

TYPICAL INFORMATION SOURCES:

Corporate/Non-Military

- Function/Task Lists
- Subject Matter Experts
- System Descriptions
- Task Descriptions

Military

- Subject Matter Experts
- Function/Task Lists (including METLs, UJTL, Service Task Lists)
- Task Descriptions

- System Descriptions

TOOLS:

- Text Editor
- Drawing/Graphics Tool
- Database

PARTICIPANTS:

Corporate/Non-Military

- Operations Manager
- Resource Manager
- Software Developers
- Trainers
- Operational Architect/Facilitator
- Subject Matter Expert

Military

- Combat Developer
- Operational Architect/Facilitator
- Subject Matter Expert
- Warfighter
- Program/Project/Product Developer
- Systems Architect
- Technical Architect
- Systems Engineer

PRODUCT DEVELOPMENT: The process to be used to develop the Operational Activity to System Function Traceability Matrix depends on the purpose for which the matrix is being developed. As stated above, there are two primary purposes for developing the matrix: to identify how well the system functionality meets the system's performance requirements as described in the Activity Model, or to document the operational activities that are associated with each system function. The specific steps to be used to create Operational Activity to System Function Traceability Matrices for each of these purposes is described below.

Developing the Operational Activity to System Function Traceability Matrix to identify how well the system functions meet the operational requirements defined in the Activity Model

1. ***List the operational activities from the Activity Model.*** The core of this form of the Operational Activity to System Function Traceability Matrix is the operational activities from the activity model. The matrix may include all activities that appear in the Activity Model, or only a subset. The activities to be listed in the matrix are those for which it is necessary or desirable to understand the degree to which they are supported by existing or developmental systems. If not listing all activities, then either list: 1) all the activities in a section of the model; 2) all activities down to a predefined level of decomposition; or 3) all activities at the lowest level of decomposition. After selecting the correct set of activities, list them by name in the first column of the matrix.
2. ***For each operational activity, list the associated system function(s).*** Extract the functions from one or more System Functionality Descriptions. Enter the functions in the matrix rows to reflect their relationships to the appropriate operational activities. Multiple functions may be associated with each activity, and individual functions may be associated with more than one activity.
3. ***Where necessary or desirable, indicate the level to which the system function(s) satisfy the requirements reflected in the operational activity.*** Use text and/or graphics to indicate whether the system function(s) fully or only partially support the operational requirements reflected in the associated activities.
4. ***Document the timeframe(s) addressed by the matrix.*** Document the timeframes associated with each operational activity and with each associated system function. As an alternative, document the timeframe of the activity-function association. The timeframe(s) may be addressed in general (e.g., as-is or to-be), relative (e.g., current, interim, or objective), or specific terms (e.g., 2010 or 2020). The temporal focus of the System Communications Description may also be described in operational terms (e.g., prior to reorganization, during reorganization, after reorganization, pre-deployment or post-deployment).
5. ***Provide the draft Operational Activity to System Function Traceability Matrix to SMEs for review and comment.*** Include information on the portions of the Operational Activity to System Function Traceability Matrix to be reviewed, the types of comments to be provided, the desired comment format, the individual(s) or organization(s) to whom/which comments are to be submitted, and the suspense for comment submission.
6. ***Update and modify the Operational Activity to System Function Traceability Matrix as necessary based upon SME comments and***

recommendations. Change the included operational activities, the system functions, the activity-function associations, or the association timeframes.
7. ***Publish the final Operational Activity to System Function Traceability Matrix.***

Developing the Operational Activity to System Function Traceability Matrix to document the operational activities associated with each system function.

1. ***List the system functions from the System Functionality Description.*** This version of the Operational Activity to System Function Traceability Matrix is built upon the functions documented in a System Functionality Description. The matrix may include all functions in the function description, or only a subset.
2. ***For each system function, list the associated operational activity or activities from the Activity Model.*** Enter into the matrix the names of the operational activity or activities that are fully or partially supported by each included system function.
3. ***Document the degree to which the functions and activities are in agreement.*** Use text and/or graphics to indicate the level to which each system function supports each associated operational activity. The level of functional support may be stated in relative (e.g., fully supports or partially supports), or objective terms (e.g., 10%, 35%, 90%).
4. ***Document the timeframe(s) addressed by the matrix.*** Document the timeframes associated with each operational activity and with each associated system function. As an alternative, document the timeframe of the activity-function association. The timeframe(s) may be addressed in general (e.g., as-is or to-be), relative (e.g., current, interim, or objective), or specific terms (e.g., 2010 or 2020). The temporal focus of the System Communications Description may also be described in operational terms (e.g., prior to reorganization, during reorganization, after reorganization, pre-deployment or post-deployment).
5. ***Provide the draft Operational Activity to System Function Traceability Matrix to SMEs for review and comment.*** Include information on the portions of the Operational Activity to System Function Traceability Matrix to be reviewed, the types of comments to be provided, the desired comment format, the individual(s) or organization(s) to whom/which comments are to be submitted, and the suspense for comment submission.
6. ***Update and modify the Operational Activity to System Function Traceability Matrix as necessary based upon SME comments and recommendations.*** Change system functions, associated operational activities, function-activity associations, or association timeframes.
7. ***Publish the final Operational Activity to System Function Traceability Matrix.***

RECOMMENDED DEVELOPMENT SEQUENCE: Following the development of the Activity Model and the System Functionality Description.

KEY RELATIONSHIPS:

- Activity Model: The operational activities shown in the Operational Activity to System Function Traceability Matrix are exactly the same as those included in the Activity Model.
- System Functionality Description: The system functions shown in the Operational Activity to System Function Traceability Matrix are exactly the same as those included in the System Functionality Description.

CRITICAL SUCCESS FACTORS:

DO'S:
— Use operational activities and system functions from existing Activity Models and System Functionality Descriptions.

— Where definitions exist for the operational activities and the system functions, base the activity-function associations on a comparison of the definitions, and not just the names.

DON'TS:
— Don't create an Activity Model simply to provide operational justification for an existing system or a System Functionality Description.

CHECKLIST: The OPERATIONAL ACTIVITY TO SYSTEM FUNCTION TRACEABILITY MATRIX

Developing the Operational Activity to System Function Traceability Matrix to identify how well the system functions meet the operational requirements defined in the Activity Model

Process Steps	Complete
1. List the operational activities from the Activity Model.	
2. For each operational activity, list the associated system function(s).	
3. Where necessary or desirable, indicate the level to which the system function(s) satisfy the requirements reflected in the operational activity.	
4. Document the timeframe(s) addressed by the matrix.	
5. Provide the draft Operational Activity to System Function Traceability Matrix to SMEs for review and comment.	
6. Update and modify the Operational Activity to System Function Traceability Matrix as necessary based upon SME comments and recommendations	
7. Publish the final Operational Activity to System Function Traceability Matrix.	

Developing the Operational Activity to System Function Traceability Matrix to document the operational activities associated with each system function.

Process Steps	Complete
1. List the system functions from the System Functionality Description.	
2. For each system function, list the associated operational activity or activities from the Activity Model.	
3. Document the degree to which the functions and activities are in agreement.	
4. Document the timeframe(s) addressed by the matrix.	
5. Provide the draft Operational Activity to System Function Traceability Matrix to SMEs for review and comment.	
6. Update and modify the Operational Activity to System Function Traceability Matrix as necessary based upon SME comments and recommendations	
7. Publish the final Operational Activity to System Function Traceability Matrix.	

CHAPTER FOURTEEN

PRODUCT NAME: SYSTEM DATA EXCHANGE MATRIX

OTHER ALIASES: System Information Exchange Matrix, System Information Exchange Requirements Matrix, System IER

PRODUCT DESIGNATION: SV-6

ARCHITECTURE VIEW: SYSTEMS

PRODUCT DEFINITION: The SYSTEM DATA EXCHANGE MATRIX describes the data elements exchanged between two or more systems.

PRODUCT DESCRIPTION: The System Data Exchange Matrix is the System Architecture/System View version of the Operational Information Exchange Matrix (OIEM). It replaces the OIEM's information exchange elements with data elements, and replaces the sending and receiving operational nodes with sending and receiving systems. Like the OIEM, it defines the qualitative and quantitative characteristics of the data exchange. Qualitative characteristics include, but are not limited to: the timeframe in which the exchange is or will be implemented, the formatted data packet/message used to effect the exchange, the exchange medium, the security classification of the data being exchanged, the precedence of the exchange, the operational impact of not conducting the exchange, the status of the exchange, and the directionality of the exchange. Quantitative characteristics include, but are not limited to: the physical size of the data packet/message to be exchanged, the frequency of the exchange, the perishability of the data being exchanged, and the required speed of service.

The actual qualitative and quantitative characteristics captured in a particular matrix are dependent on the uses to which the matrix will be put. For some common uses, standard matrix formats have already been established. For other uses, the format should be defined cooperatively by the producer(s) of the matrix and the expected user(s).

PRODUCT FORMAT: Best presented as a Database, but may be a table or spreadsheet.

USERS & USES:

USERS:

Corporate/Non-Military

- Operations Manager
- Information Manager
- Quality Assurance Manager
- Facilities Manager
- Security Manager
- Supervisors
- Workers
- Software Developers
- Research and Development

Military

- Combat Developer
- Program/Project/Product Developer
- Operational Architect
- Systems Architect
- Technical Architect
- Systems Engineer
- Software Developer
- Manufacturer
- Test & Evaluation Community
- Modeling & Simulation Community
- Training Developer
- Warfighter

USES:

Corporate/Non-Military

- Development of Procedures Guides and User's Manuals
- Business Process Reengineering
- Development/validation of SOPs
- Quality Control/Quality Management
- Description of Required System Capabilities
- Database Design
- Identification of Operational Issues
- Allocation Of Communication Assets
- Communications Network Burden Assessment
- Wargaming Alternatives
- Design of Human-Computer Interface
- Performance of Cost/Benefits Analysis

Military

- Identification of Operational Issues
- Standardization of Processes, Activities and Tasks
- Development/Validation Of Tactics, Techniques & Procedures (TTPs)
- Development/Validation Of SOPs
- Identification Of Functional Information Requirements
- Identification of IERs
- Development/Validation Of Models & Simulations
- Allocation Of Communication Assets
- Planning For System Tests
- Network Burden Assessment
- Identification of OPFAC Hardware Requirements
- Data Modeling
- Standardization of Data Elements
- Development Of System Software
- Comparing User's Vision To Developer's Implementation
- Wargaming Alternatives
- Providing Roadmap For System Improvement
- Battlefield/Business Process Reengineering

- Development of Procedures Guides and User's Manuals
- Design of Human-Computer Interface
- Performance of Cost/Benefits Analysis

TYPICAL INFORMATION SOURCES:

Corporate/Non-Military

- Subject Matter Experts
- System Descriptions
- Task Descriptions

Military

- Subject Matter Experts
- Policy and Procedures Guides
- Function/Task Lists (including METLs, UJTL, Service Task Lists)
- Task Descriptions
- Standing Operating Procedures (SOPs)
- Interface Descriptions
- System Descriptions

TOOLS:

- Text Editor
- Drawing/Graphics Tool
- Database
- Object Modeling Tool

PARTICIPANTS:

Corporate/Non-Military

- Operations Manager
- Information Manager
- Security Manager
- Supervisors
- Workers

- Software Developers
- Operational Architect/Facilitator
- Subject Matter Expert

Military

- Combat Developer
- Operational Architect/Facilitator
- Subject Matter Expert
- Warfighter
- Program/Project/Product Developer
- Systems Architect
- Technical Architect
- Systems Engineer

PRODUCT DEVELOPMENT:
The procedure to be used to develop the System Data Exchange Matrix is dependent on the existence or absence of other specific operational and/or system architecture products. The matrix may be developed based upon a pre-existing System Data Exchange Matrix created for another architecture. It may be developed from information presented in a System Interface Description or a System Communications Description. It may be created from a crosswalk of two or more System Functionality Descriptions. A Logical or Physical Data Model may serve as the basis for producing the matrix. If neither of these architecture products is available, the matrix may be created based on information gained from SMEs or extracted from available system documentation.

Developing the System Data Exchange Matrix based on an existing System Data Exchange Matrix

1. ***Identify an existing System Data Exchange Matrix to be used as a template.*** Matrices that were developed as a part of other architectures are candidates for reuse. The best candidates are those developed for the same system as that being architected, but under different environmental or operational conditions. Other good candidates are those developed for similar systems under the same or similar environmental or operational conditions. First, identify System Data Exchange Matrices developed for other architectures. Next, review the identified matrices for applicability to the systems being architected. Finally, select a matrix to use as a template.
2. ***Save and rename a copy of the existing matrix.***
3. ***Identify reusable portions of the saved matrix.*** Determine the data exchange elements, sending and receiving system names/identifiers, producing or consuming functions, or qualitative and quantitative technical

exchange parameters from the saved matrix that can be reused as-is or with minor modifications to support the system being architected. Delete from the matrix all information that cannot be reused.
4. ***Modify reused portions of the matrix as necessary.***
   a. ***Modify data exchange elements.*** Change the names of data exchange elements to more accurately reflect the architecture being developed and the system being architected.
   b. ***Modify sending and receiving systems.*** Update the receiving system name for incoming data exchanges and the sending system name for outgoing data exchanges to reflect the name of the systems being architected. Also update external sending and receiving systems as required.
   c. ***Modify producing and consuming functions.*** Update the system function names to match the modified sending and receiving system names.
   d. ***Modify qualitative and quantitative technical exchange characteristics.*** Change the saved qualitative and quantitative technical exchange parameters to reflect the actual nature of the exchanges.
5. ***Add new information to the matrix.*** Incorporate additional data exchange elements and associated sending and receiving systems, producing and consuming functions, ad qualitative and quantitative technical exchange parameters not included in the original System Data Exchange Matrix that was copied to produce the new matrix.
6. ***Provide the draft System Data Exchange Matrix to SMEs for review and comment.*** Include information on the portions of the System Data Exchange Matrix to be reviewed, the types of comments to be provided, the desired comment format, the individual(s) or organization(s) to whom/which comments are to be submitted, and the suspense for comment submission.
7. ***Update and modify the System Data Exchange Matrix based on SME comments and recommendations.*** Review comments and recommendations for validity and appropriateness. Incorporate into the matrix all accepted change recommendations.
8. ***Publish the final System Data Exchange Matrix.***

Developing the System Data Exchange Matrix based on a single System Functionality Description

1. ***Identify the external information exchanges required by the System Functionality Description.*** In a System Functionality Description that includes information exchanges, a portion of those exchanges may reflect interfaces with external systems. The externally exchanged information elements provide the basis for the development of the System Data Exchange Matrix. Identify and record those of the System Functionality Description's information elements that are, or must be, exchanged with external systems.

2. ***Determine the physical and/or logical data elements of which the system information exchange elements are composed.*** Some of the information elements extracted from the System Functionality Description reflect single elements of data. Others are composed of multiple related data elements. As much as possible, the System Data Exchange Matrix should include single data elements, not composite information elements. For this reason, most composite information elements must be decomposed into their elemental data elements before being entered into the matrix. The exception is that some elemental data elements are never used or exchanged individually but are always combined with one or more other elemental data elements. Review the names and definitions of the information elements identified in Step 1 to determine the elemental data elements of which they are formed. Every person, place, thing, event, concept, or idea mentioned in the information element name or definition is a candidate data element for inclusion in the matrix.
3. ***Develop the data exchange matrix:***
   a. ***Record the data exchange element name.*** Create or adopt a name for the data exchange element that reflects the nature of the element, is easily recognizable by users of the matrix, and is in accordance with any existing naming standards. Enter the name in the first column of the System Data Exchange Matrix.
   b. ***Identify the sending and receiving systems by name.*** List in the appropriate columns of the matrix the standard name(s) or designation(s) of the internal and external systems that produce and consume each exchanged data element. At least one sending system name/designation and at least one receiving system name/designation must be entered for each exchanged data element. Multiple systems also may be recorded in either or both columns.
   c. ***Identify the producing and consuming system functions.*** List in the appropriate column of the matrix the name of the function from the System Functionality Description that produces each outgoing data element or that receives and consumes each incoming data element. Where appropriate, it may be advantageous or desirable to list multiple sending and/or receiving functions for a data exchange element. When the System Data Exchange Matrix is developed from a single System Functionality Description, each row of the matrix (which represents a description of a single data exchange element) will include an entry in either the Sending System column or the Receiving System column, but not both.
   d. ***Document the qualitative and quantitative technical characteristics of the data exchange.*** Qualitative characteristics include, but are not limited to: the timeframe in which the exchange is or will be implemented, the formatted data packet/message used to effect the exchange, the exchange medium, the security classification of the data being exchanged, the precedence of the exchange, the operational impact of not conducting the exchange, the status of the exchange, and the directionality of the exchange. Quantitative characteristics include, but are not limited to: the

physical size of the data packet/message to be exchanged, the frequency of the exchange, the perishability of the data being exchanged, and the required speed of service.
4. **Provide the draft System Data Exchange Matrix to SMEs for review and comment.** Include information on the portions of the System Data Exchange Matrix to be reviewed, the types of comments to be provided, the desired comment format, the individual(s) or organization(s) to whom/which comments are to be submitted, and the suspense for comment submission.
5. **Update and modify the System Data Exchange Matrix as necessary based upon SME comments and recommendations.** Add, delete, or modify the included data exchange elements, the sending or receiving systems, the sending or receiving functions, or the qualitative or quantitative exchange characteristics.
6. **Publish the final System Data Exchange Matrix.**

Developing the System Data Exchange Matrix based on System Functionality Descriptions for two interfacing systems.

1. **Crosswalk the System Functionality Descriptions of the two interfacing systems.** For those external interfaces for which a System Functionality Description of both interfacing systems exists, conduct of a crosswalk of the two Function Descriptions. Ideally, the developers of the Function Descriptions for both interfacing systems, or other individuals knowledgeable of the contents of the descriptions and the meanings of the functions and information elements contained in them, should participate in the crosswalks. An acceptable, though not desirable, alternative is for a single individual who is knowledgeable of at least one of the descriptions to conduct an independent crosswalk.

In conducting the crosswalk, the external outputs from one interfacing system are compared to the external inputs of the other system to identify information element correspondences and/or disconnects. The comparisons are made on three levels. First, information element names are compared, and identical or similar names are tentatively associated with each other. For example, if both Function Descriptions contain information elements named "Reports", then those information elements are tentatively associated with each other. Also, if one Function Description contains an input named "Weather Information" and the other contains an output named "Environmental Condition Report", those two information elements would be tentatively associated. Next, the information element definitions are compared to further refine the tentative associations. Finally, the contexts within which the information elements are used are compared, as the level of detail contained in the definitions may vary widely, and the real intent of a definition may be ambiguous until it is examined in context. This three-level analysis should result in a good understanding of information element

correspondences between the two System Functionality Descriptions, which are documented in the first column of the System Data Exchange Matrix.
2. ***Determine the physical and/or logical data elements of which the system information exchange elements are composed.*** Some of the information elements extracted from the System Functionality Descriptions reflect single elements of data. Others are composed of multiple related data elements. As much as possible, the System Data Exchange Matrix should include single data elements, not composite information elements. For this reason, most composite information elements must be decomposed into their elemental data elements before being entered into the matrix. The exception is that some elemental data elements are never used or exchanged individually but are always combined with one or more other elemental data elements. These composite data elements may be entered in the matrix as is. Review the names and definitions of the information elements identified in Step 1 to determine the elemental data elements of which they are formed. Every person, place, thing, event, concept, or idea mentioned in the information element name or definition is a candidate data element for inclusion in the matrix.
3. ***Develop the data exchange matrix:***
    a. ***Record the data exchange element name.*** Create or adopt a name for the data exchange element that reflects the nature of the element, is easily recognizable by users of the matrix, and is in accordance with any existing naming standards. Enter the name in the first column of the System Data Exchange Matrix.
    b. ***Identify the sending and receiving systems by name.*** List in the appropriate columns of the matrix the standard name(s) or designation(s) of the internal and external systems that produce and consume each exchanged data element. At least one sending system name/designation and at least one receiving system name/designation must be entered for each exchanged data element. Multiple systems also may be recorded in either or both columns.
    c. ***Identify the producing and consuming system functions.*** List in the appropriate column of the matrix the name of the function from the System Functionality Description that produces each outgoing data element or that receives and consumes each incoming data element. Where appropriate, it may be advantageous or desirable to list multiple sending and/or receiving functions for a data exchange element. When the System Data Exchange Matrix is developed from a single System Functionality Description, each row of the matrix (which represents a description of a single data exchange element) will include an entry in either the Sending System column or the Receiving System column, but not both.
    d. ***Document the qualitative and quantitative technical characteristics of the data exchange.*** Qualitative characteristics include, but are not limited to: the timeframe in which the exchange is or will be implemented, the formatted data packet/message used to effect the exchange, the exchange medium, the security classification of the data being exchanged,

the precedence of the exchange, the operational impact of not conducting the exchange, the status of the exchange, and the directionality of the exchange. Quantitative characteristics include, but are not limited to: the physical size of the data packet/message to be exchanged, the frequency of the exchange, the perishability of the data being exchanged, and the required speed of service.
4. ***Provide the draft System Data Exchange Matrix to SMEs for review and comment.*** Include information on the portions of the System Data Exchange Matrix to be reviewed, the types of comments to be provided, the desired comment format, the individual(s) or organization(s) to whom/which comments are to be submitted, and the suspense for comment submission.
5. ***Update and modify the System Data Exchange Matrix as necessary based upon SME comments and recommendations.*** Add, delete, or modify the included data exchange elements, the sending or receiving systems, the sending or receiving functions, or the qualitative or quantitative exchange characteristics.
6. ***Publish the final System Data Exchange Matrix.***

Developing the System Data Exchange Matrix based on a System Interface Description

1. ***Identify the information exchanges required by the System Interface Description.*** The System Interface Description includes a high level description of the information exchanged among and between systems. These high-level information elements can serve as the basis for development of the System Data Exchange Matrix. It may be necessary to decompose the high-level information elements into more specific elements in order to provide the appropriate level of detail in the System Data Exchange Matrix.
2. ***Determine the physical and/or logical data elements of which the system information exchange elements are composed.*** Most of the information elements extracted from the System Interface Description are composed of multiple related data elements. As much as possible, the System Data Exchange Matrix should include single data elements, not composite information elements. For this reason, most composite information elements must be decomposed into their elemental data elements before being entered into the matrix. The exception is that some elemental data elements are never used or exchanged individually but are always combined with one or more other elemental data elements. These composite data elements may be entered in the matrix as is. Review the names of the information elements identified in Step 1 to determine the elemental data elements of which they are formed.
3. ***Develop the data exchange matrix:***
    a. ***Record the data exchange element name.*** Create or adopt a name for the data exchange element that reflects the nature of the element, is

easily recognizable by users of the matrix, and is in accordance with any existing naming standards. Enter the name in the first column of the System Data Exchange Matrix.

   b. ***Identify the sending and receiving systems by name.*** List in the appropriate columns of the matrix the standard name(s) or designation(s) of the internal and external systems that produce and consume each exchanged data element. At least one sending system name/designation and at least one receiving system name/designation must be entered for each exchanged data element. Multiple systems also may be recorded in either or both columns.

   c. ***Identify the producing and consuming system functions.*** List in the appropriate column of the matrix the name of the function from the System Functionality Description that produces each outgoing data element or that receives and consumes each incoming data element. Where appropriate, it may be advantageous or desirable to list multiple sending and/or receiving functions for a data exchange element. When the System Data Exchange Matrix is developed from a single System Functionality Description, each row of the matrix (which represents a description of a single data exchange element) will include an entry in either the Sending System column or the Receiving System column, but not both.

   d. ***Document the qualitative and quantitative technical characteristics of the data exchange.*** Qualitative characteristics include, but are not limited to: the timeframe in which the exchange is or will be implemented, the formatted data packet/message used to effect the exchange, the exchange medium, the security classification of the data being exchanged, the precedence of the exchange, the operational impact of not conducting the exchange, the status of the exchange, and the directionality of the exchange. Quantitative characteristics include, but are not limited to: the physical size of the data packet/message to be exchanged, the frequency of the exchange, the perishability of the data being exchanged, and the required speed of service.

4. ***Provide the draft System Data Exchange Matrix to SMEs for review and comment.*** Include information on the portions of the System Data Exchange Matrix to be reviewed, the types of comments to be provided, the desired comment format, the individual(s) or organization(s) to whom/which comments are to be submitted, and the suspense for comment submission.

5. ***Update and modify the System Data Exchange Matrix as necessary based upon SME comments and recommendations.*** Add, delete, or modify the included data exchange elements, the sending or receiving systems, the sending or receiving functions, or the qualitative or quantitative exchange characteristics.

6. ***Publish the final System Data Exchange Matrix.***

Developing the System Data Exchange Matrix based on an existing Data Model

1. ***Identify data elements from the Data Model that are applicable to the system.*** Using data elements from the Data Model eliminates the need to decompose system information elements into their component data elements. Based on the purpose for which it was developed, the Data Model may contain many data elements that are applicable to the system being architected, and many that are not. The critical task performed in this step is to identify those data elements that are applicable to the system.
2. ***Determine which of the applicable data elements are exchanged by the system.*** Select, from the data elements applicable to the system, those that are exchanged with external systems.
3. ***Determine the system functions supported by the exchanged data elements.*** Identify system functions that receive and consume incoming data elements and functions that produce outgoing data elements.
4. ***Develop the data exchange matrix:***
    a. ***Record the data exchange element name.*** Create or adopt a name for the data exchange element that reflects the nature of the element, is easily recognizable by users of the matrix, and is in accordance with any existing naming standards. Enter the name in the first column of the System Data Exchange Matrix.
    b. ***Identify the sending and receiving systems by name.*** List in the appropriate columns of the matrix the standard name(s) or designation(s) of the internal and external systems that produce and consume each exchanged data element. At least one sending system name/designation and at least one receiving system name/designation must be entered for each exchanged data element. Multiple systems also may be recorded in either or both columns.
    c. ***Identify the producing and consuming system functions.*** List in the appropriate column of the matrix the name of the function from the System Functionality Description that produces each outgoing data element or that receives and consumes each incoming data element. Where appropriate, it may be advantageous or desirable to list multiple sending and/or receiving functions for a data exchange element. When the System Data Exchange Matrix is developed from a single System Functionality Description, each row of the matrix (which represents a description of a single data exchange element) will include an entry in either the Sending System column or the Receiving System column, but not both.
    d. ***Document the qualitative and quantitative technical characteristics of the data exchange.*** Qualitative characteristics include, but are not limited to: the timeframe in which the exchange is or will be implemented, the formatted data packet/message used to effect the exchange, the exchange medium, the security classification of the data being exchanged, the precedence of the exchange, the operational impact of not conducting the exchange, the status of the exchange, and the directionality of the

exchange. Quantitative characteristics include, but are not limited to: the physical size of the data packet/message to be exchanged, the frequency of the exchange, the perishability of the data being exchanged, and the required speed of service.

5. **Provide the draft System Data Exchange Matrix to SMEs for review and comment.** Include information on the portions of the System Data Exchange Matrix to be reviewed, the types of comments to be provided, the desired comment format, the individual(s) or organization(s) to whom/which comments are to be submitted, and the suspense for comment submission.
6. ***Update and modify the System Data Exchange Matrix as necessary based upon SME comments and recommendations.*** *Add, delete, or modify the included data exchange elements, the sending or receiving systems, the sending or receiving functions, or the qualitative or quantitative exchange characteristics.*
7. **Publish the final System Data Exchange Matrix.**

Developing the System Data Exchange Matrix based on SME input.

1. **Gather SME input through the conduct of interviews or workshops, or through the use of surveys and questionnaires.** Conduct one-on-one interviews with SMEs or conduct information collection workshops involving multiple SMEs. Interviews and workshops may be supplemented by surveys or questionnaires sent to SMEs who are cannot be interviewed and who are unable to participate in workshops.
2. **Resolve conflicts in information provided by different SMEs.** As the information provided by different SMEs may not be in total agreement, it will sometimes be necessary to resolve inconsistencies in the information collected from two or more different SMEs. One possible resolution method is to identify and adopt the information that is provided by the majority of SMEs. A secondary resolution strategy is to adopt the information that is most consistent with other information included in the architecture. Another method is to bring together the providers of conflicting information so that they may collectively reach a consensus.
3. **Consolidate SME input to produce an initial System Data Exchange Matrix.** Enter information provided by SMEs into the appropriate rows, columns, and cells of the System Data Exchange Matrix.
4. **Solicit additional SME input to fill in gaps in the matrix.** Identify to the same SMEs who originally provided input, or to a different set of SMEs, the elements of information needed to complete the System Data Exchange Matrix, and request that they provide the needed information. Specific elements of information may be solicited from specific SMEs—those best qualified to provide the appropriate information.
5. **Provide the complete draft System Data Exchange Matrix to SMEs for review and comment.** Include information on the portions of the System Data Exchange Matrix to be reviewed, the types of comments to be provided,

the desired comment format, the individual(s) or organization(s) to whom/which comments are to be submitted, and the suspense for comment submission.
6. ***Update and modify the System Data Exchange Matrix based on SME comments and recommendations.*** Add, delete, or modify the included data exchange elements, the sending or receiving systems, the sending or receiving functions, or the qualitative or quantitative exchange characteristics.
7. ***Provide the updated System Data Exchange Matrix to SMEs for approval.*** Once appropriate change recommendations have been incorporated into the matrix, provide the updated matrix to SMEs for additional comment or final approval.
8. ***Publish the final System Data Exchange Matrix.***

Developing the System Data Exchange Matrix based on non-architectural system documentation.

1. ***Review documentation to identify and collect information related to system data exchanges.*** First, identify available documentation that might contain information related to the exchange of data among systems. Next, extract and document appropriate information from the source documents. Categorize the extracted information by System Data Exchange Matrix column; e.g., consolidate candidate data exchange elements into one group, sending and receiving system names in another, and producing and consuming functions in another. This information categorization will facilitate identifying conflicts in information extracted from different documents.
2. ***Identify and resolve conflicts in the information collected from different source documents.*** Review the collected information to uncover **substantive** differences in the information extracted from different source documents, or from different portions of the same document. Substantive differences include disagreements in the data to be exchanged, the systems being exchanged, or the characteristics of the exchange. By contrast, trivial differences may include the use in different documentation sources of slightly different names for data exchange elements, systems, or functions that are easily identified as the same (e.g., "status data" versus "status report", "car" versus "automobile", or "Maintenance Operations" versus "Repair Operations").
3. ***Consolidate collected information to produce an initial System Data Exchange Matrix.*** Enter the consolidated, deconflicted information into the correct row, column, and cell of the System Data Exchange Matrix.
4. ***Fill in information gaps in the initial matrix.*** First, identify the elements of information needed to complete the matrix. Second, search already available documentation sources, attempting to find the missing information. Enter into the matrix any information uncovered as a result of this documentation search. Third, attempt to identify additional documentation sources for information still missing from the matrix. Only after exhausting all possible

documentation sources, use your own professional judgement to fill in any remaining information gaps.
5. ***Provide the draft System Data Exchange Matrix to SMEs for review and comment.*** Include information on the portions of the System Data Exchange Matrix to be reviewed, the types of comments to be provided, the desired comment format, the individual(s) or organization(s) to whom/which comments are to be submitted, and the suspense for comment submission.
6. ***Update and modify the draft System Data Exchange Matrix based on SME comments and recommendations.*** Add, delete, or modify the included data exchange elements, the sending or receiving systems, the sending or receiving functions, or the qualitative or quantitative exchange characteristics.
7. ***Publish the final System Data Exchange Matrix.***

RECOMMENDED DEVELOPMENT SEQUENCE:
Following the development of the System Functionality Description and the Operational Information Exchange Matrix.

KEY RELATIONSHIPS:

- Operational Information Exchange Matrix: The System Data Exchange Matrix should be directly traceable to the OIEM, as it reflects the system implementation of the operational requirements captured in the OIEM. Each data exchange element in the System Data Exchange Matrix should be directly traceable to one or more information exchange elements from the OIEM. The sending and receiving system nodes identified in the System Data Exchange Matrix should be a subordinate component of or directly traceable to one or more sending or receiving operational nodes, systems, elements, or organizations identified in the OIEM.
- Logical Data Model: The data exchange elements included in the System Data Exchange Matrix should be the same as those captured in the Logical Data Model.
- Physical Data Model: The data exchange elements included in the System Data Exchange Matrix should be the same as those captured in the Physical Data Model.
- System Interface Description: The System Data Exchange Matrix should provide a detailed technical description of the nature of the data exchanges identified in the System Interface Description.
- System Communications Description: The system data exchange elements detailed in the System Data Exchange Matrix should be consistent with and directly traceable to one or more inter-system interfaces captured on the System Communication Description. If high-level data exchange element names appear on the System Communications Description, they should be the

same as or directly traceable to one or more system data exchange elements included in the System Data Exchange Matrix.
- System^2 Matrix: The system data exchange elements defined in the System Data Exchange Matrix should support the system to system relationship types reflected in the System^2 Matrix.

CRITICAL SUCCESS FACTORS:

DO'S:
- Ensure that the data exchange elements identified in the System Data Exchange Matrix are consistent with the data elements defined in the Logical or Physical Data Model, if one exists.
- Ensure that the sending and receiving systems identified in the System Data Exchange Matrix are consistent with those shown on the System Interface Description and/or the System Communications Description.
- Ensure that the qualitative and quantitative technical exchange parameters defined in the System Data Exchange Matrix are consistent with the information captured in the System Communications Description.
- Ensure that the data exchanges depicted in the System Data Exchange Matrix are consistent with the information exchanges depicted in the Operational Information Exchange Matrix.
- Validate the System Data Exchange Matrix by having it reviewed by persons responsible for producing or using external sending and receiving systems.

DON'TS:
- Don't include notional sending and receiving systems in the matrix without clearly indicating their notional nature.
- Don't include producing and consuming functions in the matrix that do not appear in the System Functionality Description, if one exists.

CHECKLIST: The SYSTEM DATA EXCHANGE MATRIX

Developing the System Data Exchange Matrix based on an existing System Data Exchange Matrix

Process Steps	Complete
1. Identify an existing System Data Exchange Matrix to be used as a template.	
2. Save and rename a copy of the existing matrix.	
3. Identify reusable portions of the existing matrix.	
4. Modify reused portions of the matrix as necessary.	
a. Modify data exchange elements.	
b. Modify sending and receiving systems.	
c. Modify producing and consuming functions.	
d. Modify qualitative and quantitative technical exchange characteristics.	
5. Add new information to the matrix.	
6. Provide the draft System Data Exchange Matrix to SMEs for review and comment.	
7. Update and modify the System Data Exchange Matrix based on SME comments and recommendations.	
8. Publish the final System Data Exchange Matrix.	

Developing the System Data Exchange Matrix based on a single System Functionality Description

Process Steps	Complete
1. Identify the information exchanges required by the System Functionality Description.	
2. Determine the physical and/or logical data elements of which the system information exchange elements are composed.	
3. Develop the data exchange matrix:	
a. Record the data exchange element name.	
b. Identify the sending and receiving systems by name.	
c. Identify the producing and consuming system functions.	
d. Document the qualitative and quantitative technical characteristics of the data exchange.	
4. Provide the draft System Data Exchange Matrix to SMEs for review and comment.	
5. Update and modify the System Data Exchange Matrix as necessary based upon SME comments and recommendations.	
6. Publish the final System Data Exchange Matrix.	

Developing the System Data Exchange Matrix based on System Functionality Descriptions for two interfacing systems.

Process Steps	Complete
1. Crosswalk the System Functionality Descriptions of the two interfacing systems.	
2. Determine the physical and/or logical data elements of which the system information exchange elements are composed.	
3. Develop the data exchange matrix:	
a. Record the data exchange element name.	
b. Identify the sending and receiving systems by name.	
c. Identify the producing and consuming system functions.	
d. Document the qualitative and quantitative technical characteristics of the data exchange.	
4. Provide the draft System Data Exchange Matrix to SMEs for review and comment.	
5. Update and modify the System Data Exchange Matrix as necessary based upon SME comments and recommendations.	
6. Publish the final System Data Exchange Matrix.	

Developing the System Data Exchange Matrix based on a System Interface Description

Process Steps	Complete
1. Identify the information exchanges required by the System Interface Description.	
2. Determine the physical and/or logical data elements of which the system information exchange elements are composed.	
3. Develop the data exchange matrix:	
a. Record the data exchange element name.	
b. Identify the sending and receiving systems by name.	
c. Identify the producing and consuming system functions.	
d. Document the qualitative and quantitative technical characteristics of the data exchange.	
4. Provide the draft System Data Exchange Matrix to SMEs for review and comment.	
5. Update and modify the System Data Exchange Matrix as necessary based upon SME comments and recommendations.	
6. Publish the final System Data Exchange Matrix.	

Developing the System Data Exchange Matrix based on an existing Data Model

Process Steps	Complete
1. Identify data elements from the Data Model that are applicable to the system.	
2. Determine which of the applicable data elements are exchanged by the system.	
3. Determine the system functions supported by the exchanged data elements.	
4. Develop the data exchange matrix:	
a. Record the data exchange element name.	
b. Identify the sending and receiving systems by name.	
c. Identify the producing and consuming system functions.	
d. Document the qualitative and quantitative technical characteristics of the data exchange.	
5. Provide the draft System Data Exchange Matrix to SMEs for review and comment.	
6. Update and modify the System Data Exchange Matrix as necessary based upon SME comments and recommendations.	
7. Publish the final System Data Exchange Matrix.	

Developing the System Data Exchange Matrix based on SME input.

Process Steps	Complete
1. Gather SME input through the conduct of interviews or workshops, or through the use of surveys and questionnaires.	
2. Resolve conflicts in information provided by different SMEs.	
3. Consolidate SME input to produce an initial System Data Exchange Matrix.	
4. Solicit additional SME input to fill in gaps in the matrix.	
5. Provide the complete draft System Data Exchange Matrix to SMEs for review and comment.	
6. Update and modify the System Data Exchange Matrix based on SME comments and recommendations.	
7. Provide the updated System Data Exchange Matrix to SMEs for approval.	
8. Publish the final System Data Exchange Matrix.	

Developing the System Data Exchange Matrix based on non-architectural system documentation.

Process Steps	Complete
1. Review documentation to identify and collect information related to system data exchanges.	
2. Identify and resolve conflicts in the information collected from different source documents.	
3. Consolidate collected information to produce an initial System Data Exchange Matrix.	
4. Fill in information gaps in the initial matrix.	
5. Provide the draft System Data Exchange Matrix to SMEs for review and comment.	
6. Update and modify the draft System Data Exchange Matrix based on SME comments and recommendations.	
7. Publish the final System Data Exchange Matrix.	

CHAPTER FIFTEEN

PRODUCT NAME: SYSTEM PERFORMANCE PARAMETERS MATRIX

OTHER ALIASES: None

PRODUCT DESIGNATION: SV-7

ARCHITECTURE VIEW: SYSTEMS

PRODUCT DEFINITION: The SYSTEM PERFORMANCE PARAMETERS MATRIX is a description of a system's level of performance within defined capability areas. It describes both current and future system performance.

PRODUCT DESCRIPTION: The System Performance Parameters Matrix provides a detailed description of the current or future performance characteristics of a system. The rows of the matrix define the various system capability areas. The matrix columns identify different time periods. The sum total of the entries in a single column of the matrix provides a snapshot of the system's capabilities at a particular point in time. Existing systems may or may not have a column describing current system capabilities. All matrices, however, will include one or more columns describing future system capabilities. Future performance characteristics in the matrix may reflect planned or projected system performance, or system performance **requirements**. Through the inclusion of multiple timeframes, the matrix may be used to describe the evolution of the system over time.

	Performance Measures		
	Time 1 (Threshold)	Time 2	Timex (Objective)
System A			
Performance Area 1			
Performance Area 2			
Performance Area 3			
Performance Area 4			
Performance Area 5			
Performance Area 6			
Performance Area 7			
Performance Area 8			
Performance Area 9			

PRODUCT FORMAT: Table or spreadsheet

USERS & USES:

USERS:

Corporate/Non-Military

- Operations Manager
- Resource Manager
- Information Manager
- Quality Assurance Manager
- Facilities Manager
- Security Manager
- Supervisors
- Workers
- Software Developers
- Research and Development
- Sales Department

Military

- Combat Developer
- Concept Developer
- Program/Project/Product Developer
- Resource Manager
- Operational Architect
- Systems Architect
- Technical Architect
- Systems Engineer
- Software Developer
- Manufacturer
- Test & Evaluation Community
- Modeling & Simulation Community
- Warfighter

USES:

Corporate/Non-Military

- Business Process Reengineering
- Development of Capital Investment Strategies
- Quality Control/Quality Management
- Description of Required System Capabilities
- Identification of Operational Issues
- Wargaming Alternatives
- Performance of Cost/Benefits Analysis

Military

- Identification of Operational Issues
- Identification/Validation of Operational Needs/Requirements
- Development/Validation Of Models & Simulations
- Allocation Of Communication Assets
- Planning For System Tests
- Identification of OPFAC Hardware Requirements
- Development Of System Software
- Wargaming Alternatives
- Providing Roadmap For System Improvement
- Battlefield/Business Process Reengineering
- Design of Human-Computer Interface

TYPICAL INFORMATION SOURCES:

Corporate/Non-Military

- Subject Matter Experts
- System Descriptions

Military

- Subject Matter Experts
- Interface Descriptions
- System Descriptions

TOOLS:

- Text Editor
- Drawing/Graphics Tool
- Database

PARTICIPANTS:

Corporate/Non-Military

- Operations Manager
- Resource Manager
- Information Manager
- Security Manager
- Supervisors
- Workers
- Software Developers
- Operational Architect/Facilitator
- Subject Matter Expert

Military

- Combat Developer
- Operational Architect/Facilitator
- Subject Matter Expert
- Warfighter
- Program/Project/Product Developer
- Systems Architect
- Technical Architect
- Systems Engineer

PRODUCT DEVELOPMENT:

1. ***Identify the system for which a System Performance Parameters Matrix will be developed.***
2. ***Determine the specific performance parameters to be captured in the matrix.*** The matrix may address all or only a subset of the system's performance parameters. The actual parameters addressed will depend on

the use(s) to which the matrix will be put. First, define the purposes for which the matrix is being developed. Second, determine the system performance parameters that best support those purposes. Finally, add rows to the matrix for each of the selected parameters.
3. ***Identify the timeframe(s) to be addressed within the matrix.*** As with the performance parameters, the timeframes addressed in the matrix are dependent on the use(s) to which the matrix will be put. First, define the purposes for which the matrix is being developed. Second, determine the timeframes that best support those purposes. Finally, add columns to the matrix for each of the selected timeframes. Matrices developed for existing systems may or may not include a column for the current timeframe that describes current system capabilities. All matrices, however, will include at least one column describing future system capabilities.
4. ***Label the rows and columns of the matrix to reflect the selected performance parameters and timeframes.***
5. ***Document (quantify) the level of performance for each parameter during each applicable timeframe.*** Use text and/or graphics to indicate the system's current, proposed, expected, or required level of performance for each performance parameter in each timeframe. If graphics are used, include a legend to define the graphical symbols.
6. ***Provide the draft System Performance Parameter Matrix to SMEs for review and comment.*** Include information on the portions of the System Performance Parameters Matrix to be reviewed, the types of comments to be provided, the desired comment format, the individual(s) or organization(s) to whom/which comments are to be submitted, and the suspense for comment submission.
7. ***Update and modify the System Performance Parameters Matrix as necessary based on SME comments and recommendations.*** Change the included performance parameters, the timeframes, or the descriptions of system capabilities based on SME input.
8. ***Publish the final System Performance Parameters Matrix.***

RECOMMENDED DEVELOPMENT SEQUENCE: Following the development of the System Functionality Description, the System Interface Description, and the Technical Architecture Profile.

KEY RELATIONSHIPS:

- System Interface Description: Selected systems shown on the System Performance Parameters Matrix should be the same as the systems shown in the System Interface Description.

- System Evolution Description: The System Evolution Description may identify how the performance of the system(s) shown in the System Performance Parameters Matrix change over time.
- System Technology Forecast: The System Technology Forecast shows how the performance of a system (as shown in the System Performance Parameters Matrix) changes over time as capabilities are added or removed.
- Technical Architecture Profile: Appropriate performance parameters described in the System Performance Parameters Matrix must be in accordance with the information processing, information exchange, information security, and human-computer interface standards defined in the Technical Architecture Profile.

CRITICAL SUCCESS FACTORS:

DO'S:
– Ensure that the system capabilities described in the System Performance Parameters Matrix are consistent with the system capabilities described in the System Functionality Description and the Technical Architecture Profile.

– Ensure that the future system capabilities described in the System Performance Parameters Matrix are consistent with the System Technology Forecast and the System Evolution Description.

DON'TS:
– Don't include non-performance related system characteristics in the System Performance Parameters Matrix.

CHECKLIST: The SYSTEM PERFORMANCE PARAMETERS MATRIX

Process Steps	Complete
1. Identify the system for which a System Performance Parameters Matrix will be developed.	
2. Determine the specific performance parameters to be captured in the matrix.	
3. Identify the timeframe(s) to be addressed within the matrix.	
4. Label the rows and columns of the matrix to reflect the selected performance parameters and timeframes.	
5. Document (quantify) the level of performance for each parameter during each applicable timeframe.	
6. Provide the draft System Performance Parameter Matrix to SMEs for review and comment.	
7. Update and modify the System Performance Parameters Matrix as necessary based on SME comments and recommendations.	
8. Publish the final System Performance Parameters Matrix.	

CHAPTER SIXTEEN

PRODUCT NAME: SYSTEM EVOLUTION DESCRIPTION

OTHER ALIASES: None

PRODUCT DESIGNATION: SV-8

ARCHITECTURE VIEW: SYSTEMS

PRODUCT DEFINITION: The SYSTEM EVOLUTION DESCRIPTION provides a graphical depiction of how system capabilities change over time.

PRODUCT DESCRIPTION: The System Evolution Description can be thought of as a less detailed, graphics-based version of the System Performance Parameters Matrix. It is normally presented as an annotated timeline. It may be developed to address the capabilities of a single system or a family of related systems.

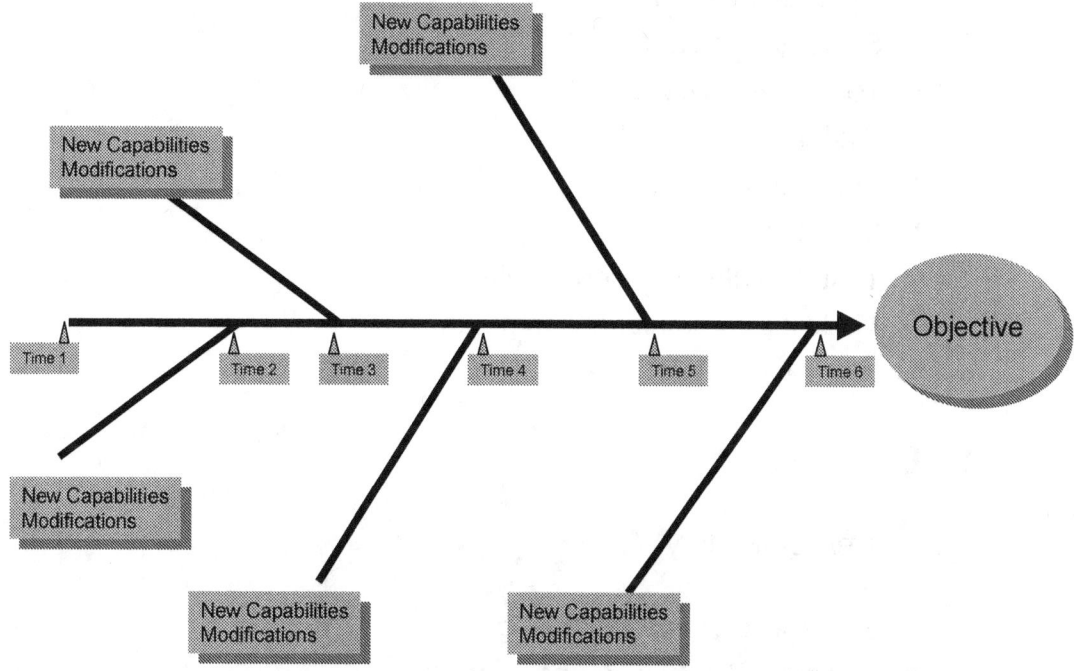

PRODUCT FORMAT: Graphical, with textual annotations

USERS & USES:

USERS:

Corporate/Non-Military

- Strategic Planner
- Operations Manager
- Resource Manager
- Information Manager
- Software Developers
- Research and Development
- Sales Department

Military

- Combat Developer
- Concept Developer
- Program/Project/Product Developer
- Resource Manager
- Operational Architect
- Systems Architect
- Technical Architect
- Systems Engineer
- Software Developer
- Manufacturer
- Test & Evaluation Community
- Modeling & Simulation Community
- Warfighter

USES:

Corporate/Non-Military

- Strategic Business Planning
- Business Process Reengineering
- Development of Capital Investment Strategies
- Identification of Operational Issues

- Allocation Of Communication Assets
- Wargaming Alternatives

Military

- Identification of Operational Issues
- Development/Validation Of Models & Simulations
- Planning For System Tests
- Development Of System Software
- Wargaming Alternatives
- Prioritizing Activities For Implementation
- Providing Roadmap For System Improvement
- Battlefield/Business Process Reengineering
- Development of Procedures Guides and User's Manuals
- Performance of Cost/Benefits Analysis

TYPICAL INFORMATION SOURCES:

Corporate/Non-Military

- Long Range Plans
- Subject Matter Experts
- System Descriptions
- Vision Statements

Military

- Subject Matter Experts
- Future Operational Capabilities (FOCs)
- Long Range Plans
- Modernization Plans
- System Descriptions

TOOLS:

- Text Editor
- Drawing/Graphics Tool
- Database

PARTICIPANTS:

Corporate/Non-Military

- Strategic Planner
- Operations Manager
- Resource Manager
- Security Manager
- Supervisors
- Workers
- Software Developers
- Trainers
- Operational Architect/Facilitator
- Subject Matter Expert

Military

- Combat Developer
- Training Developer
- Operational Architect/Facilitator
- Subject Matter Expert
- Warfighter
- Program/Project/Product Developer
- Systems Architect
- Technical Architect
- Systems Engineer

PRODUCT DEVELOPMENT:

1. ***Select the system(s) to be covered.*** Identify the individual system or family of systems to be addressed based on the purpose(s) for which the System Evolution Description is being developed.
2. ***Identify the period of time to be addressed by the System Evolution description timeline.*** Based on the proposed use(s) of the System Evolution Description, determine the appropriate start and end times for the timeline that forms the core of the product.
3. ***Construct the base timeline.*** *Label key points along the timeline, to include the start and end date-time and significant interim time points.*

4. ***Determine the system lifecycle milestones to be captured on the System Evolution Description.*** The timeline may address all system lifecycle milestones. However, doing so may make it overly detailed and difficult to use as it contains more information than is necessary to support the purposes for which it is being developed. Instead of incorporating all system lifecycle milestones, it may be preferable to include a limited set of milestones tailored to the specific use(s) to which the product will be put. Determine the specific system lifecycle milestones (e.g., system or version fielding, operational tests, hardware and software upgrades, incorporation of new capabilities, or retirement from service) based on required or desired system use(s). Enter the selected milestone events along the timeline.
5. ***Identify on the timeline the points in time when each system lifecycle milestone event will take place.*** Mark and label the dates associated with each milestone event.
6. ***Provide the draft System Evolution Description to SMEs for review and comment.*** Include information on the portions of the System Evolution Description to be reviewed, the types of comments to be provided, the desired comment format, the individual(s) or organization(s) to whom/which comments are to be submitted, and the suspense for comment submission.
7. ***Update and modify the System Evolution Description as necessary based on SME comments and recommendations.*** Change the timeline start or end dates, add or delete system lifecycle milestones, or modify milestone dates as necessary to implement accepted SME comments and recommendations.
8. ***Publish the final System Evolution Description.***

RECOMMENDED DEVELOPMENT SEQUENCE: No recommendation.

KEY RELATIONSHIPS:

- System Functionality Description: The System Evolution Description may describe how the functions performed by a particular system (as shown in the System Functionality Description) change over time.
- System Performance Parameters Matrix: The System Evolution Description may identify how the performance of the system(s) shown in the System Performance Parameters Matrix change over time.
- System Technology Forecast: Both the System Technology Forecast and the System Evolution Description can be used to show how the technical standards implemented by systems change over time.
- Technical Architecture Profile: The System Evolution Description provides a description of the time-phased implementation of the standards identified in the Technical Architecture Profile.

- Standards Technology Forecast: The changes to the system, as documented in the System Evolution Description, should be consistent with the mandated/acceptable standards defined in the Standards Technology Forecast.

CRITICAL SUCCESS FACTORS:

DO'S:
- Ensure that the performance related system lifecycle milestones are consistent with the System Performance Parameters Matrix.
- Ensure that technical system lifecycle milestones are consistent with the technical standards contained in the Technical Architecture Profile and the Standards Technology Forecast.
- Ensure that planned or projected system changes are consistent with the future technical standards presented in the Systems Technology Forecast.

DON'TS: None.

CHECKLIST: The SYSTEM EVOLUTION DESCRIPTION

Process Steps	Complete
1. Select the system(s) to be covered.	
2. Identify the period of time to be addressed by the System Evolution description timeline.	
3. Construct the base timeline. Label key points along the timeline, to include the start and end date-time and significant interim time points.	
4. Determine the system lifecycle milestones to be captured on the System Evolution Description.	
5. Capture the selected system lifecycle milestones on the timeline.	
6. Identify on the timeline the points in time when each system lifecycle milestone event will take place.	
7. Provide the draft System Evolution Description to SMEs for review and comment.	
8. Update and modify the System Evolution Description as necessary based on SME comments and recommendations.	
9. Publish the final System Evolution Description.	

CHAPTER SEVENTEEN

PRODUCT NAME: SYSTEM FUNCTION SEQUENCE & TIMING DESCRIPTION

OTHER ALIASES: System Process Model, System Mission Thread, System State Transition Diagram

PRODUCT DESIGNATION: SV-10a, b, c

ARCHITECTURE VIEW: SYSTEMS

PRODUCT DEFINITION: The SYSTEM FUNCTION SEQUENCE & TIMING DESCRIPTION describes the time sequencing of system functions and processes.

PRODUCT DESCRIPTION: The System Function Sequence and Timing Description provides a means for describing or defining the time based behavior of a system. It can link individual functions from the System Functionality Description together to describe end-to-end processes. It can show the required, preferred, or prescribed sequence of functions. It can be used to define or document the timing and duration of functions and processes. It can also be used to identify critical functions (e.g., functions that must be completed before subsequent functions may be initiated) within processes.

There are two general categories of System Function Sequence and Timing Descriptions—task based and information exchange based. The difference between the two is the nature of the building blocks used to produce an individual sequence and timing description. In a task-based description, the basic building blocks are operational functions, tasks, missions, actions, or activities. In information exchange based descriptions, the basic building blocks are individual information exchange actions (e.g., transmissions, retransmissions, message deliveries, transmission acknowledgments, etc.).

Both categories of System Function Sequence and Timing Description can be documented using one of three types of models. These three model types are:

- System Rules Model

- System State Transition Description

- System Event/Trace Description

The System Rules Model captures the "business rules" associated with elements of the architecture. The rules may prescribe the conditions under which actions or tasks are initiated, performed, continued, resumed, or terminated. Other rules may control or constrain the types or quantities of outputs produced by system functions. These rules may take the form of algorithms, mathematical formulae, decision trees, "if/then" statements, Boolean statements, or statements and assertions in plain English.

The System State Transition Description describes how enterprise components (i.e., systems and information/data) are modified as a result of the performance of functions and processes.

The System Event/Trace Description is the most familiar of the three model types. It shows the sequencing of individual functions, events, and actions. An example System Event /Trace Description diagram is shown below.

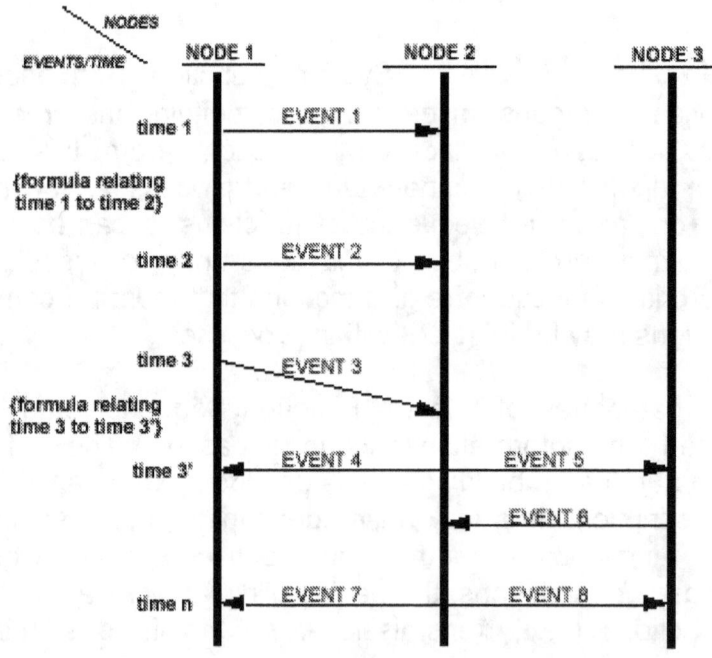

PRODUCT FORMAT: Graphical, with textual annotations

USERS & USES:

USERS:

Corporate/Non-Military

- Operations Manager
- Information Manager
- Quality Assurance Manager
- Security Manager
- Supervisors
- Workers
- Software Developers
- Trainers
- Research and Development
- Policy Writers

Military
- Combat Developer
- Concept Developer
- Trainer
- Training Developer
- Program/Project/Product Developer
- Operational Architect
- Systems Architect
- Technical Architect
- Systems Engineer
- Software Developer
- Manufacturer
- Test & Evaluation Community
- Modeling & Simulation Community
- Warfighter

USES:

Corporate/Non-Military

- Strategic Business Planning
- Development of Procedures Guides and User's Manuals
- Business Process Reengineering
- Development/validation of SOPs
- Quality Control/Quality Management
- Description of Required System Capabilities
- Baselining of Functionality
- Functional Allocation
- Database Design
- Identification of Operational Issues
- Wargaming Alternatives
- Performance of Cost/Benefits Analysis
- Development of Training Materials

Military

- Development/Modification of Operational Concepts
- Identification of Operational Issues
- Identification/Validation of Operational Needs/Requirements
- Standardization of Processes, Activities and Tasks
- Development/Validation Of Tactics, Techniques & Procedures (TTPs)
- Development/Validation Of SOPs
- Development/Validation Of Models & Simulations
- Development/Validation Of Mission Training Plans
- Planning For Organization Exercises
- Planning For System Tests
- Development Of System Software
- Baselining Of Functionality
- Wargaming Alternatives
- Battlefield/Business Process Reengineering
- Development of Procedures Guides and User's Manuals
- Design of Human-Computer Interface
- Performance of Cost/Benefits Analysis

- Development of Training Materials

TYPICAL INFORMATION SOURCES:

Corporate/Non-Military

- Function/Task Lists
- Long Range Plans
- Organization Descriptions
- Operational Concepts
- Policy and Procedures Guides
- Standing Operating Procedures (SOPs)
- Strategic Plans
- Subject Matter Experts
- System Descriptions
- Task Descriptions
- Vision Statements
- Business Plans
- Corporate Brochures

Military

- Subject Matter Experts
- Policy and Procedures Guides
- Doctrinal Publications
- Operational Concepts
- Operational and Organizational Plans
- Vision Statements
- Function/Task Lists (including METLs, UJTL, Service Task Lists)
- Task Descriptions
- Standing Operating Procedures (SOPs)
- Interface Descriptions

TOOLS:

- Text Editor
- Drawing/Graphics Tool

- Function/Process Modeling Tool
- Object Modeling Tool
- Flow Charting Tool

PARTICIPANTS:

Corporate/Non-Military

- Strategic Planner
- Operations Manager
- Human Resource Manager
- Resource Manager
- Information Manager
- Quality Assurance Manager
- Facilities Manager
- Security Manager
- Supervisors
- Workers
- Trainers
- Policy Writers
- Operational Architect/Facilitator
- Subject Matter Expert

Military

- Combat Developer
- Concept & Doctrine Developer
- Training Developer
- Operational Architect/Facilitator
- Subject Matter Expert
- Warfighter
- Program/Project/Product Developer
- Systems Architect
- Technical Architect
- Systems Engineer

PRODUCT DEVELOPMENT:

Develop System Rules Model

8. ***Identify critical processes for which System Rules Models are needed.***
9. ***For each identified critical process, determine the type(s) of rules to be captured.*** Determine whether the System Rules Model is meant to (1) describe the conditions under which actions or tasks are initiated, performed, continued, resumed, or terminated, or (2) to define the rules that control or constrain the types or quantities of outputs produced by system functions.
10. ***Document the System rules in the appropriate format(s).*** Define the appropriate rules in the form of algorithms, mathematical formulae, decision trees, "if/then" statements, Boolean statements, or statements and assertions in plain English.

> 1. If the value of Attribute 1 equals zero (0), then set the value of Attribute 2 to equal zero (0).
> 2. If the value of Attribute 1 is greater than or equal to one (1), then set the value of Attribute 2 equal to five (5) times the value of Attribute 1.
> 3. If the value of Attribute 2 is an even integer, then set the value of Attribute 3 to "No". Otherwise, set the value of Attribute 3 to "Yes".

11. ***Provide the System Rules Model to SMEs for review and comment.*** Include information on the portions of the event/trace description to be reviewed, the types of comments to be provided, the desired comment format, the individual(s) or organization(s) to whom/which comments are to be submitted, and the suspense for comment submission.
12. ***Modify and update the System Rules Model based on SME comments.*** Alter the model as necessary to incorporate recommended changes.
13. ***Publish the System Rules Model.***
14. ***Repeat the steps as necessary to develop additional System Rules Model for other critical processes.***

Develop System State Transition Description

12. ***Identify critical processes for which System State Transition Descriptions are needed.*** Select functions or processes for which it is important to understand or describe the nature of the change in state, or the conditions under which the state transition occurs.
13. ***Identify the specific function that results in a change of state.*** Where possible, reuse a function or a mission/task previously defined in the System Functionality Description. Adopt the name of the function or mission as the title of the System State Transition Description.

14. ***Define the initial state.*** Determine how the architecture component (e.g., the node, organization, system, and information element) looks prior to the performance of the function.
15. ***Define the specific conditions under which the state transition occurs.*** Determine whether the state transition is time or event driven, i.e., whether it occurs at a specified time (or time interval) or as a result of a predefined action or event. Also consider state transitions that are initiated as a result of external environmental conditions (e.g., weather, visibility, or illumination) rather than clearly defined events.
16. ***Define the final state.*** Determine the way that the architecture component is expected to look after the state transition is completed.
17. ***Identify and document interim state transitions included in the larger state transition chain.*** Define any intermediate states between the initial and end state, or any "nested" state transition processes that are a part of the larger state transition process being described.
18. ***Build System State Transition Description diagram.***
    - Depict the initial, interim, and end states as rounded corner boxes. Label the boxes to define/describe the state being depicted.
    - Connect the boxes with one-way arrows that reflect the events or activities that result in the transition from one state to the next.
    - Add start and stop terminators to show the beginning and end of the process. The start terminator is depicted by a single dot with an arrow pointing to the box for the beginning state. The end terminator is shown by an arrow pointing from the end state box to a circle with a dot at its center.
    - Label the end terminator arrow to indicate the final result of the state transition process being described.

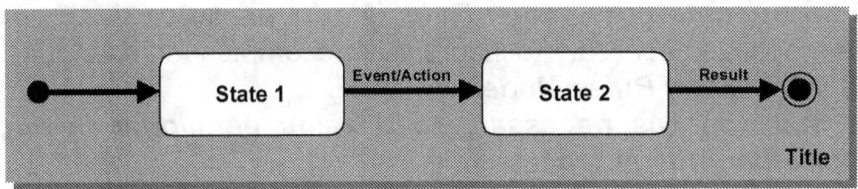

19. ***Provide the System State Transition Description to SMEs for review and comment.*** Include information on the portions of the System State Transition Description to be reviewed, the types of comments to be provided, the desired comment format, the individual(s) or organization(s) to whom/which comments are to be submitted, and the suspense for comment submission.
20. ***Modify and update the System State Transition Description based on SME comments.***
21. ***Publish the System State Transition Description.***
22. ***Repeat the steps as necessary to develop additional System State Transition Descriptions for other critical processes.***

Develop System Event/Trace Description

1. ***Identify critical processes for which System Event/Trace Descriptions are needed.*** Select processes for which the correct timing and sequencing of included functions and tasks is essential to mission success, those for which the sequencing and timing of functions has not been determined, or those for which a more efficient or effective sequencing and timing of system functions is desired.
2. ***For each identified critical process, determine whether it should be captured as a function based or information exchange based process.*** Consider the primary use to which the product is to be put. Identify the primary questions that the System Event/Trace Description is expected to answer or the information that it is meant to illustrate.

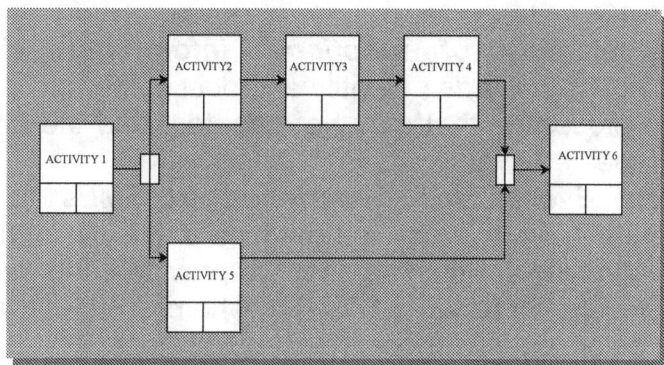

3. ***Identify functions or information exchanges included in the event/trace description.*** For function based event/trace descriptions, identify appropriate functions from the System Functionality Description to be incorporated into the model(s). Identify information exchanges to be included in information exchange based even/trace descriptions by reviewing the System Data Exchange Matrix, the System Interface Description, or the System Communications Description.
4. ***Determine function or information exchange sequencing.*** Place icons representing the selected functions or information exchange events in the order in which the functions or information exchanges are, or should be, performed.
5. ***Identify function or information exchange relationships.*** Determine the relationships among the functions or information exchange events included in the event/trace descriptions. Relationship types include, but are not limited to, precedence, concurrence, or alternatives. Precedence relationships are those in which one function or information exchange must always be initiated or completed before a subsequent function or information exchange event can take place. Concurrence relationships are those in which two or more functions or information exchanges may be performed simultaneously. Alternative relationships are those in which any one (but only one) of two or more equivalent functions or information exchanges may be activated upon

the completion of a preceding function or information exchange. Connect pairs of functions or information exchange events using connectors that indicate the types of relationships between them.
6. ***Define subordinate process threads that are included in larger event/trace descriptions.*** The process described in the event/trace description may include within it subordinate processes that encompass a smaller number of function or information exchanges.
7. ***Define the timing of activities or information exchanges.*** Capture either function or information exchange duration (i.e., the total time that it takes to complete a function, information exchange, or process) or start/execution time. Functions or information exchanges may be initiated either at a specified time or at a specified interval.
8. ***Identify function or information exchange triggers.*** Define the events, actions, or conditions that cause functions or information exchanges to be initiated.
9. ***Determine repeatability of functions, information exchanges, or subordinate process threads.*** Identify and document functions, information exchanges, and processes that may be repeated, and the conditions under which they are repeated.
10. ***Provide System Event/Trace Description to SMEs for review and comment.*** Include information on the portions of the event/trace description to be reviewed, the types of comments to be provided, the desired comment format, the individual(s) or organization(s) to whom/which comments are to be submitted, and the suspense for comment submission.
11. ***Modify and update System Event/Trace Description based on SME comments.***
12. ***Publish the System Event/Trace Description.***
13. ***Repeat the steps as necessary to document other critical processes.***

RECOMMENDED DEVELOPMENT SEQUENCE:
Following the development of the System Functionality Description and the Operational Activity Sequence & Timing Description.

KEY RELATIONSHIPS:

- Operational Activity Sequence & Timing Description: Each System Functionality Sequence and Timing Description may be developed as the system implementation of one or more Operational Activity Sequence and Timing Descriptions.
- System Functionality Description: The system functions depicted in the System Functionality Sequence and Timing Description should be the same as or directly traceable to functions included in the System Functionality Description.

CRITICAL SUCCESS FACTORS:

DO'S:
- Reuse missions, functions and tasks from the System Functionality Description to develop System Function Sequence and Timing Descriptions.
- Select the type of System Function Sequence and Timing Description model based on the type of information to be described and the uses to which the finished product will be put.

DON'TS:
- Don't create new functions, tasks, events, or actions when acceptable ones already exist as a part of the System Functionality Description.

CHECKLIST: The OPERATIONAL ACTIVITY SEQUENCE AND TIMING DESCRIPTION

Develop System Rules Model

Process Steps	Complete
1. Identify critical processes for which System Rules Models are needed.	
2. For each identified critical process, determine the type(s) of rules to be captured.	
3. Document the system rules in the appropriate format(s).	
4. Provide the System Rules Model to SMEs for review and comment.	
5. Modify and update the System Rules Model based on SME comments.	
6. Publish the System Rules Model.	
7. Repeat the steps as necessary to develop additional System Rules Model for other critical processes.	

Develop System State Transition Description

Process Steps	Complete
1. Identify critical processes for which System State Transition Descriptions are needed.	
2. Identify the specific function that results in a change of state.	
3. Define the initial state.	
4. Define the specific conditions under which the state transition occurs.	
5. Define the final state.	
6. Identify and document interim state transitions included in the larger state transition chain	
7. Build System State Transition Description diagram.	
8. Provide the System State Transition Description to SMEs for review and comment.	
9. Modify and update the System State Transition Description based on SME comments.	
10. Publish the System State Transition Description.	
11. Repeat the steps as necessary to develop additional System State Transition Descriptions for other critical processes.	

Develop System Event/Trace Description

Process Steps	Complete
1. Identify critical processes for which System Event/Trace Descriptions are needed.	
2. For each identified critical process, determine whether it should be captured as a function based or information exchange based process.	
3. Identify functions or information exchanges included in the event/trace description.	
4. Determine function or information exchange sequencing.	
5. Identify function or information exchange relationships.	
6. Define subordinate process threads that are included in larger event/trace descriptions.	
7. Define the timing of functions or information exchanges.	
8. Identify function or information exchange triggers.	
9. Determine repeatability of functions, information exchanges, or subordinate process threads.	
10. Provide System Event/Trace Description to SMEs for review and comment.	
11. Modify and update System Event/Trace Description based on SME comments.	
12. Publish the System Event/Trace Description.	
13. Repeat the steps as necessary to document other critical processes.	

CHAPTER EIGHTEEN

PRODUCT NAME: SYSTEM TECHNOLOGY FORECAST

OTHER ALIASES: None

PRODUCT DESIGNATION: SV-9

ARCHITECTURE VIEW: SYSTEMS

PRODUCT DEFINITION: The SYSTEM TECHNOLOGY FORECAST identifies emerging technologies that may be applied to the system(s) within an enterprise at some time in the future.

PRODUCT DESCRIPTION: The System Technology Forecast describes how a system/enterprise will evolve over time in terms of the technical standards that are incorporated into the system design. The forecast is typically presented as a matrix that includes three categories of information: the rows of the matrix reflect hardware and software technology areas associated with the system, the columns of the matrix reflect critical system lifecycle milestones, and the cells of the matrix identify the actual technical standards expected to be applied to the system in each technology area during each timeframe.

System Name

Technology Area	Current Standard	FY20XX	FY20XX
Kernel			
Shell and Utilities			
Programming Languages			
Client Service Operations			
Object Definition and Management			
Window Management			
Dialogue Support			
Data Management			
Data Interchange			
Electronic Data Interchange			
Graphics			

Because the matrix can contain columns for multiple timeframes, each row of the matrix can illustrate the adoption of different technical standards within a single technology area over time. Likewise, each column of the matrix describes the collection of technical standards that will be implemented by the system at a particular point in time.

PRODUCT FORMAT: Table or spreadsheet

USERS & USES:

USERS:

Corporate/Non-Military

- Strategic Planner
- Operations Manager
- Resource Manager
- Information Manager
- Facilities Manager
- Security Manager
- Supervisors
- Workers
- Software Developers
- Research and Development

Military

- Combat Developer
- Program/Project/Product Developer
- Resource Manager
- Operational Architect
- Systems Architect
- Technical Architect
- Systems Engineer
- Software Developer
- Manufacturer
- Test & Evaluation Community
- Modeling & Simulation Community

USES:

Corporate/Non-Military

- Strategic Business Planning
- Business Process Reengineering
- Development of Capital Investment Strategies
- Quality Control/Quality Management
- Description of Required System Capabilities
- Database Design
- Identification of Operational Issues
- Communications Network Burden Assessment
- Wargaming Alternatives
- Performance of Cost/Benefits Analysis

Military

- Identification of Operational Issues
- Allocation Of Communication Assets
- Planning For System Tests
- Network Burden Assessment
- Data Modeling
- Standardization of Data Elements
- Comparing User's Vision To Developer's Implementation
- Wargaming Alternatives
- Providing Roadmap For System Improvement
- Battlefield/Business Process Reengineering

TYPICAL INFORMATION SOURCES:

Corporate/Non-Military

- Long Range Plans
- Subject Matter Experts
- System Descriptions

Military

- Subject Matter Experts
- Future Operational Capabilities (FOCs)
- Long Range Plans
- Modernization Plans
- Master Plans
- Interface Descriptions
- System Descriptions

TOOLS:

- Text Editor
- Drawing/Graphics Tool
- Database

PARTICIPANTS:

Corporate/Non-Military

- Strategic Planner
- Operations Manager
- Resource Manager
- Information Manager
- Security Manager
- Supervisors
- Workers
- Software Developers
- Operational Architect/Facilitator
- Subject Matter Expert

Military

- Combat Developer
- Operational Architect/Facilitator
- Subject Matter Expert
- Program/Project/Product Developer
- Systems Architect

- Technical Architect
- Systems Engineer

PRODUCT DEVELOPMENT:

1. ***Identify technology areas applicable to the system(s) for which the architecture is being developed.*** Select hardware and software technology areas that will be applicable to the system(s) in the future. For existing systems, include as a minimum those technology areas within which the system currently operates.
2. ***Discover available emerging standards for each identified technology area.*** Conduct research and document reviews to identify developmental (i.e., emerging) military and/or commercial technical standards within each technology area. Emerging standards are those that are in limited use, but have not received wide acceptance. Examples include operational prototypes of hardware, "beta" test versions of software, and draft versions of standards documentation.
3. ***Select from among the emerging standards those that are most likely to be applied to the system(s) in the future.*** Selection criteria include, but are not limited to: availability of the technology, potential operational benefit to the system, expected costs of implementing the standard, the current level of maturity of the technology standard, the relative ease of implementing the standard, the current level of community acceptance of the standard, and the compatibility of the standard with other standards implemented by the system.
4. ***Build the System Technology Forecast as a matrix.*** Add rows to the matrix for each technology area. The columns of the matrix reflect key future time periods. Select matrix timeframes to correspond to critical system lifecycle milestones. Enter the selected technical standards in the cells of the matrix.
5. ***Add a legend to define symbols and terms used in the matrix.*** The legend should include definitions for each term, abbreviation, acronym, and graphical symbol used in the matrix.
6. ***Provide the draft System Technology Forecast to SMEs for review and comment.*** Include information on the portions of the System Technology Forecast to be reviewed, the types of comments to be provided, the desired comment format, the individual(s) or organization(s) to whom/which comments are to be submitted, and the suspense for comment submission.
7. ***Modify the System Technology Forecast based on SME comments and recommendations.*** Update the technology areas, timeframes, or actual technical standards as necessary to accommodate approved SME comments and recommendations.
8. ***Publish final System Technology Forecast.***

RECOMMENDED DEVELOPMENT SEQUENCE: Following the development of the Technical Architecture Profile and the Standards Technology Profile.

KEY RELATIONSHIPS:

- Logical Data Model: The technical standards identified in the System Technology Forecast may influence the structure and characteristics of the data elements captured in the Logical Data Model. For example, the adoption of a specific technical standard for reporting time may effect the way that time based data elements are captured in the Logical Data Model. Likewise, the structure and characteristics of data elements in the Logical Data Model may influence which technical standards are adopted for inclusion in the System Technology Forecast.
- Physical Data Model: The future technical standards identified in the System Technology Forecast may influence the structure and characteristics of the data elements captured in the Physical Data Model. For example, the adoption of a specific technical standard for reporting time may affect the way that time based data elements are captured in the Physical Data Model. Likewise, the structure and characteristics of data elements in the Physical Data Model may influence which technical standards are adopted for inclusion in the System Technology Forecast.
- System Performance Parameters Matrix: The System Technology Forecast shows how the performance of a system (as shown in the System Performance Parameters Matrix) changes over time as capabilities are added or removed.
- System Evolution Description: Both the System Technology Forecast and the System Evolution Description can be used to show how the technical standards implemented by systems change over time.
- Technical Architecture Profile: The System Technology Forecast identifies how the system standards defined in the Technical Architecture Profile will evolve over time.
- Standards Technology Forecast: The changes to the technical standards implemented by a system, as documented in the System Technology Forecast, must be consistent with the mandated and/or acceptable standards identified in the Standards Technology Forecast.

CRITICAL SUCCESS FACTORS:

DO'S:
- Ensure that the standards identified in the System Technology Forecast are consistent with the System Evolution Description.

- Ensure that the System Technology Forecast addresses hardware and software technologies, not physical characteristics or operational capabilities.

DON'TS:

- Don't include technical standards in the System Technology Forecast that are not included as future standards in the Standards Technology Forecast.

CHECKLIST: The SYSTEM TECHNOLOGY FORECAST

Process Steps	Complete
1. Identify technology areas applicable to the system(s) for which the architecture is being developed.	
2. Discover available emerging standards for each identified technology area.	
3. Select from among the emerging standards those that are most likely to be applied to the system(s) in the future.	
4. Build the System Technology Forecast as a matrix.	
5. Add a legend to define symbols and terms used in the matrix.	
6. Provide the draft System Technology Forecast to SMEs for review and comment.	
7. Modify the System Technology Forecast based on SME comments and recommendations.	
8. Publish final System Technology Forecast.	

CHAPTER NINETEEN

PRODUCT NAME: PHYSICAL DATA MODEL

OTHER ALIASES: Data Model, Data Description, Data Element Description, Class Diagram, Entity Relationship Diagram, Entity Relationship Model

PRODUCT DESIGNATION: SV-11

ARCHITECTURE VIEW: SYSTEMS

PRODUCT DEFINITION: The PHYSICAL DATA MODEL defines the physical data elements and structures associated with enterprise concepts, missions, tasks, and components.

PRODUCT DESCRIPTION: The Physical Data Model describes how data is, will be, or should be implemented in actual systems. It differs from the Logical Data Model in that the logical model describes the data independent of how it will be stored, managed, or used, while the physical model reflects the way in which the data will be stored and accessed by the target database management system (DBMS). The Physical Data Model may be developed without the prior creation of a Logical Data Model, or it may be developed as an extension or extract of an existing Logical Data Model. If an enterprise Logical Data Model exists, the data elements and structures must be traceable to the logical elements and structures.

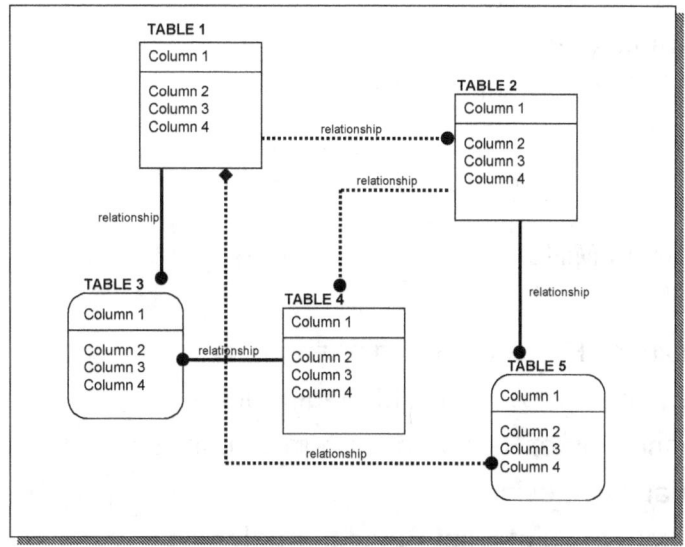

PRODUCT FORMAT: Graphics and text

USERS & USES:

USERS:

Corporate/Non-Military

- Information Manager
- Quality Assurance Manager
- Security Manager
- Workers
- Software Developers
- Research and Development

Military

- Combat Developer
- Concept Developer
- Program/Project/Product Developer
- Operational Architect
- Systems Architect
- Technical Architect
- Systems Engineer
- Software Developer
- Manufacturer
- Modeling & Simulation Community

USES:

Corporate/Non-Military

- Business Process Reengineering
- Quality Control/Quality Management
- Description of Required System Capabilities
- Database Design
- Performance of Cost/Benefits Analysis

- Development of Training Materials

Military

- Standardization of Processes, Activities and Tasks
- Development/Validation Of Tactics, Techniques & Procedures (TTPs)
- Identification of IERs
- Development/Validation Of Models & Simulations
- Planning For System Tests
- Data Modeling
- Standardization of Data Elements
- Development/Modification Of Standard Messages
- Development Of System Software
- Comparing User's Vision To Developer's Implementation
- Providing Roadmap For System Improvement
- Battlefield/Business Process Reengineering
- Development of Procedures Guides and User's Manuals
- Design of Human-Computer Interface

TYPICAL INFORMATION SOURCES:

Corporate/Non-Military

- Function/Task Lists
- Long Range Plans
- Organization Descriptions
- Operational Concepts
- Policy and Procedures Guides
- Standing Operating Procedures (SOPs)
- Strategic Plans
- Subject Matter Experts
- System Descriptions
- Task Descriptions
- Vision Statements
- Business Plans
- Corporate Brochures

- Annual Reports

Military

- Subject Matter Experts
- Policy and Procedures Guides
- Doctrinal Publications
- Operational Concepts
- Operational and Organizational Plans
- Organization Descriptions (including TOEs, MTOEs, TDAs)
- Function/Task Lists (including METLs, UJTL, Service Task Lists)
- Task Descriptions
- Standing Operating Procedures (SOPs)
- Interface Descriptions
- System Descriptions

TOOLS:

- Text Editor
- Drawing/Graphics Tool
- Data Modeling Tool
- Database
- Object Modeling Tool

PARTICIPANTS:

Corporate/Non-Military

- Operations Manager
- Human Resource Manager
- Resource Manager
- Information Manager
- Facilities Manager
- Security Manager
- Supervisors
- Workers
- Software Developers
- Operational Architect/Facilitator

- Subject Matter Expert

Military

- Combat Developer
- Concept & Doctrine Developer
- Training Developer
- Force Developer
- Operational Architect/Facilitator
- Subject Matter Expert
- Warfighter
- Program/Project/Product Developer
- Systems Architect
- Technical Architect
- Systems Engineer

PRODUCT DEVELOPMENT: There are four primary methods for developing an enterprise Physical Data Model. The model may be developed from the ground up, starting with a blank sheet. An existing Logical Data Model may be modified and extended to include physical data elements and metadata associated with its physical implementation. An existing Physical Data Model may be expanded to incorporate enterprise unique physical data elements and relationships. Finally, an existing system database may be reverse engineered to produce the data model. The method to be used depends on the time available for model development, the availability and usability of an existing data model, or the availability of an enterprise related database. The process steps involved in each of the development methodologies identified above are outlined below.

Full Model Development

Under this method, the Physical Data Model can be created in one of two ways: by a single individual or small group of SMEs working closely together, or by a larger group of individuals conducting facilitated modeling workshops.

Individual/Small Team Development of a New Data Model

1. **Determine and document enterprise data requirements.** Determine the data elements necessary to fulfill enterprise data requirements as those requirements are defined, documented, or implied in enterprise Operational Concept Descriptions, Activity Models, Operational Information Exchange Matrices, or other non-architecture documents and products.

a. ***Decompose Activity Model ICOMs to the data element level.*** If a well-developed Activity Model exists, with well-defined ICOMs, extract enterprise data elements from the ICOMs. Potential data elements may be explicitly specified in the ICOM name or definition, or they may only be implied by the ICOM definition or functional context. To decompose an ICOM into candidate data elements:
   - Record the ICOM name.
   - Record and review the ICOM definition.
   - Identify in the ICOM definition all mentions of, or references to persons, places, things, events, or concepts. Each of these represents a potential data element.
   - Determine whether each of the candidate elements represents a single piece of data (i.e., it cannot be broken down further) or a composite of multiple data elements.
   - Further decompose each composite data element until it cannot be decomposed further.
   - Record all identified basic data elements.
   - Identify any relationships among and between identified data elements.
b. ***Develop Data Requirement Worksheets (DRW) to document data needs.*** If no Activity Model exists, if one exists but is relatively immature, or if the model ICOMs are not well defined, then it will not be possible to define data requirements using the ICOM decomposition method. In these situations, data requirements may be defined through the development of data requirements worksheets. To develop a DRW:
   - Identify an activity, operational concept, or functional/subject area to be analyzed.
   - Define the activity, operational concept, or functional/subject area.
   - Establish the activity, operational concept, or functional/subject area scope and viewpoint.
   - Identify any operational rules, assumptions, or constraints associated with the activity, operational concept, or functional/subject area.
   - Identify data elements associated with the selected activity, operational concept, or functional area.
   - Determine business rules that define the relationships among and between identified data elements.
c. ***"Mine" data from available source documents.*** Data "mining" is not a single process, but includes all techniques used to extract data elements from a wide variety of source documents. Candidates for data mining include organization and system description documents, organization SOPs, operations manuals, operational requirements documents, system specifications, interface descriptions, standardized message catalogs, and data element dictionaries. Mine data from these documents by identifying references to enterprise related persons, places, things, events, and concepts.

Document all data requirements identified through either Activity Model ICOM decomposition, development of DRWs, or data mining.
2. ***Submit candidate data requirements to SMEs for review and comment.*** Provide the decomposed Activity Model ICOMs, DRWs, or lists of mined data elements to reviewers with instructions on the type of review required, the format in which to provide comments and recommendations, and the suspense for providing input.
3. ***Update/modify data requirements based on SME comments.*** Add or delete candidate data elements, change data element names, and adjust data element relationships based on the comments and recommendations provided by SME reviewers.
4. ***Compare data requirements (candidate data elements) to existing data elements.*** Attempt to find approved data elements in existing Data Models or data repositories that match or nearly match enterprise data requirements.
5. ***Adopt appropriate data elements to meet data requirements.*** Capture the adopted data elements in an initial enterprise Physical Data Model.
6. ***Modify adopted data elements to meet enterprise data needs.*** Make changes to data element names, definitions, and relationships to more accurately reflect enterprise data requirements. Modify logical data structures and combine logical data elements as necessary to match physical data storage and access requirements.
7. ***Develop new data elements (tables and columns) where none exist.***
   a. ***Create new data entities (tables).*** Name and define new entities/tables and identify appropriate key attributes/columns.
   b. ***Add non-key data attributes/columns to new entities/tables.*** Include the attribute/column name, definition, and data type (e.g., character string, integer, or time).
   c. ***Identify indexed non-key attributes/columns.*** Define those attributes/columns that may be used to access or sort each entity/table.
   d. ***Add entity/table relationships.*** Graphically and textually depict the relationship type (e.g., identifying, non-identifying, mandatory, non-mandatory, or many-to-many), directionality, verb phrase, and cardinality.
8. ***Add physical metadata.*** Enter metadata values appropriate to the target database management system (DBMS). Physical metadata values include, but are not limited to:
   - Datatype
   - Minimum and maximum acceptable data values
   - Data field length
   - Unit(s) of measure
   - Data validation rule(s)
   - Data processing algorithm(s)
   - Valid values list
   - Decimal place count
   - Required data accuracy

9. **Combine new data elements and adopted data elements to produce an enterprise Physical Data Model.**
10. **Normalize the Physical Data Model.**
11. **Submit the data model/data elements to SMEs for review and comment.** Provide to most reviewers the model data dictionary (i.e., data element names and definitions) for review and comment. For those reviewers with a good working knowledge of data modeling syntax, provide the actual Data Model.
12. **Update/modify the Physical Data Model/data elements based on SME comments.** Add or delete data elements, change data element names, and adjust data element relationships based on the comments and recommendations provided by SME reviewers.
13. **Publish the Physical Data Model.**

Conduct of Data Modeling Workshops

1. Identify and gather resources and references required to support model development.
2. Identify and notify SMEs. Development of the model may require the participation of several groups of SMEs:
- Those who will participate in the modeling sessions.
- Those who will not participate in the modeling sessions, but will provide input via face-to-face interviews with facilitators/modelers.
- Those who will review and provide comment on drafts and the final model.
- Those whose knowledge of a specific subject area will be solicited only when needed.

3. Conduct face-to-face interviews with SMEs not participating in the working sessions.
4. Conduct the modeling session. During the modeling session, the facilitator will guide and direct the discussion, but the main source of information and input will be the SMEs in attendance.
   a. *Create new data entities/tables.* Name and define new entities/tables and identify appropriate key attributes/columns.
   b. *Add non-key data attributes/columns to new entities/tables.* Include the attribute/table name, definition, and data type (e.g., character string, integer, or time).
   c. *Add entity/table relationships.* Graphically and textually depict the relationship type (e.g., identifying, non-identifying, mandatory, non-mandatory, or many-to-many), directionality, verb phrase, and cardinality.
   d. *Add physical metadata.* Enter metadata values appropriate to the target database management system (DBMS). Physical metadata values include, but are not limited to:

- Datatype
- Minimum and maximum acceptable data values
- Data field length
- Unit(s) of measure
- Data validation rule(s)
- Data processing algorithm(s)
- Valid values list
- Decimal place count
- Required data accuracy

  e. *Review results of the modeling session.* Ensure that all modeling session participants agree on what was accomplished during the session, what actions are to be performed between sessions and what goals are to be established for the next session.
  f. *Identify any outstanding issues from the modeling session.*
  g. *Assign outstanding issues to selected participants for resolution.*

5. Update the model by incorporating the results of the modeling session. This is primarily the job of the facilitator and modeler(s) between modeling sessions. It includes making all agreed to changes to the model and "cleaning up" the model for publication/distribution.

6. Publish and distribute the updated model to modeling session participants and other specified reviewers for review and/or comment. Include information on the portions of the Physical Data Model to be reviewed, the types of comments to be provided, the desired comment format, the individual(s) or organization(s) to whom/which comments are to be submitted, and the suspense for comment submission. If no comments or recommended changes are received, go to step 10 below.

7. Receive, review and respond to recommended changes to the draft model.

8. Incorporate approved changes into an updated model draft.

9. Repeat from step 4.

10. Conduct additional modeling sessions as necessary.

11. Finalize the model.

12. Publish the final Physical Data Model.

Expansion of an Existing Logical Data Model

If an enterprise Logical Data Model exists, it may serve as the basis for the development of a Physical Data Model. Many of the data elements and structures included in the Logical Data Model may be retained in the Physical Data Model with the addition of appropriate physical data elements and structures.

1. **Modify adopted data elements to meet enterprise data needs.** Make changes to data element names, definitions, and relationships to reflect more

accurately enterprise data requirements. Modify logical data structures and combine logical data elements as necessary to match physical data storage and access requirements.
2. ***Develop new data elements (tables and columns) where none exist.***
   a. ***Create new data entities (tables).*** Name and define new entities/tables and identify appropriate key attributes/columns.
   b. ***Add non-key data attributes/columns to new entities/tables.*** Include the attribute/column name, definition, and data type (e.g., character string, integer, or time).
   c. ***Identify indexed non-key attributes/columns.*** Define those attributes/columns that may be used to access or sort each entity/table.
   d. ***Add entity/table relationships.*** Graphically and textually depict the relationship type (e.g., identifying, non-identifying, mandatory, non-mandatory, or many-to-many), directionality, verb phrase, and cardinality.
3. ***Add physical metadata.*** Enter metadata values appropriate to the target database management system (DBMS). Physical metadata values include, but are not limited to:
   - Datatype
   - Minimum and maximum acceptable data values
   - Data field length
   - Unit(s) of measure
   - Data validation rule(s)
   - Data processing algorithm(s)
   - Valid values list
   - Decimal place count
   - Required data accuracy
4. ***Normalize the Physical Data Model.***
5. ***Submit the data model/data elements to SMEs for review and comment.*** Provide to most reviewers the model data dictionary (i.e., data element names and definitions) for review and comment. For those reviewers with a good working knowledge of data modeling syntax, provide the actual Data Model.
6. ***Update/modify the Physical Data Model/data elements based on SME comments.*** Add or delete data elements, change data element names, and adjust data element relationships based on the comments and recommendations provided by SME reviewers.
7. ***Publish the Physical Data Model.***

Expansion of an Existing Physical Data Model

An existing physical data model may be adopted and modified to create an enterprise Physical Data Model.

1. ***Adopt usable data elements from selected Data Model or subject area view.*** Identify individual data entities/tables, attributes/columns, and relationships from the selected Data Model to be retained in the enterprise Physical Data Model. Include both those that can be used as they are and those that may require relatively minor changes to accurately reflect enterprise data requirements.
2. ***Delete unneeded data elements from the existing Data Model.*** Remove from the selected Data Model all data entities/tables, attributes/columns, and relationships that are not applicable to enterprise data requirements.
3. ***Modify adopted data elements as necessary to meet fully enterprise physical data requirements.*** Where necessary to more accurately reflect enterprise data requirements, modify data entity/table, attribute/column, and relationship names and/or definitions. Add new relationships as needed. Modify logical data elements and structures to reflect physical data storage and access requirements.
4. ***Produce a new/modified Physical Data Model.*** Change Data Model descriptive information to identify it as a new model. This includes renaming the model and updating the model purpose, scope, and viewpoint.
5. ***Provide the Physical Data Model to SMEs for review and comment.*** Review of the Physical Data Model should focus on the names and definitions of entities/tables, attributes/columns, and relationships as well as on the level to which they fulfill known enterprise data requirements. Provide to each reviewer the data dictionary (i.e., list of entity/table, attribute/column, and relationship names and definitions) and the list of enterprise data requirements. Where possible, indicate the Data Model that was modified to create the enterprise Data Model, and highlight the modifications that were made. Provide to selected reviewers the actual Physical Data Model diagram(s) for review.
6. ***Update the Physical Data Model based on SME comments.*** Review submitted comments and recommendations to determine which should be accepted and which should not. Identify and resolve any conflicts in comments and recommendations received (i.e., the change recommended in one comment is inconsistent with or counter to the change that is recommended in another). Modify the Physical Data Model in accordance with all accepted comments.
7. ***Publish the final version of the Physical Data Model.***

Reverse Engineering of an Existing System Database

Reverse engineering is simply using the IDEF1X data modeling format and syntax to document an existing physical database. Reverse engineering is probably the least time and resource intensive method for developing a Physical Data Model. The main shortcoming of this development methodology is that it assumes that the existing database accurately reflects all enterprise data requirements. If the reverse engineered database is missing critical data elements then those same data elements likely will be missing from the resultant Physical Data Model.

Combination

Any two or more of the four data modeling methodologies described above may be combined to produce composite methodologies that take maximum advantage of the amount of development time available, and the availability and usefulness of resources and SMEs.

RECOMMENDED DEVELOPMENT SEQUENCE: After the Logical Data Model.

KEY RELATIONSHIPS:

- Operational Concept Description: The data elements in the Physical Data Model should be based upon or directly traceable to the missions, tasks, activities, nodes, and organizations described in the Operational Concept Description. Any information exchanges depicted in the Operational Concept Description should be supported by data elements in the Physical Data Model.
- Operational Information Exchange Matrix: The information exchange elements and sending and receiving nodes captured in the Operational Information Exchange Matrix should be supported by data elements in the Physical Data Model. The technical and performance parameters associated with the information exchange elements in the Operational Information Exchange Matrix should be reflected in the attributes of the appropriate data elements in the Physical Data Model.
- Activity Model: The data elements in the Physical Data Model should be based upon or directly traceable to Activity Model ICOMs.
- System Data Exchange Matrix: The data exchange elements included in the System Data Exchange Matrix should be the same as those captured in the Physical Data Model.
- Logical Data Model: The Physical Data Model may be developed directly from the Logical Data Model by adding implementation-specific data characteristics. The Physical Data Model may also be developed independent of the Logical Data Model, but its physical data elements should be traceable to the logical data elements described in the Logical Data Model.
- Technical Architecture Profile: The technical standards identified in the Technical Architecture Profile may influence the structure and characteristics of the data elements captured in the Physical Data Model. For example, the adoption of a specific technical standard for reporting time may affect the way that time based data elements are captured in the Physical Data Model. Likewise, the structure and characteristics of data elements in the Physical

Data Model may influence which technical standards are adopted for inclusion in the Technical Architecture Profile.
- System Technology Forecast: The future technical standards identified in the System Technology Forecast may influence the structure and characteristics of the data elements captured in the Physical Data Model. For example, the adoption of a specific technical standard for reporting time may affect the way that time based data elements are captured in the Physical Data Model. Likewise, the structure and characteristics of data elements in the Physical Data Model may influence which technical standards are adopted for inclusion in the System Technology Forecast.

CRITICAL SUCCESS FACTORS:

DO'S:
- Base physical data elements on information elements described in the Activity Model and logical data elements and structures defined in the Logical Data Model.
- Reuse existing approved data elements whenever possible.
- Identify data element relationships two data elements at a time.
- Define all new data elements as they are developed.
- Identify the source of adopted data elements.
- Use role names to reflect enterprise unique names for adopted data elements.

DON'TS:
- Don't develop new data elements when existing data elements can be used as they are or modified slightly to meet enterprise physical data storage and access requirements.
- Don't rename adopted data elements simply to reflect enterprise unique terminology.
- Don't assume that an existing database accurately reflects all enterprise data requirements.

CHECKLIST: The PHYSICAL DATA MODEL

Full Model Development

Individual/Small Team Development of a New Data Model

Process Steps	Complete
1. Determine and document enterprise data requirements.	
a. Decompose Activity Model ICOMs to the data element level.	
− Record the ICOM name.	
− Record and review the ICOM definition.	
− Identify in the ICOM definition all mentions of, or references to persons, places, things, events, or concepts	
− Determine whether each of the candidate elements represents a single piece of data (i.e., it cannot be broken down further) or a composite of multiple data elements.	
− Further decompose each composite data element until it cannot be decomposed further.	
− Record all identified basic data elements.	
− Identify any relationships among and between identified data elements.	
b. Develop Data Requirement Worksheets (DRW) to document data needs.	
− Identify an activity, operational concept, or functional/subject area to be analyzed.	
− Define the activity, operational concept, or functional/subject area.	
− Establish the activity, operational concept, or functional/subject area scope and viewpoint.	
− Identify any operational rules, assumptions, or constraints associated with the activity, operational concept, or functional/subject area.	
− Identify data elements associated with the selected activity, operational concept, or functional area.	
− Determine business rules that define the relationships among and between identified data elements.	
"Mine" data from available source documents.	
2. Submit candidate data requirements to SMEs for review and comment.	
3. Update/modify data requirements based on SME comments.	
4. Compare data requirements (candidate data elements) to existing data elements.	

5. Adopt appropriate data elements to meet data requirements.	
6. Modify adopted data elements to meet enterprise data needs	
7. Develop new data elements (tables and columns) where none exist.	
a. Create new data entities (tables).	
b. Add non-key data attributes/columns to new entities/tables.	
c. Identify indexed non-key attributes/columns.	
d. Add entity/table relationships.	
e. Add physical metadata.	
8. Combine new data elements and adopted data elements to produce an enterprise Physical Data Model.	
9. Normalize the Physical Data Model.	
10. Submit the data model/data elements to SMEs for review and comment.	
11. Update/modify the Physical Data Model/data elements based on SME comments.	
12. Publish the Physical Data Model.	

Conduct of Data Modeling Workshops

Process Steps	Complete
1. Identify and gather resources and references required to support model development.	
2. Identify and notify SMEs.	
3. Conduct face-to-face interviews with SMEs not participating in the working sessions.	
4. Conduct the modeling session.	
a. Create new data entities/tables.	
b. Add non-key data attributes/columns to new entities/tables.	
c. Add entity/table relationships.	
d. Add physical metadata.	
e. Review results of the modeling session.	
f. Identify any outstanding issues from the modeling session.	
g. Assign outstanding issues to selected participants for resolution.	
5. Update the model by incorporating the results of the modeling session.	
6. Publish and distribute the updated model to modeling session participants and other specified reviewers for review and/or comment.	
7. Receive, review and respond to recommended changes to the draft model.	
8. Incorporate approved changes into an updated model draft.	
9. Repeat from step 4.	
10. Conduct additional modeling sessions as necessary.	
11. Finalize the model.	
12. Publish the final Physical Data Model.	

Expansion of an Existing Logical Data Model

Process Steps	Complete
1. Modify adopted data elements to meet enterprise data needs.	
2. Develop new data elements (tables and columns) where none exist.	
a. Create new data entities (tables).	
b. Add non-key data attributes/columns to new entities/tables.	
c. Identify indexed non-key attributes/columns.	
d. Add entity/table relationships.	
e. Add physical metadata.	
3. Normalize the Physical Data Model.	
4. Submit the data model/data elements to SMEs for review and comment.	
5. Update/modify the Physical Data Model/data elements based on SME comments.	
6. Publish the Physical Data Model.	

Expansion of an Existing Physical Data Model

Process Steps	Complete
1. Adopt usable data elements from selected Data Model or subject area view.	
2. Delete unneeded data elements from the existing Data Model.	
3. Modify adopted data elements as necessary to meet fully enterprise physical data requirements.	
4. Produce a new/modified Physical Data Model.	
5. Provide the Physical Data Model to SMEs for review and comment.	
6. Update the Physical Data Model based on SME comments.	
7. Publish the final version of the Physical Data Model.	

CHAPTER TWENTY

PRODUCT NAME: TECHNICAL ARCHITECTURE PROFILE

OTHER ALIASES: None

PRODUCT DESIGNATION: TV-1

ARCHITECTURE VIEW: TECHNICAL

PRODUCT DEFINITION: The TECHNICAL ARCHITECTURE PROFILE lists those technical standards that are applicable to the architecture and its components.

PRODUCT DESCRIPTION: The Technical Architecture Profile is the primary technical architecture product. It identifies the technical standards that are or will be adhered to in the development of the architecture or implemented by systems, organizations, or operational nodes that comprise the enterprise being architected. A technical standard describes how a process is to be performed, how a system is to operate, or how information is to be processed and presented. The purposes of the standards in the Technical Architecture Profile are two-fold – to facilitate the understanding of architecture information through the use of common modeling and information presentation techniques, and to ensure interoperability among systems within and external to the enterprise being architected through the use of common information processing, exchange, security, and human computer interface schemes. The standards captured in the Technical Architecture Profile fall into six general categories: information processing standards, information transfer standards, information modeling and exchange standards, human-computer interface standards, and information security standards. The Technical Architecture Profile will identify not only mandated standards that are applicable to the system or enterprise, but also non-mandatory standards that are adopted for use. It will include both currently available technical standards and emerging or future standards. A Technical Architecture Profile may be developed for individual enterprise components and elements or for the enterprise as a whole.

TECHNICAL AREA	STANDARDS AREA	STANDARD
Information Processing	Programming Language	Mandated Standard
Information Transfer	Internet Protocol	Selected Standard
Information Modeling	Process Modeling	Mandated Standard
Information and Data Exchange	Communications Means	Selected Standard
Information Security	Information Encryption	Mandated Standard
Human-Computer Interface	Information Presentation	Selected Standard

PRODUCT FORMAT: Table or spreadsheet

USERS & USES:

USERS:

Corporate/Non-Military

- Operations Manager
- Resource Manager
- Information Manager
- Quality Assurance Manager
- Security Manager
- Supervisors
- Workers
- Software Developers
- Research and Development
- Policy Writers

Military

- Combat Developer
- Program/Project/Product Developer
- Resource Manager
- Operational Architect
- Systems Architect
- Technical Architect
- Systems Engineer
- Software Developer

- Manufacturer
- Modeling & Simulation Community

USES:

Corporate/Non-Military

- Strategic Business Planning
- Business Process Reengineering
- Development of Capital Investment Strategies
- Quality Control/Quality Management
- Description of Required System Capabilities
- Database Design
- Identification of Operational Issues
- Design of Human-Computer Interface
- Performance of Cost/Benefits Analysis
- Development/Validation of SOPs

Military

- Development/Validation of SOPs
- Identification of Operational Issues
- Data Modeling
- Development/Modification Of Standard Messages
- Development Of System Software
- Comparing User's Vision To Developer's Implementation
- Providing Roadmap For System Improvement

TYPICAL INFORMATION SOURCES:

Corporate/Non-Military

- Long Range Plans
- Operational Concepts
- Policy and Procedures Guides
- Standing Operating Procedures (SOPs)
- Subject Matter Experts

- System Descriptions
- Task Descriptions

Military

- Subject Matter Experts
- Future Operational Capabilities (FOCs)
- Long Range Plans
- Strategic Plans
- Modernization Plans
- Master Plans
- Interface Descriptions
- System Descriptions

TOOLS:

- Text Editor
- Drawing/Graphics Tool
- Database

PARTICIPANTS:

Corporate/Non-Military

- Information Manager
- Security Manager
- Workers
- Software Developers
- Operational Architect/Facilitator
- Subject Matter Expert

Military

- Subject Matter Expert
- Program/Project/Product Developer
- Systems Architect
- Technical Architect
- Systems Engineer

PRODUCT DEVELOPMENT:

1. *Decide whether the Technical Architecture Profile is being developed for a single system or for a functional area or Family of Systems.* Determine the focus of the profile based on the purpose and scope of the architecture and the use(s) to which the product will be put. To support system acquisition, modification, or upgrade, develop the Technical Architecture Profile for a single system.
2. *Identify mandated technical standards applicable to the system or enterprise.*
3. *Specify non-mandatory technical standards that are or will be implemented by the system, in the architecture, or within the enterprise.* Select technical standards to be implemented within those areas for which no standard has been mandated for use. Document the selected standards in the Technical Architecture Profile matrix.
4. *Document the temporal nature of the standards included in the Technical Architecture Profile.* Annotate the mandated and selected non-mandatory standards as either current, future, emerging, or interim to specify when they are to be implemented. As an alternative, indicate the actual date, month, and/or year that each standard will be applied or available.
5. *Submit the Technical Architecture Profile to SMEs for review and comment.* Include information on the portions of the Technical Architecture Profile to be reviewed, the types of comments to be provided, the desired comment format, the individual(s) or organization(s) to whom/which comments are to be submitted, and the suspense for comment submission.
6. *Update the Technical Architecture Profile based on comments received.* Modify the Technical Architecture Profile as necessary to incorporate approved change recommendations resulting from the SME review.
7. *Publish the final Technical Architecture Profile.*

RECOMMENDED DEVELOPMENT SEQUENCE:
This product may be developed at any point in the architecture development process. Ideally, it is developed prior to the Activity Model, the Operational Information Exchange Matrix, and the Logical and Physical Data Models, as it prescribes standards that govern the development of these products.

KEY RELATIONSHIPS:

- Operational Information Exchange Matrix: The information exchange media identified in the Operational Information Exchange Matrix must be in accordance with the information exchange standards defined in the Technical Architecture Profile.

- System Interface Description: The system and node interface media identified in the System Interface Description must be in accordance with the information exchange standards defined in the Technical Architecture Profile.
- Logical Data Model: The Logical Data Model must be developed in accordance with the information modeling and exchange standards defined in the Technical Architecture Profile.
- Physical Data Model: The Physical Data Model must be developed in accordance with the information modeling and exchange standards defined in the Technical Architecture Profile. The data processing algorithms and rules described in the Physical Data Model must be in accordance with the information processing standards defined in the Technical Architecture Profile.
- System Communications Description: The communications media identified in the System Communications Description must be in accordance with the information exchange standards defined in the Technical Architecture Profile.
- System Performance Parameters Matrix: Appropriate performance parameters described in the System Performance Parameters Matrix must be in accordance with the information processing, information exchange, information security, and human-computer interface standards defined in the Technical Architecture Profile.
- System Evolution Description: The System Evolution Description provides a description of the time-phased implementation of the standards identified in the Technical Architecture Profile.
- System Technology Forecast: The System Technology Forecast identifies how the system standards defined in the Technical Architecture Profile will evolve over time.
- Standards Technology Forecast: The Standards Technology Forecast identifies how current standards from the Technical Architecture Profile will be replaced by emerging and future standards.

CRITICAL SUCCESS FACTORS:

DO'S:
- Adopt mandated technical standards for use within the enterprise.
- Select appropriate standards from among the approved list of alternatives in those technical areas where no standard has been mandated.
- Identify the when each standard will be implemented.

DON'TS:
- Don't adopt a technical standard different from the mandated standard (or the approved list of alternatives).

- Don't document standards in the Technical Architecture Profile that are not actually being implemented by systems within the enterprise.

CHECKLIST: The TECHNICAL ARCHITECTURE PROFILE

Process Steps	Complete
1. Decide whether the Technical Architecture Profile is being developed for a single system or for a functional area or Family of Systems.	
2. Identify mandated technical standards applicable to the system or enterprise.	
3. Specify non-mandatory technical standards that are or will be implemented by the system, in the architecture, or within the enterprise.	
4. Document the temporal nature of the standards included in the Technical Architecture Profile.	
5. Submit the Technical Architecture Profile to SMEs for review and comment.	
6. Update the Technical Architecture Profile based on comments received.	
7. Publish the final Technical Architecture Profile.	

CHAPTER TWENTY ONE

PRODUCT NAME: STANDARDS TECHNOLOGY FORECAST

OTHER ALIASES: None

PRODUCT DESIGNATION: TV-2

ARCHITECTURE VIEW: TECHNICAL

PRODUCT DEFINITION: A STANDARDS TECHNOLOGY FORECAST is a detailed description of emerging technology standards relevant to the systems and business processes covered by the architecture.

PRODUCT DESCRIPTION: The Standards Technology Forecast identifies the emerging technical standards that will be applied in the development of future architectures or implemented by systems, organizations, or operational nodes that comprise the enterprise being architected. A technical standard describes how a process is to be performed, how a system is to operate, or how information is to be processed and presented. An emerging technical standard is one that is under development, or one that has been developed but has not yet received wide acceptance or use. The purposes of the standards in the Standards Technology Forecast are two-fold – to facilitate the understanding of architecture information through the use of common modeling and information presentation techniques, and to ensure interoperability among systems within and external to the enterprise being architected through the use of common information processing, exchange, security, and human-computer interface schemes. The standards captured in the Standards Technology Forecast fall into six general categories: information processing standards, information transfer standards, information modeling and exchange standards, human-computer interface standards, and information security standards.

The Standards Technology Forecast describes how the technical standards applicable to an enterprise or architecture will evolve over time. The forecast is typically presented as a matrix that includes three categories of information: the rows of the matrix reflect hardware and software technology areas associated with the system, the columns of the matrix reflect critical system lifecycle milestones, and the cells of the matrix identify the actual technical standards expected to be applied to the system in each technology area during each timeframe.

Because the matrix can contain columns for multiple timeframes, each row of the matrix can illustrate the adoption of different technical standards within a single technology area over time. Likewise, each column of the matrix describes the collection of technical standards that may be implemented by the system at a particular point in time.

Technology Area	Current Standard	FY20XX	FY20XX
Kernel			
Shell and Utilities			
Programming Languages			
Client Service Operations			
Object Definition and Management			
Window Management			
Dialogue Support			
Data Management			
Data Interchange			
Electronic Data Interchange			
Graphics			

PRODUCT FORMAT: Table or spreadsheet

USERS & USES:

USERS:

Corporate/Non-Military

- Strategic Planner
- Information Manager
- Security Manager
- Software Developers
- Research and Development

Military

- Combat Developer
- Program/Project/Product Developer
- Resource Manager

- Operational Architect
- Systems Architect
- Technical Architect
- Systems Engineer
- Software Developer
- Manufacturer
- Test & Evaluation Community
- Modeling & Simulation Community

USES:

Corporate/Non-Military

- Strategic Business Planning
- Description of Required System Capabilities
- Database Design
- Identification of Operational Issues
- Wargaming Alternatives
- Design of Human-Computer Interface

Military

- Identification of Operational Issues
- Data Modeling
- Development Of System Software
- Wargaming Alternatives
- Providing Roadmap For System Improvement
- Battlefield/Business Process Reengineering
- Design of Human-Computer Interface

TYPICAL INFORMATION SOURCES:

Corporate/Non-Military

- Long Range Plans
- Subject Matter Experts
- Standards Documents

Military

- Subject Matter Experts
- Future Operational Capabilities (FOCs)
- Standards Documents

TOOLS:

- Text Editor
- Drawing/Graphics Tool
- Database

PARTICIPANTS:

Corporate/Non-Military

- Strategic Planner
- Operations Manager
- Resource Manager
- Information Manager
- Security Manager
- Software Developers
- Operational Architect/Facilitator
- Subject Matter Expert

Military

- Combat Developer
- Operational Architect/Facilitator
- Subject Matter Expert
- Program/Project/Product Developer
- Systems Architect
- Technical Architect
- Systems Engineer

PRODUCT DEVELOPMENT: The Standards Technology Forecast is developed from the Technical Architecture Profile.

1. *Determine the timeframe(s) to be addressed by the Standards Technology Forecast.* Timeframes addressed in this product are not tied to any particular system, organization, or architecture product but are related to the enterprise or architecture as a whole. Timeframes may be selected to provide "snapshots" of the status of technical architecture standards at regular intervals (e.g., every six months or every two years) or to highlight points in time when major changes in applicable standards are expected to take place. To simplify the development of the Standards Technology Forecast, the timeframes that it addresses should match those addressed in the Technical Architecture Profile wherever possible.
2. *Identify technology areas that will be applicable to the enterprise or architecture.* As a minimum, include the technology areas that are included in the Technical Architecture Profile. Where possible and necessary, add new and emerging technology areas that will be applied to the enterprise/architecture in the future, but that were not included in the Technical Architecture Profile.
3. *Select from among the future and emerging technical standards identified in the Technical Architecture Profile, those that will be applied to the enterprise or architecture.* If the Technical Architecture Profile identifies only one acceptable technical standard for a particular technology area during a particular timeframe, that standard should be transferred directly to the Standards Technology Forecast for the corresponding technology area and timeframe. Where the Technical Architecture Profile allows for a selection from among two or more alternative technical standards, then select one or more of the acceptable alternatives for inclusion in the Standards Technology Forecast.
4. *Identify technical standards for technology areas not addressed in the Technical Architecture Profile.* This includes technology areas added to the Standards Technology Forecast that were not a part of the Technical Architecture Profile or technology areas that were included in the Technical Architecture Profile, but for which no technical standard was specified or recommended.
5. *Build the Standards Technology Forecast as a matrix. .* Add rows to the matrix for each technology area. The columns of the matrix reflect key future time periods. Select matrix timeframes to correspond to critical system lifecycle milestones. Enter the selected technical standards in the cells of the matrix.
6. *Add a legend to define symbols and terms used in the matrix.* The legend should include definitions for each term, abbreviation, acronym, and graphical symbol used in the matrix.
7. *Provide the draft Standards Technology Forecast to SMEs for review and comment.* Include information on the portions of the Standards Technology Forecast to be reviewed, the types of comments to be provided,

the desired comment format, the individual(s) or organization(s) to whom/which comments are to be submitted, and the suspense for comment submission.
8. ***Modify the Standards Technology Forecast based on SME comments and recommendations.*** Update the technology areas, timeframes, or actual technical standards as necessary to accommodate approved SME comments and recommendations.
9. ***Publish the final Standards Technology Forecast.***

RECOMMENDED DEVELOPMENT SEQUENCE:
Following the development of the Technical Architecture Profile, and prior to the development of the System Technology Forecast.

KEY RELATIONSHIPS:

- Operational Information Exchange Matrix: The technical and performance parameters shown in the OIEM may include allowances for the implementation of future technical standards as described in the Standards Technology Forecast. If such future standards are included in the OIEM, they should be identified clearly, to include the timeframe within which they are expected to be implemented. For example, an information exchange using an exchange medium that will not be available or acquired until 2010 should be identified as a future requirement and further annotated with an indication that the exchange is expected to be effective after 2010.
- System Evolution Description: The changes to the system, as documented in the System Evolution Description, should be consistent with the mandated/acceptable standards defined in the Standards Technology Forecast.
- System Technology Forecast: The changes to the technical standards implemented by a system, as documented in the System Technology Forecast, must be consistent with the mandated and/or acceptable standards identified in the Standards Technology Forecast.
- Technical Architecture Profile: The Standards Technology Forecast identifies how current standards from the Technical Architecture Profile will be replaced by emerging and future standards.

CRITICAL SUCCESS FACTORS:

DO'S:
– Ensure that the technology areas and the technical standards identified in the Standards Technology Forecast are consistent with those in the Technical Architecture Profile.
– Ensure that proprietary commercial standards included in the Standards Technology Forecast are clearly identified.

- Where necessary, identify the potential impact to the enterprise or architecture of adopting a particular technical standard.
- Indicate obsolete technical standards that will be retained for use within the enterprise or architecture to support operational requirements.

DON'TS: None.

CHECKLIST: The STANDARDS TECHNOLOGY FORECAST

Process Steps	Complete
1. Determine the timeframe(s) to be addressed by the Standards Technology Forecast.	
2. Identify technology areas that will be applicable to the enterprise or architecture.	
3. Select from among the future and emerging technical standards identified in the Technical Architecture Profile those that will be applied to the enterprise or architecture.	
4. Identify technical standards for technology areas not addressed in the Technical Architecture Profile.	
5. Build the Standards Technology Forecast as a matrix.	
6. Add a legend to define symbols and terms used in the matrix.	
7. Provide the Standards Technology Forecast to SMEs for review and comment.	
8. Modify the Standards Technology Forecast based on SME comments and recommendations.	
9. Publish the final Standards Technology Forecast.	

CHAPTER TWENTY TWO

PRODUCT NAME: OVERVIEW & SUMMARY INFORMATION

OTHER ALIASES: None

PRODUCT DESIGNATION: AV-1

ARCHITECTURE VIEW: ALL[4]

PRODUCT DEFINITION: OVERVIEW & SUMMARY INFORMATION provides general, descriptive information about the architecture as a whole.

PRODUCT DESCRIPTION: The Overview & Summary Information is different from other architecture products in that it doesn't actually describe any aspect of the enterprise being architected. Instead, it provides information that describes the architecture and the products it contains. The Overview & Summary Information is initially developed in the early stages of architecture development, and is updated through the development process to incorporate information about each product as it is produced. The initial version of the Overview and Summary Information provides a guide for architecture and product development in that it defines the enterprise being architected; the products to be included; the purpose, scope, and viewpoint of the architecture; and the timeframe addressed by the architecture. The final Overview & Summary Information provides an introduction to and description of the architecture for users. Along with the Integrated Dictionary, the Overview & Summary Information pulls together the many disparate products developed for an architecture into a single, coherent whole and allows it to be read and used without referencing other documents.

PRODUCT FORMAT: Text (may include graphics to augment the text).

---

[4] "All View" architecture products are so designated because they are to be included in all Operational, System, or Technical architectures

USERS & USES:

USERS:

Corporate/Non-Military

- Strategic Planner
- Operations Manager
- Human Resource Manager
- Resource Manager
- Information Manager
- Quality Assurance Manager
- Facilities Manager
- Security Manager
- Supervisors
- Workers
- Software Developers
- Trainers
- Research and Development
- Policy Writers
- Public Relations Department
- Sales Department

Military

- Combat Developer
- Concept Developer
- Trainer
- Training Developer
- Force Developer
- Program/Project/Product Developer
- Resource Manager
- Operational Architect
- Systems Architect
- Technical Architect
- Systems Engineer
- Software Developer
- Manufacturer

- Test & Evaluation Community
- Modeling & Simulation Community
- Warfighter

USES:

- Describing the architecture

TYPICAL INFORMATION SOURCES:

- Subject Matter Experts
- Architects
- Architecture Products

TOOLS:

- Text Editor
- Drawing/Graphics Tool

PARTICIPANTS:

Corporate/Non-Military

- Operational Architect/Facilitator
- Subject Matter Expert

Military

- Combat Developer
- Concept & Doctrine Developer
- Operational Architect/Facilitator
- Subject Matter Expert
- Warfighter
- Program/Project/Product Developer
- Systems Architect
- Technical Architect

PRODUCT DEVELOPMENT:

1. **Identify the architecture.** Provide a unique but descriptive name or designation for the architecture. Indicate whether the architecture is a modification to or an updated version of a pre-existing architecture. The name of the architecture should include the name/designation of the system, organization, functional area, or family of systems being described and may also indicate the architecture timeframe and/or the use(s) to which the architecture is to be put.
2. **Identify the developers of the architecture.** List all individuals and organizations involved in the development or review of the architecture or its products. Include modelers, facilitators, observers, controllers, system operators, SMEs, and reviewers. Describe the nature and extent of each individual's or organization's participation.
3. **Define the purpose(s) for developing the architecture**. Describe the reasons why the architecture was or is being developed. List and describe the primary users of the architecture and the uses to which it is expected to be put. Indicate the questions that the architecture is meant to answer, the problems that the architecture is meant to solve, or the information that the architecture is meant to provide. Where possible, also identify other potential users of the architecture beyond the primary intended users, and other potential uses of the architecture beyond the primary intended uses.
4. **Define the architecture scope.** Describe the type of architecture (operational, system, or technical) being developed. Identify the specific products to be included in the architecture. Define what will be covered (i.e., the depth and breadth of the missions, activities, operational nodes, information and information exchanges) in the architecture. It may also be advantageous to specify what **will not** be covered in the architecture. Also identify the temporal nature of the architecture. Describe the temporal nature of the architecture using relative (e.g., as-is, to-be, current, near-term, interim, or objective), or absolute terms (e.g., 2005, 2010). Identify the period of time during which the information within the architecture is valid (e.g., "The information in this architecture is considered valid until the year 2015 or until superseded by a newer architecture.").
5. **Identify the viewpoint of the architecture.** Define the perspective from which the architecture is depicted.
6. **Define the environmental context of the architecture.** Identify and document the external conditions, constraints, and assumptions that exert an influence on the architecture. Describe the operational environment in which all architecture missions and tasks are performed. For military architectures, this includes an indication of those strategic theaters within which tasks are or are expected to be performed. Also include an indication of those levels of conflict [e.g., peace, stability and sustainment operations (SASO), small scale contingency operations (SSCO), and major theater war (MTW)] that are

supported by the enterprise, functional area, or FoS. Identify the physical conditions that promote or are required for the performance of tasks as well as those that constrain or prevent task performance. List the doctrinal, regulatory, or guidance documents that govern the development and contents of the architecture. Other aspects of the operational environment that may be captured are the socio-political considerations--requirements, limitations, and constraints—that influence the performance of architecture missions and tasks. Include a description of key external elements, nodes, and organizations that support or are the objects of architecture tasks and actions. Among those external elements, nodes, and organizations for a military architecture are the threats that are countered by elements of the architecture. Also identify other related architectures and state how they are related to the subject architecture.

7. ***Document architecture findings, conclusions, and recommendations.*** Document the findings that resulted from the development of the architecture, the conclusions that can be drawn from those findings and any recommendations based on those conclusions. Findings and conclusions usually fall into two categories: issues that require a solution, and opportunities for improvement in current processes and structures. Architecture recommendations should identify how the issues may be resolved or how the improvement opportunities may be exploited.
8. ***Identify architecture development tools and file formats.*** Identify the software tools and techniques used to develop architecture products. Identify the file formats used to document each product.
9. ***Describe how the architecture is stored and accessed.*** Identify how and where the architecture and its various products are stored, and how and by whom they may be accessed and downloaded.
10. ***Provide the Overview & Summary Information to SMEs for review and comment.*** Include information on the portions of the product to be reviewed, the types of comments to be provided, the desired comment format, the individual(s) or organization(s) to whom/which comments are to be submitted, and the suspense for comment submission.
11. ***Update Overview & Summary Information based on comments received.*** Modify the Overview & Summary Information as necessary to incorporate approved change recommendations resulting from the SME review.
12. ***Publish the final Overview & Summary Information.***

RECOMMENDED DEVELOPMENT SEQUENCE:
Begin development of this product early (even first) in the architecture development process. Complete the development of the Overview & Summary Information as the last architecture product.

KEY RELATIONSHIPS:

- All: The Overview & Summary Information product contains information from (and/or about) every other architecture product.

CRITICAL SUCCESS FACTORS:

DO'S:
- Begin development of the Overview & Summary Information early in the architecture development process.
- Include information from (and/or about) every architecture product in the Overview and Summary Information.
- Define the scope of the architecture in terms of the products to be produced.

DON'TS:
- Don't include too much detailed architectural information in the Overview & Summary Information. Capture detailed information in the appropriate architecture product.

CHECKLIST: The OVERVIEW & SUMMARY INFORMATION

Process Steps	Complete
1. Identify the architecture.	
2. Identify the developers of the architecture.	
3. Define the purpose(s) for developing the architecture.	
4. Define the architecture scope.	
5. Identify the viewpoint of the architecture.	
6. Define the environmental context of the architecture.	
7. Document architecture findings, conclusions, and recommendations.	
8. Identify architecture development tools and file formats.	
9. Describe how the architecture is stored and accessed.	
10. Provide the Overview & Summary Information to SMEs for review and comment.	
11. Update Overview & Summary Information based on comments received	
12. Publish the final Technical Architecture Profile.	

CHAPTER TWENTY THREE

PRODUCT NAME: INTEGRATED DICTIONARY

OTHER ALIASES: None

PRODUCT DESIGNATION: AV-2

ARCHITECTURE VIEW: ALL

PRODUCT DEFINITION: The INTEGRATED DICTIONARY provides definitions for all the terms, labels, acronyms and abbreviations used in the architecture.

PRODUCT DESCRIPTION: Every architecture product, to include those that are primarily graphical in nature, contain words, terms, symbols, abbreviations, and acronyms that may be unfamiliar to some architecture users. In order to allow users and reviewers to understand and use the architecture most effectively, these unfamiliar words, terms, symbols, abbreviations, and acronyms must be defined. Many architecture products (e.g., the Activity Model, the Data Model, and the Operational Activity Sequence & Timing Description) include definitions and descriptions of the key terms contained within them. Other products include legends that define terms, abbreviations, symbols, and labels included in or on them. The Integrated Dictionary provides a consolidated list of the dictionary, legend, and glossary type information contained in each product, as well as definitions for and descriptions of other terms that are not used in any product, but are required for a complete understanding of the architecture.

Architects should use standard terms where possible (i.e., terms from existing, approved dictionaries and lexicons). However, in some cases, new terms and/or modified definitions for existing terms will be needed. This can happen when a given architecture is at a lower level of detail than existing architectures or lexicons, or when new concepts are devised for objective architectures. In those cases, the new terms contained in a given architecture's Integrated Dictionary should be submitted to the maintainer of the approved dictionaries. All definitions that originate in existing dictionaries should reference the source document.

Along with the Overview & Summary Information, the Integrated Dictionary provides information that allows the architecture to be read and understood without reference to other documents.

PRODUCT FORMAT: Text

USERS & USES:

USERS:

Corporate/Non-Military

- Strategic Planner
- Operations Manager
- Human Resource Manager
- Resource Manager
- Information Manager
- Quality Assurance Manager
- Facilities Manager
- Security Manager
- Supervisors
- Workers
- Software Developers
- Trainers
- Research and Development
- Policy Writers
- Public Relations Department
- Sales Department

Military

- Combat Developer
- Concept Developer
- Trainer
- Training Developer
- Force Developer
- Program/Project/Product Developer
- Resource Manager
- Operational Architect

- Systems Architect
- Technical Architect
- Systems Engineer
- Software Developer
- Manufacturer
- Test & Evaluation Community
- Modeling & Simulation Community
- Warfighter

USES:

- Defining and describing architecture elements.

TYPICAL INFORMATION SOURCES:

Corporate/Non-Military

- Function/Task Lists
- Long Range Plans
- Organization Descriptions
- Operational Concepts
- Policy and Procedures Guides
- Standing Operating Procedures (SOPs)
- Strategic Plans
- Subject Matter Experts
- System Descriptions
- Task Descriptions
- Vision Statements
- Business Plans
- Corporate Brochures
- Annual Reports

Military

- Subject Matter Experts
- Policy and Procedures Guides
- Doctrinal Publications

- Operational Concepts
- Operational and Organizational Plans
- Vision Statements
- Future Operational Capabilities (FOCs)
- Long Range Plans
- Strategic Plans
- Modernization Plans
- Master Plans
- Organization Descriptions (including TOEs, MTOEs, TDAs)
- Function/Task Lists (including METLs, UJTL, Service Task Lists)
- Task Descriptions
- Standing Operating Procedures (SOPs)
- Interface Descriptions
- System Descriptions
- Architecture Products

TOOLS:

- Text Editor
- Database

PARTICIPANTS:

Corporate/Non-Military

- Operational Architect/Facilitator
- Subject Matter Expert

Military

- Combat Developer
- Concept & Doctrine Developer
- Operational Architect/Facilitator
- Subject Matter Expert
- Warfighter
- Program/Project/Product Developer
- Systems Architect
- Technical Architect

- Systems Engineer

PRODUCT DEVELOPMENT:

1. ***Document and define key terms from architecture products.*** Review all architecture products to identify key terms for inclusion in the Integrated Dictionary. If the terms are defined in the architecture product, then copy the definition into the Integrated Dictionary. For terms that are not defined in the architecture products, adopt definitions from approved source documents such as dictionaries, doctrinal publications, operational concepts, or existing architectures and products whenever possible. Modify adopted definitions as necessary to accurately reflect unique aspects of the enterprise. Create new definitions only when no appropriate definition can be adopted from an existing source document. Include in the Integrated Dictionary such terms as:
   - Concepts, missions, tasks, operational nodes, and information exchange elements from the Operational Concept Description;
   - Activities and ICOMs from the Activity Model;
   - Operational nodes from the Node Connectivity Description and the Organizational Relationships Chart;
   - Operational nodes and information exchange elements from the Operational Information Exchange Matrix;
   - Activities, events, information exchanges, and triggers from the Operational Activity Sequence and Timing Description;
   - Entities, attributes, and relationships from the Logical Data Model;
   - Tables and columns from the Physical Data Model;
   - Systems and nodes from the System Interface Description.
2. ***Document and define key abbreviations and acronyms from architecture products.*** Identify and extract abbreviations and acronyms used in each architecture product. Copy available definitions from the architecture products for inclusion in the Integrated Dictionary.
3. ***Define architecture products.*** List the architecture products included in the architecture and add the standard definitions for each product. Where necessary, add to the standard definition to describe any unique aspects of, or non-standard modifications to any product.
4. ***List, define, and describe architecture product components and elements.*** Add to the Integrated Dictionary terms that describe the component parts of each architecture product. Adopt standard definitions for these product components from service or joint architecture guidance documents or commercial standards (e.g., IEEE 1320.1A for IDEF0 Activity Modeling). Include entries for:
   - Diagram types (i.e., Context, Decomposition, Node Tree, and For Exposition Only (FEO)), and ICOM types (i.e., Input, Control, Output, Mechanism, and Control) used in the Activity Model.

— Entity types (i.e., Independent, Dependent, and Associative), relationship types (i.e., Identifying, Non-Identifying, Mandatory, Non-Mandatory, Recursive, Many-to-Many, and Category), and relationship cardinality types used in the Logical and Physical Data Models;

— Column headings used in the Operational Information Exchange Matrix and codes used to represent valid values for filling the matrix columns; and

— Relationship and interface types shown in the Operational Concept Description, the Organizational Relationships Chart, the Node Connectivity Description, and the System Interface Description.

5. ***Define and describe graphical elements used in architecture products.*** Review all architecture products and extract all graphical icons, symbols and product elements. Describe what the graphical element represents or how it is used in the architecture. Include entries for:

— Geometric shapes (e.g., squares, circles, ovals, rectangles, and triangles) used to represent activities, operational nodes, or systems;

— Icons and pictograms used to represent operational nodes and systems; and

— Lines and arrows used to represent relationships among and between operational nodes and systems.

6. ***Provide the Integrated Dictionary to SMEs for review and comment.*** Include information on the portions of the product to be reviewed, the types of comments to be provided, the desired comment format, the individual(s) or organization(s) to whom/which comments are to be submitted, and the suspense for comment submission.

7. ***Update Integrated Dictionary based on comments received.*** Modify the Integrated Dictionary entries as necessary to incorporate approved change recommendations resulting from the SME review.

8. ***Publish the final Integrated Dictionary.***

RECOMMENDED DEVELOPMENT SEQUENCE:

Begin the development of this product early in the architecture development process. Add terms and definitions as architecture products are developed. Finalize the Integrated Dictionary after the last architecture product is completed.

KEY RELATIONSHIPS:

- All: The Integrated Dictionary includes definitions and descriptions of words, terms, abbreviations, acronyms, symbols, and labels contained in every architecture product.

CRITICAL SUCCESS FACTORS:

DO'S:
- Include in the Integrated Dictionary entries for graphical as well as textual architecture elements.
- Whenever possible, reuse approved definitions from existing documentation and architectures.
- Update reused definitions only to the extent necessary to address unique aspects of the architecture.

DON'TS:
- Don't create new definitions for terms that already have widely accepted, approved definitions.
- Don't use the Integrated Dictionary as a replacement for providing required definitions in appropriate products like the Activity Model and the Data Model.

CHECKLIST: The INTEGRATED DICTIONARY

Process Steps	Complete
1. Document and define key terms from architecture products.	
2. Document and define key abbreviations and acronyms from architecture products.	
3. Define architecture products.	
4. List, define, and describe architecture product components and elements.	
5. Define and describe graphical elements used in architecture products.	
6. Provide the Integrated Dictionary to SMEs for review and comment.	
7. Update the Integrated Dictionary based on comments received.	
8. Publish the final Integrated Dictionary.	

Section Three: ARMY UNIQUE PRODUCTS

Army Unique Products

CHAPTER TWENTY FOUR

PRODUCT NAME: OPERATIONAL FACILITY (OPFAC) EQUIPMENT DESCRIPTION

OTHER ALIASES: OPFAC

PRODUCT DESIGNATION: None

ARCHITECTURE VIEW: ARMY INSTITUTIONAL

PRODUCT DEFINITION: The OPERATIONAL FACILITY (OPFAC) EQUIPMENT DESCRIPTION lists the command, control, communications, and computer (C4) equipment associated with a particular operational element.

PRODUCT DESCRIPTION: An OPFAC Equipment Description is a way to describe individuals as an integrated unit performing one or more related C2 tasks. The OPFAC Equipment Description identifies the operational element and the associated C4ISR and related equipment. Validated OPFAC Equipment Descriptions contain the information necessary to support the development of TOEs/MTOEs and to modify basis of issue plans (BOIPs). For the Army, the OPFAC Equipment Description is one of several products used to identify and document the equipment to be acquired for and fielded to an organization.

PRODUCT FORMAT: Text. May be presented as a Table or Spreadsheet

USERS & USES:

USERS:

- Combat Developer
- Concept Developer
- Training Developer
- Force Developer
- Program/Project/Product Developer
- Resource Manager

- Operational Architect
- Systems Architect
- Technical Architect
- Test & Evaluation Community
- Modeling & Simulation Community
- Warfighter

USES:

- Identification of IERs
- Development/Validation Of Models & Simulations
- Allocation Of Communication Assets
- Planning For Organization Exercises
- Network Burden Assessment
- Identification of OPFAC Hardware Requirements
- Wargaming Alternatives
- Battlefield/Business Process Reengineering
- Development of Procedures Guides and User's Manuals
- Performance of Cost/Benefits Analysis
- Development of Training Materials

TYPICAL INFORMATION SOURCES:

- Subject Matter Experts
- Policy and Procedures Guides
- Doctrinal Publications
- Operational Concepts
- Operational and Organizational Plans
- Organization Descriptions (including TOEs, MTOEs, TDAs)
- Function/Task Lists (including METLs, UJTL, Service Task Lists)
- Task Descriptions
- Standing Operating Procedures (SOPs)
- Interface Descriptions
- System Descriptions

TOOLS:

- Text Editor
- Database

PARTICIPANTS:

- Combat Developer
- Concept & Doctrine Developer
- Force Developer
- Operational Architect/Facilitator
- Subject Matter Expert
- Warfighter
- Program/Project/Product Developer
- Systems Architect
- Technical Architect
- Systems Engineer

PRODUCT DEVELOPMENT:
Once the activities and information exchanges for an organization have been identified and captured, a next step is the creation or modification of OPFAC Equipment Descriptions. The OPFAC Equipment Description associates specific C4 equipment with particular operational elements. This may involve either updating existing OPFAC Equipment Descriptions to reflect the requirements captured in other architecture products or creating new OPFAC Equipment Descriptions where none currently exist.

1. ***Identify operational elements included in the architecture that are required to perform C4ISR tasks or exchange information and via automated communications means.*** Based on information contained in the Operational Concept Description, the Node Connectivity Description, or the Activity Model, determine whether the target operational element is involved in the performance of command and control or coordination functions, or is expected to execute automated information exchanges.
2. ***Determine whether an OPFAC Equipment Description template has already been developed for each operational element.*** Review the list of approved OPFAC Equipment Descriptions to identify any that have been developed for similar operational elements.
3. ***If an OPFAC Equipment Description template already exists for the target operational element, determine whether it is sufficient to meet the requirements of the operational element included in the architecture.***

a. Compare the capabilities of the equipment associated with the existing OPFAC Equipment Description to the capabilities required of the target operational element.
- Identify any missing equipment or capabilities.
- Identify any excess equipment or capabilities.

b. Modify the equipment list to match the requirements of the target operational element.
- Add required systems by name, nomenclature, and quantity.
- Delete excess equipment.

c. Create a new OPFAC Equipment Description number.
- Add a designator to identify the proponent for the new OPFAC Equipment Description.
- Add an echelon identifier to indicate the operational level at which the operational element resides or will reside.
- For operational elements that occur more than once in a single organization, add an identifier to indicate the specific instance of the operational element being described.

4. ***If no OPFAC Equipment Description template exists for the type of operational element being considered, develop a new rule.***

    a. Create the new OPFAC Equipment Description number.
    - Establish a unique, two-digit designator for the target operational element.
    - Add an echelon identifier to indicate the operational level at which the operational element resides or will reside.
    - Add a designator to identify the proponent for the new OPFAC Equipment Description.
    - For operational elements that occur more than once in a single organization, add an identifier to indicate the specific instance of the operational element being described.

    b. Fill the new OPFAC Equipment Description with appropriate C4ISR equipment.
    - List required C4ISR systems by name and nomenclature.
    - Specify the quantities of each type of system.

5. ***Provide the OPFAC Equipment Description to SMEs for review and comment.*** Include information on the portions of the product to be reviewed, the types of comments to be provided, the desired comment format, the individual(s) or organization(s) to whom/which comments are to be submitted, and the suspense for comment submission.

6. ***Update OPFAC Equipment Description based on comments received.*** Modify the OPFAC Equipment Description as necessary to incorporate approved change recommendations resulting from the SME review.

7. ***Submit the final OPFAC Equipment Description for service approval.***

RECOMMENDED DEVELOPMENT SEQUENCE: Following the development of the Operational Concept Description, the Activity Model, the Node Connectivity Description and the Operational Information Exchange Matrix.

KEY RELATIONSHIPS:

- Activity Model: The operational element and the C4ISR equipment included in the OPFAC Equipment Description should be the same as or directly traceable to one or more mechanisms described in the Activity Model. The equipment listed in the OPFAC Equipment Description should be the equipment required to perform the activities and effect the information exchanges shown in the Activity Model.
- Organizational Relationships Chart: The operational element reflected in the OPFAC Equipment Description should be the same as or directly traceable to an operational node shown on the Organizational Relationships Chart.
- System Interface Description: The OPFAC Equipment Description is the textual equivalent of an operational node shown graphically on the System Interface Description. The operational element reflected in the OPFAC Equipment Description should be the same as or directly traceable to an operational node shown on the System Interface Description. The C4ISR equipment included in the OPFAC Equipment Description should match the systems included as components of the corresponding operational node on the System Interface Description.
- System Communications Description: The operational element reflected in the OPFAC Equipment Description should be the same as or directly traceable to an operational node shown on the System Communications Description. The C4ISR equipment included in the OPFAC Equipment Description should match the systems included as components of the corresponding operational node on the System Communications Description.
- System^2 Matrix: The C4ISR equipment included in the OPFAC Equipment Description should match systems included in the System^2 Matrix.
- Core Systems & Quantities Inventory: The C4ISR equipment included in the OPFAC Equipment Description should match systems included in the Core Systems & Quantities Inventory.
- Horseblanket: The C4ISR equipment included in the OPFAC Equipment Description should match systems shown on the Horseblanket.

CRITICAL SUCCESS FACTORS:

DO'S:
– Adopt existing OPFAC Equipment Description templates whenever possible and modify them to meet the requirements of the enterprise being architected.

DON'TS:
– Don't create new OPFAC Equipment Descriptions when usable ones have already been approved.
– Don't include excessive quantities of C4ISR equipment. Include only the types and quantities of equipment necessary to perform required functions and effect required information exchanges.

CHECKLIST: The OPERATIONAL FACILITY (OPFAC) EQUIPMENT DESCRIPTION

Process Steps	Complete
1. Identify operational elements included in the architecture that are required to perform C4ISR tasks or exchange information and via automated communications means.	
2. Determine whether an OPFAC Equipment Description template has already been developed for each operational element.	
3. If an OPFAC Equipment Description template already exists for the target operational element, determine whether it is sufficient to meet the requirements of the operational element included in the architecture.	
a. Compare the capabilities of the equipment associated with the existing OPFAC Equipment Description to the capabilities required of the target operational element.	
– Identify any missing equipment or capabilities.	
– Identify any excess equipment or capabilities.	
b. Modify the equipment list to match the requirements of the target operational element.	
– Add required systems by name, nomenclature, and quantity.	
– Delete excess equipment.	
c. Create a new OPFAC Equipment Description number.	
– Add a designator to identify the proponent for the new OPFAC Equipment Description.	
– Add an echelon identifier to indicate the operational level at which the operational element resides or will reside.	
– For operational elements that occur more than once in a single organization, add an identifier to indicate the specific instance of the operational element being described.	
4. If no OPFAC Equipment Description template exists for the type of operational element being considered, develop a new rule.	
a. Create the new OPFAC Equipment Description number.	
– Establish a unique, two-digit designator for the target operational element.	
– Add an echelon identifier to indicate the operational level at which the operational element resides or will reside.	
– Add a designator to identify the proponent for the new OPFAC Equipment Description.	
– For operational elements that occur more than once in a single organization, add an identifier to indicate the specific	

instance of the operational element being described.	
b. Fill the new OPFAC Equipment Description with appropriate C4ISR equipment.	
– List required C4ISR systems by name and nomenclature.	
– Specify the quantities of each type of system.	
8. Provide the OPFAC Equipment Description to SMEs for review and comment.	
9. Update OPFAC Equipment Description based on comments received.	
10. Submit the final OPFAC Equipment Description for service approval.	

CHAPTER TWENTY FIVE

PRODUCT NAME: CORE SYSTEMS & QUANTITIES INVENTORY

OTHER ALIASES: None

PRODUCT DESIGNATION: None

ARCHITECTURE VIEW: ARMY INSTITUTIONAL

PRODUCT DEFINITION: The CORE SYSTEMS & QUANTITIES INVENTORY is a textual list of hardware and software that will be fielded to a single organization.

PRODUCT DESCRIPTION: The Core Systems & Quantities Inventory provides a consolidated listing of the types and quantities of equipment and software available within an organization. It lists equipment and software by nomenclature and by version. It also shows how the hardware and software within an organization changes over time. Within the Army, the Core Systems & Quantities Inventory is one of several products used to identify and document the equipment to be acquired for and fielded to an organization.

SYSTEM ID	Configuration or Time Period	Configuration or Time Period	Configuration or Time Period	Configuration or Time Period
System A	Quantity	Quantity	Quantity	Quantity
System B	Quantity	Quantity	Quantity	Quantity
System C	Quantity	Quantity	Quantity	Quantity
System D	Quantity	Quantity	Quantity	Quantity
System E	Quantity	Quantity	Quantity	Quantity
System F	Quantity	Quantity	Quantity	Quantity

PRODUCT FORMAT: Table or spreadsheet

USERS & USES:

USERS:

- Combat Developer
- Training Developer
- Force Developer
- Resource Manager
- Operational Architect
- Systems Architect
- Technical Architect
- Test & Evaluation Community
- Modeling & Simulation Community
- Warfighter

USES:

- Development/Validation Of Models & Simulations
- Allocation Of Communication Assets
- Planning For Organization Exercises
- Network Burden Assessment
- Identification of OPFAC Hardware Requirements
- Wargaming Alternatives
- Battlefield/Business Process Reengineering

TYPICAL INFORMATION SOURCES:

- Subject Matter Experts
- Operational and Organizational Plans
- Organization Descriptions (including TOEs, MTOEs, TDAs)
- Function/Task Lists (including METLs, UJTL, Service Task Lists)
- System Descriptions

TOOLS:

- Text Editor

- Database

PARTICIPANTS:

- Combat Developer
- Operational Architect/Facilitator
- Subject Matter Expert
- Warfighter
- Systems Architect
- Systems Engineer

PRODUCT DEVELOPMENT:

1. **List all hardware and software associated with the target organization.**
2. **Group hardware and software items by type/category.** List related hardware and software items together on the matrix. Related items are those that are of the same type (e.g., all communications systems), or that perform the same or similar functions.
3. **Define the timeframes to be included in the Core Systems & Quantities Inventory.** Select the timeframes to coincide with the times when new systems or software are expected to be fielded, when major upgrades to critical systems or software are expected to be delivered, or when major systems or software are to be retired.
4. **Indicate the versions and quantities of each hardware and software item available within the target organization in each time period.**
5. **Provide the Core Systems & Quantities Inventory to SMEs for review and comment.** Include information on the portions of the product to be reviewed, the types of comments to be provided, the desired comment format, the individual(s) or organization(s) to whom/which comments are to be submitted, and the suspense for comment submission.
6. **Update the Core Systems & Quantities Inventory based on comments received.** Modify the Core Systems & Quantities Inventory as necessary to incorporate approved change recommendations resulting from the SME review.
7. **Publish the final Core Systems & Quantities Inventory.**

RECOMMENDED DEVELOPMENT SEQUENCE: Following the development of the architecture OPFAC Equipment Descriptions.

KEY RELATIONSHIPS:

- OPFAC Equipment Description: The C4ISR systems included in the Core Systems & Quantities Inventory should match the C4SIR equipment addressed in all the architecture OPFAC Equipment Descriptions.
- Horseblanket: The Horseblanket provides a graphical depiction of the information shown textually in the Core Systems & Quantities Inventory.
- System Interface Description: The C4ISR systems included in the Core Systems & Quantities Inventory should match the C4SIR equipment addressed in the System Interface Description.
- System Communications Description: The C4ISR systems included in the Core Systems & Quantities Inventory should match the C4SIR equipment addressed in the System Communications Description.
- System^2 Matrix: The C4ISR systems included in the Core Systems & Quantities Inventory should match the C4SIR equipment addressed in the System^2 Matrix.

CRITICAL SUCCESS FACTORS:

DO'S:
− Ensure that the C4ISR systems identified in the Core Systems & Quantities Inventory are consistent with the systems and quantities identified in the OPFAC Equipment Descriptions.

DON'TS:
− Don't include systems in the Core Systems & Quantities Inventory that are not documented in the organization's TOE/MTOE.

CHECKLIST: The CORE SYSTEMS & QUANTITIES INVENTORY

Process Steps	Complete
1. List all hardware and software associated with the target organization.	
2. Group hardware and software items by type/category.	
3. Define the timeframes to be included in the Core Systems & Quantities Inventory.	
4. Indicate the versions and quantities of each hardware and software item available within the target organization in each time period.	
5. Provide the Core Systems & Quantities Inventory to SMEs for review and comment.	
6. Update the Core Systems & Quantities Inventory based on comments received.	
7. Publish the final Core Systems & Quantities Inventory.	

CHAPTER TWENTY SIX

PRODUCT NAME: HORSEBLANKET

OTHER ALIASES: None

PRODUCT DESIGNATION: None

ARCHITECTURE VIEW: ARMY INSTITUTIONAL

PRODUCT DEFINITION: The HORSEBLANKET provides a graphical representation of an organization's equipment.

PRODUCT DESCRIPTION: The HORSEBLANKET is a graphical depiction of an organization's Table of Organization and Equipment (TOE) or Modified TOE (MTOE). It shows, for each TOE/MTOE paragraph, the associated C4 and power generation equipment and vehicles. The C4 equipment shown on the "Horseblanket" should be taken from the Core Systems & Quantities Inventory and/or the organization OPFAC Equipment Descriptions. The power generation equipment and vehicles shown on the "Horseblanket" should match the information contained on the organization's TOE/MTOE, if one exists. There may be instances when the "Horseblanket" is used to describe changes required to an existing TOE/MTOE, or to define the structure and equipment of a new organization for which no TOE/MTOE exists. Within the Army, the Horseblanket is one of several products used to identify and document the equipment to be acquired for and fielded to and organization.

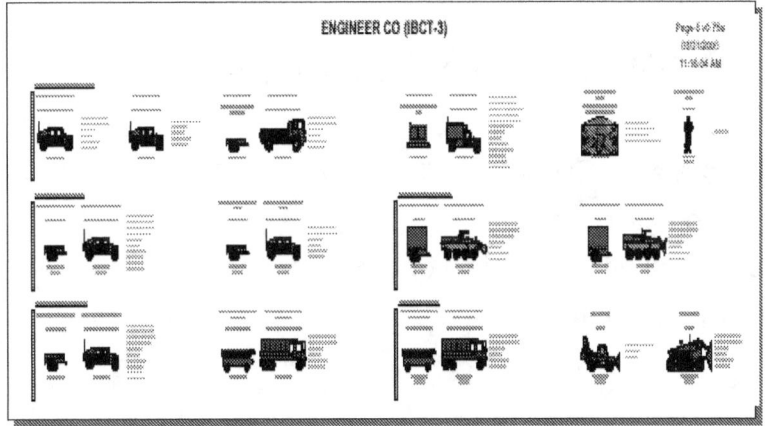

PRODUCT FORMAT: Graphical, with textual annotations

USERS & USES:

USERS:

- Combat Developer
- Force Developer
- Operational Architect
- Systems Architect
- Technical Architect
- Test & Evaluation Community
- Modeling & Simulation Community
- Warfighter

USES:

- Identification of Personnel Requirements
- Development/Validation Of Models & Simulations
- Allocation Of Communication Assets
- Planning For Organization Exercises
- Network Burden Assessment
- Identification of OPFAC Hardware Requirements
- Wargaming Alternatives
- Battlefield/Business Process Reengineering
- Comparing User's Vision to Developer's Implementation

TYPICAL INFORMATION SOURCES:

- Subject Matter Experts
- Operational Concepts
- Operational and Organizational Plans
- System Descriptions

TOOLS:

- Text Editor
- Drawing/Graphics Tool

PARTICIPANTS:

- Combat Developer
- Operational Architect/Facilitator
- Subject Matter Expert
- Warfighter
- Systems Architect
- Technical Architect
- Systems Engineer

PRODUCT DEVELOPMENT:
The process used to develop the Horseblanket depends on whether or not a TOE or MTOE already exists for the organization.

If a TOE/MTOE exists

1. ***Review the organization's TOE/MTOE to identify included C4ISR and power generation equipment, vehicles, shelters, and trailers.*** Identify and document specified equipment items from all TOE/MTOE paragraphs. Record the TOE/MTOE paragraph number associated with each equipment item.
2. ***Select graphical icons to represent the organization's C4ISR and power generation equipment, vehicles, shelters, and trailers.*** Where possible, use pictures or drawings of the actual equipment item. Otherwise, use generic icons to represent classes of equipment.
3. ***Group the icons by TOE/MTOE paragraph.***
4. ***Label the icons to indicate the equipment item(s) represented.***
5. ***Provide the Horseblanket to SMEs for review and comment.*** Include information on the portions of the product to be reviewed, the types of comments to be provided, the desired comment format, the individual(s) or organization(s) to whom/which comments are to be submitted, and the suspense for comment submission.
6. ***Update Horseblanket based on comments received.*** Modify the Horseblanket as necessary to incorporate approved change recommendations resulting from the SME review.
7. ***Publish the final Horseblanket.***

If no TOE/MTOE exists

1. **Identify organizational C4ISR and power generation equipment, vehicle, shelter, and trailer requirements.** Collect information from available sources such as the Operational Concept Description, the Node Connectivity Description, the Core Systems & Quantities Inventory, the OPFAC Equipment Descriptions, the System Interface Description, and the System Communications Description to determine what C4ISR and power generation equipment and vehicles, trailers and shelters are required by the organization. Document all identified equipment requirements.
2. **Select graphical icons to represent the organization's C4ISR and power generation equipment, vehicles, shelters, and trailers.** Where possible, use pictures or drawings of the actual equipment item. Otherwise, use generic icons to represent classes of equipment.
3. **Group the icons by operational element.** Use information from the OPFAC Equipment Descriptions and the System Interface Description to associate equipment items with the organization's operational elements.
4. **Label the icons to indicate the equipment item(s) represented.**
5. **Provide the Horseblanket to SMEs for review and comment.** Include information on the portions of the product to be reviewed, the types of comments to be provided, the desired comment format, the individual(s) or organization(s) to whom/which comments are to be submitted, and the suspense for comment submission.
6. **Update the Horseblanket based on comments received.** Modify the Core Systems & Quantities Inventory as necessary to incorporate approved change recommendations resulting from the SME review.
7. **Publish the final Horseblanket.**

RECOMMENDED DEVELOPMENT SEQUENCE: Following the development of the architecture OPFAC Equipment Descriptions.

KEY RELATIONSHIPS:

- OPFAC Equipment Description: The C4ISR systems included in the Horseblanket should match the C4SIR equipment addressed in all the architecture OPFAC Equipment Descriptions.
- Core Systems & Quantities Inventory: The Horseblanket provides a graphical depiction of the information shown textually in the Core Systems & Quantities Inventory.
- System Interface Description: The systems included in the Horseblanket should match the equipment addressed in the System Interface Description.
- System Communications Description: The systems included in the Horseblanket should match the equipment addressed in the System Communications Description.
- $System^2$ Matrix: The systems included in the Horseblanket should match the equipment addressed in the $System^2$ Matrix.

CRITICAL SUCCESS FACTORS:

DO'S:
- Ensure that the Horseblanket is consistent with the organization's TOE/MTOE, if one exists.
- Ensure that the Horseblanket is consistent with the information shown in the Core Systems & Quantities Inventory.
- Use information from the organization's OPFAC Equipment Descriptions to associate equipment items with operational elements.

DON'TS:
- Don't include equipment items on the Horseblanket that are not documented in the organization's TOE/MTOE, if one exists.

CHECKLIST: The HORSEBLANKET

If a TOE/MTOE exists

Process Steps	Complete
1. Review the organization's TOE/MTOE to identify included C4ISR and power generation equipment, vehicles, shelters, and trailers.	
2. Select graphical icons to represent the organization's C4ISR and power generation equipment, vehicles, shelters, and trailers.	
3. Group the icons by TOE/MTOE paragraph.	
4. Label the icons to indicate the equipment item(s) represented.	
5. Provide the Horseblanket to SMEs for review and comment.	
6. Update the Horseblanket based on comments received	
7. Publish the final Horseblanket.	

If no TOE/MTOE exists

Process Steps	Complete
1. Identify organizational C4ISR and power generation equipment, vehicles, shelters, and trailers.	
2. Select graphical icons to represent the organization's C4ISR and power generation equipment, vehicles, shelters, and trailers.	
3. Group the icons by operational element.	
4. Label the icons to indicate the equipment item(s) represented.	
5. Provide the Horseblanket to SMEs for review and comment.	
6. Update the Horseblanket based on comments received.	
7. Publish the final Horseblanket.	

CHAPTER TWENTY SEVEN

NON-STANDARD ARCHITECTURE PRODUCTS

This chapter describes a set of non-standard information products that complement the standard architecture products. These non-standard products are, for the most part, matrices, lists, and descriptions in plain English. Some of these non-standard products merely repackage information presented in standard architecture products in order to make that information more accessible and understandable. Other non-standard products provide information that is not available in any standard product.

These non-standard products may be developed as an aid to or as a result of architecture analysis. As an aid to analysis, they can expose architecture details that may be less than obvious when presented in standard architecture products. When used to document the results of architecture analysis, they can also expose hidden architecture details as well as integrate related elements of information captured in multiple standard products.

Activity to Organization Applicability Matrix

This matrix identifies which of the organizations or elements within an enterprise perform or support each of the activities captured in the Activity Model or the Operational Activity Sequence & Timing Description. In addition to or in lieu of the activities in the Activity Model or the Operational Activity Sequence & Timing Description, the matrix may address those identified in the Operational Concept Description and/or the Node Connectivity Description.

	Organization/ Element 1	Organization/ Element 2	Organization/ Element 3	Organization/ Element 4	Organization/ Element 5	Organization/ Element 6
Activity A						
Activity B						
Activity C						
Activity D						
Activity E						
Activity F						

Activity to System Applicability Matrix

This matrix is the System Architecture version of the Activity to Organization Applicability Matrix. It identifies which of the systems within the enterprise perform or support the activities defined in the Activity Model or the Operational Activity Sequence & Timing Description.

	System 1	System 2	System 3	System 4	System 5	System 6
Function A						
Function B						
Function C						
Function D						
Function E						
Function F						

System to Organization Matrix

This matrix identifies the systems owned, controlled, or used by each of the organizations or elements within an enterprise.

	System 1	System 2	System 3	System 4	System 5	System 6
Organization/Element A						
Organization/Element B						
Organization/Element C						
Organization/Element D						
Organization/Element E						
Organization/Element F						

Activity to System to Organization Crosswalk Matrix

This matrix identifies which system(s) is/are used by each organization or element to perform each activity within the enterprise. It can show that different systems are used by different organizations/elements to perform the same activity, that the same system is used by different organizations/elements to perform the same activity, that a single organization uses the same system to perform multiple activities, or that a single organization/element uses multiple systems to perform a single activity.

Information to Organization Applicability Matrix

This matrix relates information elements to organizations or elements within the enterprise. The information elements captured in the matrix may be those defined in the Activity Model or those identified in the Operational Information Exchange Matrix. In addition to or in lieu of the information elements from the Activity Model or the Operational Information Exchange Matrix, this matrix may include the high-level information elements shown in the Operational Concept Description and/or the Node Connectivity Description.

	Organization/ Element 1	Organization/ Element 2	Organization/ Element 3	Organization/ Element 4	Organization/ Element 5	Organization/ Element 6
Information Element A						
Information Element B						
Information Element C						
Information Element D						
Information Element E						
Information Element F						

Information to System Applicability Matrix

This matrix relates information elements to the systems that produce or use them. The included information elements may be those defined in the Activity Model or those identified in the Operational Information Exchange Matrix. In addition to or in lieu of the information elements from the Activity Model or the Operational Information Exchange Matrix, this matrix may include the high-level information elements shown in the Operational Concept Description and/or the Node Connectivity Description. If the matrix included data elements instead of information elements, they may be those identified in either the Logical or Physical Data Models or in the System Data Exchange Matrix.

	System 1	System 2	System 3	System 4	System 5	System 6
Information Element A						
Information Element B						
Information Element C						
Information Element D						
Information Element E						
Information Element F						

Organization to System to Information Crosswalk Matrix

This matrix identifies the specific system(s) used by each organization or element to produce or process each element of information. It can show that different systems are used by different organizations/elements to produce or process the same information, that the same system is used by different organizations or elements to produce or process the same information, that a single organization uses the same system to produce or process multiple information elements, or that a single organization/element uses multiple systems to produce or process the same element of information.

Architecture Product Status Matrix

This matrix documents the status of each of the products included in an architecture, to include the actual or projected product completion date.

	Current Product Status	Completion Date	Remarks
Product A			
Product B			
Product C			
Product D			
Product E			
Product F			

Product to Architecture View Applicability Matrix

This matrix identifies the specific products included in, or to be included in, each view or version of an architecture. The different views are each a part of a single enterprise architecture.

	As-Is Architecture	Interim Architecture	Objective Architecture
Product A			
Product B			
Product C			
Product D			
Product E			
Product F			

Architecture to Architecture Product Crosswalk Matrix

This matrix relates the products in one architecture to the same or similar products in another architecture. The two architectures may be part of different enterprise architectures, or they may be sub-architectures that are part of the same parent enterprise architecture.

Activity/Function to Requirements Crosswalk Matrix

This matrix crosswalks activities (from the Activity Model or Operational Activity Sequence & Timing Description) and/or functions (from the System Functionality Description or the System Function Sequence & Timing Description) to required capabilities defined in operational, functional, or technical requirements documents. The matrix shows the extent to which the requirements are being met, or will be met, by organizations, elements, or systems that comprise the enterprise. Requirements may be documented in formal operational or technical requirements documents, needs statements, vision statements, long range plans, or modernization plans.

	Requirement 1	Requirement 2	Requirement 3	Requirement 4	Requirement 5	Requirement 6	Requirement 7	Requirement 8	Requirement 9	Requirement 10	Requirement 11	Requirement 12
Activity A												
Activity B												
Activity C												
Activity D												
Activity E												
Activity F												
Function A												
Function B												
Function C												
Function D												
Function E												
Function F												

Information Element to Data Element Crosswalk

This product relates information elements from the Activity Model, the Operational Concept Description, the Node Connectivity Description, the Operational Information Exchange Matrix, or the Operational Activity Sequence & Timing Description to data elements included in the Logical or Physical Data Models or the System Data Exchange Matrix. The matrix can be used to illustrate the level to which system data exchanges meet the operational information exchange requirements as those requirements are documented in available OA products.

Organization Activities List

The Organization Activities List is a simple textual list of all the activities performed or supported by a single organization or organizational element. The basic list may be augmented by activity definitions or by implementation schedules.

System Functions List

The System Functions List is a simple textual list of all the functions performed or supported by a single system, system component, sub-system, or family of systems. The basic list may be augmented by function definitions or by implementation schedules.

Organization Description

This product is a textual description of an organization or organizational element. The description may include the name or designation of the organization, the organization type, primary and secondary organizational roles and missions, organizational relationships, and other pertinent information.

System Description

This product is a textual description of a single system. The description may include the name or designation of the system, the type of system, system components and sub-systems, system functions, and other pertinent information. The System Description may also include technical drawings or schematics.

Section Four: PRODUCT RELATIONSHIPS

CHAPTER TWENTY EIGHT

KEY RELATIONSHIPS

This chapter recaps the KEY RELATIONSHIPS portion of Chapters Two through Twenty-Six, and provides a single table summarizing the information contained in those sections. It supports an architecture developer in ensuring that the information contained within different products is consistent. It also may be used as a guideline or checklist for evaluating completed architectures or architecture products.

OPERATIONAL CONCEPT DESCRIPTION

- Node Connectivity Description: The nodes depicted on the Node Connectivity Description should be the same as, or at least directly traceable to the operational elements, nodes, and organizations described in the textual operational concept and the OPCON graphic.
- Organizational Relationships Chart: The nodes and the command and control relationships depicted on the Organizational Relationships Chart should be the same as or directly traceable to those described in the textual operational concept and the OPCON graphic.
- Operational Information Exchange Matrix: The sending and receiving nodes, connectivities, and exchanged information elements captured in the Operational Information Exchange Matrix should be the same as or directly traceable to those described in the textual operational concept and the OPCON graphic.
- Activity Model: The activities contained in the Activity Model should be directly traceable to the functions, missions, and tasks described in the textual operational concept and the OPCON graphic. The information exchanges defined in the Activity model should be the same as or directly traceable to those described in the textual operational concept and the OPCON graphic. If the Activity Model defines the elements, nodes, and organizations that perform the activities, they should be the same as or directly traceable to those described in the textual operational concept or shown on the OPCON graphic.
- Operational Activity Sequence & Timing Description: The activities contained in the Operational Activity Sequence & Timing Description should be directly traceable to the functions, missions, and tasks described in the textual operational concept and the OPCON graphic.
- Logical Data Model: The data elements contained in the Logical Data Model should be traceable to the nodes, elements, organizations, interfaces,

information exchanges, functions, missions, and tasks described in the textual operational concept or depicted on the OPCON graphic.
- OPFAC Equipment Description: The operational element depicted in an OPFAC Equipment Description should be the same as or directly traceable to an element, node, or organization described in the textual operational concept or shown on the OPCON graphic.

ACTIVITY MODEL

- Operational Concept Description: The functions/activities/tasks captured in the Activity Model should be directly traceable to the high level missions, tasks and activities described in the Operational Concept Description. The ICOMs in the Activity Model should be traceable to the information exchanges shown in the Operational Concept Description. The Activity Model scope should be consistent with the scope of the Operational Concept. The Activity Model mechanisms (if they are included) should be the same as or directly traceable to the operational elements, nodes, and systems described in the Operational Concept Description.
- Node Connectivity Description: The ICOMs in the Activity Model should be traceable to the information exchanges shown in the Node Connectivity Description. The Activity Model mechanisms (if they are included) should be the same as or directly traceable to the operational elements, nodes, and systems described in the Node Connectivity Description.
- Operational Information Exchange Matrix: The ICOMs in the Activity Model should be traceable to the information exchanges shown in the Operational Information Exchange Matrix. The Activity Model mechanisms (if they are included) should be the same as or directly traceable to the sending and receiving nodes in the Operational Information Exchange Matrix.
- Organizational Relationships Chart: The Activity Model mechanisms (if they are included) should be the same as or directly traceable to the operational elements, nodes, and systems shown in the Organizational Relationships Chart.
- Operational Activity Sequence & Timing Description: The Operational Activity Sequence and Timing Description tasks and information elements should be the same as the Activity Model activities and ICOMs. Ideally, the Operational Activity Sequence and Timing Description should be created using the same activities and information elements captured in the Activity Model.
- Logical Data Model: The data entities and attributes included in the Logical Data Model should be traceable to the ICOMs from the Activity Model. The ICOMs from the Activity Model should be decomposed into the basic elements of data of which they are composed. These basic elements of data then become the basis for defining data model entities and attributes.

- Physical Data Model: The data entities and attributes included in the Logical Data Model should be traceable to the ICOMs from the Activity Model.
- System Interface Description: The high level systems/nodes that are decomposed on the System Interface Description should be directly traceable to Activity Model mechanisms (if they are included).
- System Function Description: The system functions captured in the System Function Description should be directly traceable to activities and tasks in the Activity Model.
- Operational Activity to System Function Traceability Matrix: The Operational Activity to System Function Traceability Matrix includes the activities/tasks from the Activity Model.
- OPFAC Equipment Description: The high level nodes that are decomposed in the OPFAC Equipment Description should be directly traceable to Activity Model mechanisms (if they are included).

NODE CONNECTIVITY DESCRIPTION

- Operational Concept Description: The operational nodes, information exchanges, and high level missions and tasks shown on the Operational Node Connectivity Description should be the same as or directly traceable to those captured in the Operational Concept Description.
- Organizational Relationships Chart: Each organizational element shown on the Organizational Relationships Chart should be traceable to an operational node depicted on the Node Connectivity Description. Every command relationship on the Organizational Relationships Chart should be reflected in one or more information exchange relationships in the Node Connectivity Description.
- Operational Information Exchange Matrix: The Node Connectivity Description should graphically condense the Operational Information Exchange Matrix. The operational nodes illustrated in the Node Connectivity Description should be the same as the sending and receiving nodes described in the Operational Information Exchange Matrix. Each pair of connected nodes on the Node Connectivity Description should be reflected by a sending node-receiving node pair on the Operational Information Exchange Matrix. The elements of information shown on the Node Connectivity Description should be directly associated with specific information exchange elements detailed in the Operational Information Exchange Matrix.
- Activity Model: The high level missions and tasks for each node shown on the Node Connectivity Description should be directly traceable to activities captured in the Activity Model. If the Activity Model includes mechanisms to represent the operational elements that perform each activity, then the operational nodes shown on the Node Connectivity Description should be directly traceable to the Activity Model mechanisms. Every information

exchange element shown on the Node Connectivity Description should be traceable to one or more information elements from the Activity Model.
- System Interface Description: The operational nodes captured on the Node Connectivity Description should be decomposed on the System Interface Description to the individual systems resident at each node. The inter-nodal information exchanges shown on the System Interface Description should be directly traceable to exchanges between nodes shown on the Node Connectivity Description.
- OPFAC Equipment Description: Each OPFAC Equipment Description should describe a single node shown on the Node Connectivity Description.

OPERATIONAL INFORMATION EXCHANGE MATRIX

- Operational Concept Description: The information exchange elements captured in the OIEM should be the same as or directly traceable to the information exchange elements captured in the Operational Concept Description. The sending and receiving nodes in the OIEM should be the same as or directly traceable to operational elements, nodes, systems, or organizations described in the Operational Concept Description.
- Node Connectivity Description: The information exchange elements captured in the OIEM should be the same as or directly traceable to the information exchange elements captured in the Node Connectivity Description. The sending and receiving nodes in the OIEM should be the same as or directly traceable to operational elements, nodes, systems, or organizations described in the Node Connectivity Description.
- Activity Model: The information exchange elements captured in the OIEM should be the same as or directly traceable to the externally exchanged ICOs captured in the Activity Model. The sending and receiving nodes shown in the OIEM should be the same as or directly traceable to the mechanisms in the Activity Model, if those mechanisms represent nodes, systems, elements, or organizations.
- Organizational Relationships Chart: The sending and receiving nodes in the OIEM should be the same as or directly traceable to operational elements, nodes, systems, or organizations described in the Organizational Relationships Chart. The information exchange elements captured in the OIEM should be consistent with the types of relationships captured in the Organizational Relationships Chart. For example, the OIEM for a relationship shown as coordination only should not include information associated with exchange of commands and orders from a higher echelon organization to a subordinate.
- Logical Data Model: The metadata associated with attributes in the Logical Data Model should be consistent with or directly traceable to the technical and performance parameters captured in the OIEM.

- Physical Data Model: The metadata associated with attributes in the Physical Data Model should be consistent with or directly traceable to the technical and performance parameters captured in the OIEM.
- System Data Exchange Matrix: The System Data Exchange Matrix should be directly traceable to the OIEM, as it reflects the system implementation of the operational requirements captured in the OIEM. Each data exchange element in the System Data Exchange Matrix should be directly traceable to one or more information exchange elements from the OIEM. The sending and receiving system nodes identified in the System Data Exchange Matrix should be a subordinate component of or directly traceable to one or more sending or receiving operational nodes, systems, elements, or organizations identified in the OIEM.
- Technical Architecture Profile: The technical and performance parameters captured in the OIEM should be in accordance with the technical standards specified in the Technical Architecture Profile.
- Standards Technology Forecast: The technical and performance parameters shown in the OIEM may include allowances for the implementation of future technical standards as described in the Standards Technology Forecast. If such future standards are included in the OIEM, they should be identified clearly, to include the timeframe within which they are expected to be implemented. For example, an information exchange using an exchange medium that will not be available or acquired until 2010 should be identified as a future requirement and further annotated with an indication that the exchange is expected to be effective after 2010.

ORGANIZATIONAL RELATIONSHIPS CHART

- Operational Concept Description: The operational nodes, relationships, and information exchanges shown on the Organizational Relationships Chart should be the same as or directly traceable to those captured in the Operational Concept Description.
- Node Connectivity Description: Each organizational element shown on the Organizational Relationships Chart should be traceable to an operational node depicted on the Node Connectivity Description. Every command relationship on the Organizational Relationships Chart should be reflected in one or more information exchange relationships in the Node Connectivity Description.
- Operational Information Exchange Matrix: The organizational nodes illustrated in the Organizational Relationships Chart should be traceable to the sending and receiving nodes described in the Operational Information Exchange Matrix.
- Activity Model: If the Activity Model includes mechanisms to represent the operational elements that perform each activity, then the organizational nodes shown on the Organizational Relationships Chart should be directly traceable to

Activity Model mechanisms. Every information exchange element shown on the Organizational Relationships Chart should be traceable to one or more information elements from the Activity Model.

- System Interface Description: The organizational nodes captured on the Organizational Relationships Chart should be decomposed on the System Interface Description to the individual systems resident at each node. The inter-nodal information exchanges shown on the System Interface Description should be directly traceable to exchanges between nodes shown on the Organizational Relationships Chart.
- OPFAC Equipment Description: Each OPFAC Equipment Description should describe a single organizational node shown on the Organizational Relationships Chart.

LOGICAL DATA MODEL

- Operational Concept Description: The data elements in the Logical Data Model should be based upon or directly traceable to the missions, tasks, activities, nodes, and organizations described in the Operational Concept Description. Any information exchanges depicted in the Operational Concept Description should be supported by data elements in the Logical Data Model.
- Operational Information Exchange Matrix: The information exchange elements and sending and receiving nodes captured in the Operational Information Exchange Matrix should be supported by data elements in the Logical Data Model. The technical and performance parameters associated with the information exchange elements in the Operational Information Exchange Matrix should be reflected in the attributes of the appropriate data elements in the Logical Data Model.
- Activity Model: The data elements in the Logical Data Model should be based upon or directly traceable to Activity Model ICOMs.
- System Data Exchange Matrix: The data exchange elements included in the System Data Exchange Matrix should be the same as those captured in the Logical Data Model.
- Physical Data Model: The Physical Data Model may be developed directly from the Logical Data Model by adding implementation-specific data characteristics. The Physical Data Model may also be developed independent of the Logical Data Model, but its physical data elements should be traceable to the logical data elements described in the Logical Data Model.
- Technical Architecture Profile: The technical standards identified in the Technical Architecture Profile may influence the structure and characteristics of the data elements captured in the Logical Data Model. For example, the adoption of a specific technical standard for reporting time may effect the way that time based data elements are captured in the Logical Data Model. Likewise, the structure and characteristics of data elements in the Logical Data

Model may influence which technical standards are adopted for inclusion in the Technical Architecture Profile.

- System Technology Forecast: The technical standards identified in the System Technology Forecast may influence the structure and characteristics of the data elements captured in the Logical Data Model. For example, the adoption of a specific technical standard for reporting time may effect the way that time based data elements are captured in the Logical Data Model. Likewise, the structure and characteristics of data elements in the Logical Data Model may influence which technical standards are adopted for inclusion in the System Technology Forecast.

OPERATIONAL ACTIVITY SEQUENCE AND TIMING DESCRIPTION

- Operational Concept Description: The processes, activities, tasks, and information exchanges captured in the Operational Activity Sequence and Timing Descriptions should be directly traceable to missions, tasks, activities, and information exchanges described in the Operational Concept Description.
- Activity Model: The activities and tasks included in activity based Operational Event/Trace Descriptions and the events/actions in Operational State Transition Descriptions should be reused from or directly traceable to the Activity Model. The information elements and exchanges depicted in information exchange based Operational Event/Trace Descriptions should be based upon or traceable to the ICOs depicted in the Activity Model.
- Operational Information Exchange Matrix: Information exchange based Operational State Transition Descriptions and Operational State Transition Descriptions should be directly traceable to information exchanges defined in the Operational Information Exchange Matrix.
- Logical Data Model: The Operational Rules Model may be developed as an IDEF1X Logical Data Model. The algorithms and formulae included in the Operational Rules Model may be incorporated into the Logical Data Model.
- Physical Data Model: The Operational Rules Model may be developed as an IDEF1X Physical Data Model. The algorithms and formulae included in the Operational Rules Model may be incorporated into the Physical Data Model.
- System Functionality Sequence & Timing Description: Each System Functionality Sequence and Timing Description may be developed as the system implementation of one or more Operational Activity Sequence and Timing Descriptions.

SYSTEM INTERFACE DESCRIPTION

- Node Connectivity Description: The Node Connectivity Description forms the basis for the System Interface Description. The nodes depicted on the System Interface Description should be the same as one or more operational nodes shown in the Node Connectivity Description. The interfaces shown on the internodal System Interface Description should be the same as those shown on the Node Connectivity Description.
- Operational Information Exchange Matrix: The system and node interfaces described in the System Interface Description should be directly traceable to one or more information exchanges captured in the Operational Information Exchange Matrix.
- Activity Model: The systems and operational nodes shown in the System Interface Description should be directly traceable to system based Activity Model mechanisms. The Interfaces defined in the System Interface Description may be traceable to information exchanges described in the Activity Model.
- Organizational Relationships Chart: The interfaces shown in internodal System Interface Descriptions may be traceable to command, control, or coordination relationships shown on the Organizational Relationships Chart.
- System Communication Description: The System Communication Description provides a more detailed description of the interfaces shown in the System Interface Description.
- System^2 Matrix: Some individual systems shown in the System^2 Matrix should be the same as those shown in the System Interface Description.
- System Data Exchange Matrix: The System Data Exchange Matrix should provide a detailed technical description of the nature of the data exchanges identified in the System Interface Description.
- System Performance Parameters Matrix: Selected systems shown on the System Performance Parameters Matrix should be the same as the systems shown in the System Interface Description.
- Technical Architecture Profile: The Technical Architecture Profile may identify technical standards implemented by the systems in the System Interface Description.
- OPFAC Equipment Description: The operational element identified in the OPFAC Equipment Description is the same as the operational node shown in the System Interface Description. The individual systems that comprise the operational element in the OPFAC Equipment Description are the same as the individual systems shown in the System Interface Description.
- Core Systems & Quantities Inventory: The individual systems depicted in the System Interface Description should also be included in the Core Systems and Quantities Inventory.
- Horseblanket: The individual systems depicted in the System Interface Description should also be included on the Horseblanket. The nodes shown in

the System Interface Description may be captured in the Horseblanket as organizational sub-elements.

SYSTEMS COMMUNICATIONS DESCRIPTION

- System Interface Description: The Systems Communication Description provides a more detailed description of the interfaces shown in the System Interface Description.
- System^2 Matrix: The systems depicted on the System Communication Description should match systems shown in the System^2 Matrix. If the System^2 Matrix is developed to include communications connectivity relationships between and among systems, then the communications connectivities shown in the System^2 Matrix should match those captured on the System Communications Description.
- System Data Exchange Matrix: The system data exchange elements detailed in the System Data Exchange Matrix should be consistent with and directly traceable to one or more inter-system interfaces captured on the System Communication Description. If high-level data exchange element names appear on the System Communications Description, they should be the same as or directly traceable to one or more system data exchange elements included in the System Data Exchange Matrix.
- Technical Architecture Profile: The communications media identified in the System Communications Description must be in accordance with the information exchange standards defined in the Technical Architecture Profile.
- OPFAC Equipment Description: The operational element reflected in the OPFAC Equipment Description should be the same as or directly traceable to an operational node (system node) shown on the System Communications Description. The individual C4ISR systems included in the OPFAC Equipment Description should match the systems included as components of the corresponding operational or system nodes on the System Communications Description.
- Core Systems & Quantities Inventory: The C4ISR systems included in the Core Systems & Quantities Inventory should match the C4ISR systems addressed in the System Communications Description.
- Horseblanket: The systems shown on the Horseblanket should match systems addressed in the System Communications Description

SYSTEMS^2 MATRIX

- System Interface Description: Some individual systems shown in the System^2 Matrix should be the same as those shown in the System Interface Description.

- System Communication Description: The systems depicted on the System Communication Description should match systems shown in the System^2 Matrix. If the System^2 Matrix is developed to include communications connectivity relationships between and among systems, then the communications connectivities shown in the System^2 Matrix should match those captured on the System Communications Description.
- System Data Exchange Matrix: The data exchange elements documented in the System Data Exchange Matrix should support the system to system relationships depicted in the System^2 Matrix.
- OPFAC Equipment Description: The C4ISR equipment included in the OPFAC Equipment Description should match C4ISR systems included in the System^2 Matrix.
- Core Systems & Quantities Inventory: The C4ISR equipment included in the Core Systems & Quantities Inventory should match the C4ISR equipment addressed in the System^2 Matrix.
- Horseblanket: The systems included on the Horseblanket should match systems addressed in the System^2 Matrix.

SYSTEMS FUNCTIONALITY DESCRIPTION

- Activity Model: The system functions captured in the System Functionality Description should be directly traceable to activities, tasks, or functions included in the Activity Model.
- Operational Activity to System Function Traceability Matrix: The system functions included in the Operational Activity to System Function Traceability Matrix are exactly the same as those captured in the System Functionality Description.
- System Function Sequence & Timing Description: Each system function shown in the functionally based System Function Sequence and Timing Description should be the same as or directly traceable to one or more system functions identified in the System Functionality Description.
- System Evolution Description: The System Evolution Description may describe how the functions performed by a particular system change over time.

OPERATIONAL ACTIVITY TO SYSTEM FUNCTION TRACEABILITY MATRIX

- Activity Model: The operational activities shown in the Operational Activity to System Function Traceability Matrix are exactly the same as those included in the Activity Model.

- System Functionality Description: The system functions shown in the Operational Activity to System Function Traceability Matrix are exactly the same as those included in the System Functionality Description.

SYSTEM DATA EXCHANGE MATRIX

- Operational Information Exchange Matrix: The System Data Exchange Matrix should be directly traceable to the OIEM, as it reflects the system implementation of the operational requirements captured in the OIEM. Each data exchange element in the System Data Exchange Matrix should be directly traceable to one or more information exchange elements from the OIEM. The sending and receiving system nodes identified in the System Data Exchange Matrix should be a subordinate component of or directly traceable to one or more sending or receiving operational nodes, systems, elements, or organizations identified in the OIEM.
- Logical Data Model: The data exchange elements included in the System Data Exchange Matrix should be the same as those captured in the Logical Data Model.
- Physical Data Model: The data exchange elements included in the System Data Exchange Matrix should be the same as those captured in the Physical Data Model.
- System Interface Description: The System Data Exchange Matrix should provide a detailed technical description of the nature of the data exchanges identified in the System Interface Description.
- System Communications Description: The system data exchange elements detailed in the System Data Exchange Matrix should be consistent with and directly traceable to one or more inter-system interfaces captured on the System Communication Description. If high-level data exchange element names appear on the System Communications Description, they should be the same as or directly traceable to one or more system data exchange elements included in the System Data Exchange Matrix.
- System^2 Matrix: The system data exchange elements defined in the System Data Exchange Matrix should support the system to system relationship types reflected in the System^2 Matrix.

SYSTEM PERFORMANCE PARAMETERS MATRIX

- System Interface Description: Selected systems shown on the System Performance Parameters Matrix should be the same as the systems shown in the System Interface Description.

- System Evolution Description: The System Evolution Description may identify how the performance of the system(s) shown in the System Performance Parameters Matrix change over time.
- System Technology Forecast: The System Technology Forecast shows how the performance of a system (as shown in the System Performance Parameters Matrix) changes over time as capabilities are added or removed.
- Technical Architecture Profile: Appropriate performance parameters described in the System Performance Parameters Matrix must be in accordance with the information processing, information exchange, information security, and human-computer interface standards defined in the Technical Architecture Profile.

SYSTEM EVOLUTION DESCRIPTION

- System Functionality Description: The System Evolution Description may describe how the functions performed by a particular system (as shown in the System Functionality Description) change over time.
- System Performance Parameters Matrix: The System Evolution Description may identify how the performance of the system(s) shown in the System Performance Parameters Matrix change over time.
- System Technology Forecast: Both the System Technology Forecast and the System Evolution Description can be used to show how the technical standards implemented by systems change over time.
- Technical Architecture Profile: The System Evolution Description provides a description of the time-phased implementation of the standards identified in the Technical Architecture Profile.
- Standards Technology Forecast: The changes to the system, as documented in the System Evolution Description, should be consistent with the mandated/acceptable standards defined in the Standards Technology Forecast.

SYSTEM FUNCTIONALITY SEQUENCE & TIMING DESCRIPTION

- Operational Activity Sequence & Timing Description: Each System Functionality Sequence and Timing Description may be developed as the system implementation of one or more Operational Activity Sequence and Timing Descriptions.
- System Functionality Description: The system functions depicted in the System Functionality Sequence and Timing Description should be the same as

or directly traceable to functions included in the System Functionality Description.

SYSTEM TECHNOLOGY FORECAST

- Logical Data Model: The technical standards identified in the System Technology Forecast may influence the structure and characteristics of the data elements captured in the Logical Data Model. For example, the adoption of a specific technical standard for reporting time may effect the way that time based data elements are captured in the Logical Data Model. Likewise, the structure and characteristics of data elements in the Logical Data Model may influence which technical standards are adopted for inclusion in the System Technology Forecast.
- Physical Data Model: The future technical standards identified in the System Technology Forecast may influence the structure and characteristics of the data elements captured in the Physical Data Model. For example, the adoption of a specific technical standard for reporting time may affect the way that time based data elements are captured in the Physical Data Model. Likewise, the structure and characteristics of data elements in the Physical Data Model may influence which technical standards are adopted for inclusion in the System Technology Forecast.
- System Performance Parameters Matrix: The System Technology Forecast shows how the performance of a system, as shown in the System Performance Parameters Matrix, changes over time as capabilities are added or removed.
- System Evolution Description: Both the System Technology Forecast and the System Evolution Description can be used to show how the technical standards implemented by systems change over time.
- Technical Architecture Profile: The System Technology Forecast identifies how the system standards defined in the Technical Architecture Profile will evolve over time.
- Standards Technology Forecast: The changes to the technical standards implemented by a system, as documented in the System Technology Forecast, must be consistent with the mandated and/or acceptable standards identified in the Standards Technology Forecast.

PHYSICAL DATA MODEL

- Operational Concept Description: The data elements in the Physical Data Model should be based upon or directly traceable to the missions, tasks, activities, nodes, and organizations described in the Operational Concept Description. Any information exchanges depicted in the Operational Concept Description should be supported by data elements in the Physical Data Model.

- Operational Information Exchange Matrix: The information exchange elements and sending and receiving nodes captured in the Operational Information Exchange Matrix should be supported by data elements in the Physical Data Model. The technical and performance parameters associated with the information exchange elements in the Operational Information Exchange Matrix should be reflected in the attributes of the appropriate data elements in the Physical Data Model.
- Activity Model: The data elements in the Physical Data Model should be based upon or directly traceable to Activity Model ICOMs.
- System Data Exchange Matrix: The data exchange elements included in the System Data Exchange Matrix should be the same as those captured in the Physical Data Model.
- Logical Data Model: The Physical Data Model may be developed directly from the Logical Data Model by adding implementation-specific data characteristics. The Physical Data Model may also be developed independent of the Logical Data Model, but its physical data elements should be traceable to the logical data elements described in the Logical Data Model.
- Technical Architecture Profile: The technical standards identified in the Technical Architecture Profile may influence the structure and characteristics of the data elements captured in the Physical Data Model. For example, the adoption of a specific technical standard for reporting time may affect the way that time based data elements are captured in the Physical Data Model. Likewise, the structure and characteristics of data elements in the Physical Data Model may influence which technical standards are adopted for inclusion in the Technical Architecture Profile.
- System Technology Forecast: The future technical standards identified in the System Technology Forecast may influence the structure and characteristics of the data elements captured in the Physical Data Model. For example, the adoption of a specific technical standard for reporting time may affect the way that time based data elements are captured in the Physical Data Model. Likewise, the structure and characteristics of data elements in the Physical Data Model may influence which technical standards are adopted for inclusion in the System Technology Forecast.

TECHNICAL ARCHITECTURE PROFILE

- Operational Information Exchange Matrix: The information exchange media identified in the Operational Information Exchange Matrix must be in accordance with the information exchange standards defined in the Technical Architecture Profile.
- System Interface Description: The system and node interface media identified in the System Interface Description must be in accordance with the information exchange standards defined in the Technical Architecture Profile.

- Logical Data Model: The Logical Data Model must be developed in accordance with the information modeling and exchange standards defined in the Technical Architecture Profile.
- Physical Data Model: The Physical Data Model must be developed in accordance with the information modeling and exchange standards defined in the Technical Architecture Profile. The data processing algorithms and rules described in the Physical Data Model must be in accordance with the information processing standards defined in the Technical Architecture Profile.
- System Communications Description: The communications media identified in the System Communications Description must be in accordance with the information exchange standards defined in the Technical Architecture Profile.
- System Performance Parameters Matrix: Appropriate performance parameters described in the System Performance Parameters Matrix must be in accordance with the information processing, information exchange, information security, and human-computer interface standards defined in the Technical Architecture Profile.
- System Evolution Description: The System Evolution Description provides a description of the time-phased implementation of the standards identified in the Technical Architecture Profile.
- System Technology Forecast: The System Technology Forecast identifies how the system standards defined in the Technical Architecture Profile will evolve over time.
- Standards Technology Forecast: The Standards Technology Forecast identifies how current standards from the Technical Architecture Profile will be replaced by emerging and future standards.

STANDARDS TECHNOLOGY FORECAST

- Operational Information Exchange Matrix: The technical and performance parameters shown in the OIEM may include allowances for the implementation of future technical standards as described in the Standards Technology Forecast. If such future standards are included in the OIEM, they should be identified clearly, to include the timeframe within which they are expected to be implemented. For example, an information exchange using an exchange medium that will not be available or acquired until 2010 should be identified as a future requirement and further annotated with an indication that the exchange is expected to be effective after 2010.
- System Evolution Description: The changes to the system, as documented in the System Evolution Description, should be consistent with the mandated/acceptable standards defined in the Standards Technology Forecast.
- System Technology Forecast: The changes to the technical standards implemented by a system, as documented in the System Technology Forecast, must be consistent with the mandated and/or acceptable standards identified in the Standards Technology Forecast.

- Technical Architecture Profile: The Standards Technology Forecast identifies how current standards from the Technical Architecture Profile will be replaced by emerging and future standards.

OVERVIEW & SUMMARY INFORMATION

- All: The Overview & Summary Information product contains information from (and/or about) every other architecture product.

INTEGRATED DICTIONARY

- All: The Integrated Dictionary includes definitions and descriptions of words, terms, abbreviations, acronyms, symbols, and labels contained in every architecture product.

OPFAC EQUIPMENT DESCRIPTION

- Activity Model: The operational element and the C4ISR equipment included in the OPFAC Equipment Description should be the same as or directly traceable to one or more mechanisms described in the Activity Model. The equipment listed in the OPFAC Equipment Description should be the equipment required to perform the activities and effect the information exchanges shown in the Activity Model.
- Organizational Relationships Chart: The operational element reflected in the OPFAC Equipment Description should be the same as or directly traceable to an operational node shown on the Organizational Relationships Chart.
- System Interface Description: The OPFAC Equipment Description is the textual equivalent of an operational node shown graphically on the System Interface Description. The operational element reflected in the OPFAC Equipment Description should be the same as or directly traceable to an operational node shown on the System Interface Description. The C4ISR equipment included in the OPFAC Equipment Description should match the systems included as components of the corresponding operational node on the System Interface Description.
- System Communications Description: The operational element reflected in the OPFAC Equipment Description should be the same as or directly traceable to an operational node shown on the System Communications Description. The C4ISR equipment included in the OPFAC Equipment Description should match

the systems included as components of the corresponding operational node on the System Communications Description.

- System^2 Matrix: The C4ISR equipment included in the OPFAC Equipment Description should match systems included in the System^2 Matrix.
- Core Systems & Quantities Inventory: The C4ISR equipment included in the OPFAC Equipment Description should match systems included in the Core Systems & Quantities Inventory.
- Horseblanket: The C4ISR equipment included in the OPFAC Equipment Description should match systems shown on the Horseblanket.

CORE SYSTEMS & QUANTITIES INVENTORY

- OPFAC Equipment Description: The C4ISR systems included in the Core Systems & Quantities Inventory should match the C4SIR equipment addressed in all the architecture OPFAC Equipment Descriptions.
- Horseblanket: The Horseblanket provides a graphical depiction of the information shown textually in the Core Systems & Quantities Inventory.
- System Interface Description: The C4ISR systems included in the Core Systems & Quantities Inventory should match the C4SIR equipment addressed in the System Interface Description.
- System Communications Description: The C4ISR systems included in the Core Systems & Quantities Inventory should match the C4SIR equipment addressed in the System Communications Description.
- System^2 Matrix: The C4ISR systems included in the Core Systems & Quantities Inventory should match the C4SIR equipment addressed in the System^2 Matrix.

HORSEBLANKET

- OPFAC Equipment Description: The C4ISR systems included in the Horseblanket should match the C4SIR equipment addressed in all the architecture OPFAC Equipment Descriptions.
- Core Systems & Quantities Inventory: The Horseblanket provides a graphical depiction of the information shown textually in the Core Systems & Quantities Inventory.
- System Interface Description: The systems included in the Horseblanket should match the equipment addressed in the System Interface Description.
- System Communications Description: The systems included in the Horseblanket should match the equipment addressed in the System Communications Description.

- System² Matrix: The systems included in the Horseblanket should match the equipment addressed in the System² Matrix.

	OV-1	OV-2	OV-3	OV-4	OV-5	OV-6	OV-7	SV-1	SV-2	SV-3	SV-4	SV-5	SV-6	SV-7	SV-8	SV-9	SV-10	SV-11	TV-1	TV-2	AV-1	AV-2	OPFAC	CSQI	HB
OV-1	■	X	X	X	X	X	X																X		
OV-2	X	■	X	X	X			X													X	X	X		
OV-3	X	X	■	X	X	X	X	X													X	X			
OV-4	X	X	X	■	X																X	X			
OV-5	X	X	X	X	■	X	X	X			X										X	X	X		
OV-6	X		X		X	■	X											X			X	X	X		
OV-7	X				X		■									X		X			X	X			
SV-1		X			X			■	X	X			X	X							X	X			
SV-2						X		X	■	X			X								X	X			
SV-3								X	X	■			X								X	X			
SV-4											■	X			X						X	X			
SV-5					X						X	■									X	X			
SV-6				X	X	X		X	X	X			■	X	X		X				X	X			
SV-7								X			X		X	■	X						X	X			
SV-8											X			X	■		X	X			X	X			
SV-9							X									■	X				X	X			
SV-10															X		■	X	X		X	X			
SV-11				X		X	X								X			■	X	X	X	X			
TV-1			X		X	X	X	X	X										■		X	X			
TV-2		X	X	X																■	X	X			
OPFAC	X							X	X	X											X	X	■	X	X
CSQI								X	X	X											X	X	X	■	X
HB								X	X	X											X	X	X	X	■

CHAPTER TWENTY NINE

RECOMMENDED ARCHITECTURE DEVELOPMENT PROCESS

Provided below is a graphical representation of the architecture development process described in chapters Two through Twenty-Six. It depicts the architecture products in the recommended development order such that information defined and documented in a product can be used to feed the development of the next product.

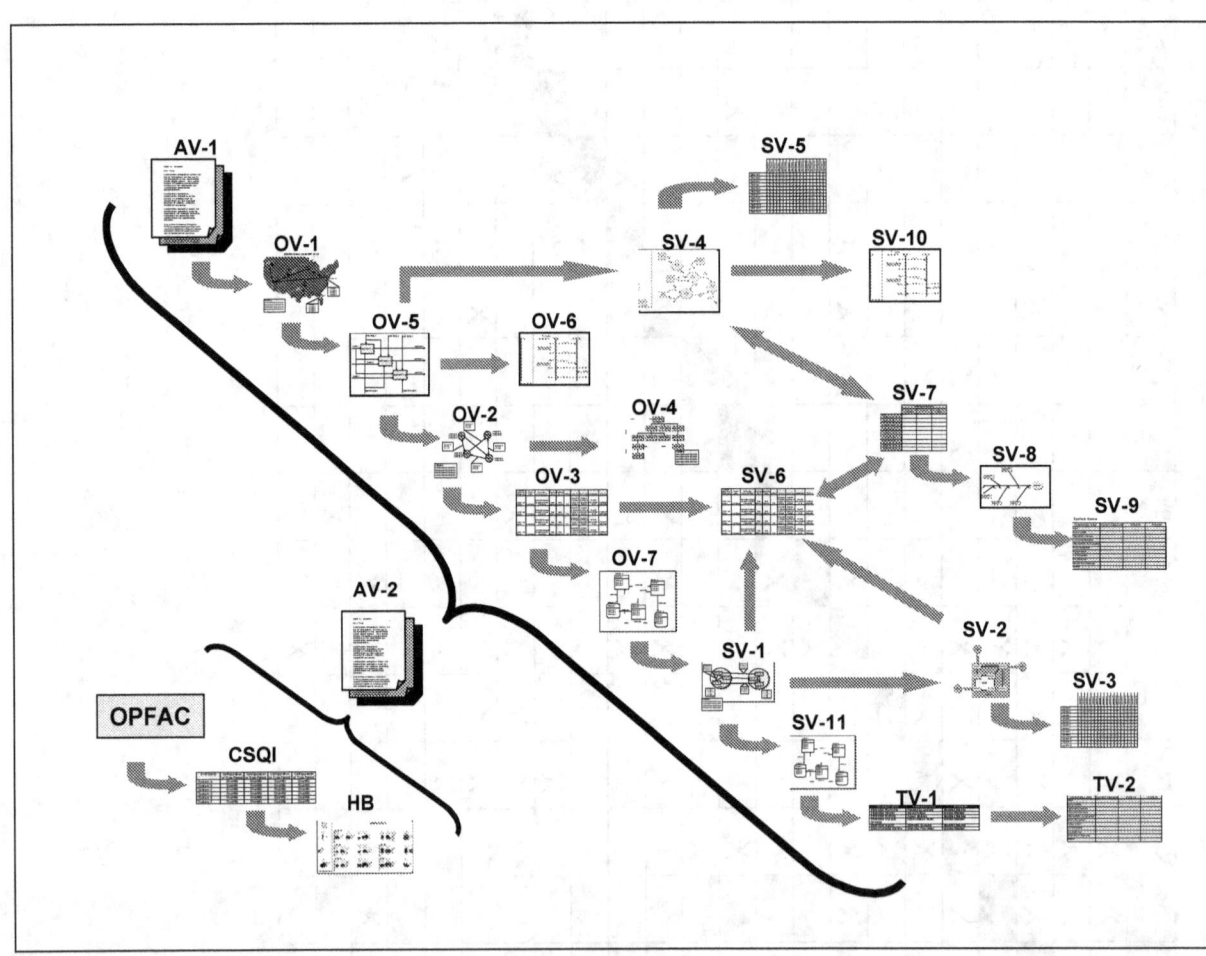

The recommended process for developing an enterprise architecture is described below. Each individual product citation within the description includes a reference to the page on which can be found a detailed methodology for producing the respective product.

Architecture Development Made Simple

1. **The Core Process**

   a. Develop the initial **Overview and Summary Information (AV-1)** *[p. 283]*
   b. Develop the **Operational Concept Description (OV-1)** *[p. 13]*
   c. Develop the **Activity Model (OV-5)** *[p. 33]*
      Go to 1.f, 1.j, 1.k, 2.b, 2.d
   d. Develop the **Node Connectivity Description (OV-2)** *[p. 65]*
      Go to 1.e, 1.g, 1.j, 1.k, 2.a
   e. Develop the **Operational Information Exchange Matrix (OV-3)** *[p. 77]*
      Go to 1.f, 1.h, 1.j, 1.k, 2.h
   f. Develop the **Logical Data Model (OV-7)** *[p. 103]*
      Go to 1.h, 1.j, 1.k
   g. Develop the **System Interface Description (SV-1)** *[p. 135]*
      Go to 1.j, 1.k, 2.f, 2.g, 2.h
   h. Develop the **Physical Data Model (SV-11)** *[p. 245]*
      Go to 1.i, 1.j, 1.k
   i. Develop the **Technical Architecture Profile (TV-1)** *[p. 263]*
      Go to 1.j, 1.k, 2.k, 2.l
   j. Develop the final **Overview and Summary Information (AV-1)** *[p. 283]*
      Go to 1.k
   k. Develop the **Integrated Dictionary (AV-2)** *[p. 291]*

2. **Additional Products**

   a. Develop the **Organizational Relationships Chart (OV-4)** *[p. 93]*
      Go to 1.j, 1.k
   b. Develop the **Operational Activity Sequence and Timing Description (OV-6)** *[p. 121]*
      Go to 1.j, 1.k, 2.e
   c. Develop the **System Functionality Description (SV-4)** *[p. 165]*
      Go to 1.j, 1.k, 2.d, 2.e, 2.h
   d. Develop the **Operational Activity to System Function Traceability Matrix (SV-5)** *[p. 175]*
      Go to 1.j, 1.k
   e. Develop the **System Function Sequence and Timing Description (SV-10)** *[p. 235]*
      Go to 1.j, 1.k
   f. Develop the **System Communications Description (SV-2)** *[p. 145]*
      Go to 1.j, 1.k, 2.g, 2.h
   g. Develop the **System2 Matrix (SV-3)** *[p. 155]*
      Go to 1.j, 1.k, 2.h
   h. Develop the **System Data Exchange Matrix (SV-6)** *[p. 185]*
      Go to 1.j, 1.k, 2.l
   i. Develop the **System Performance Parameters Matrix (SV-7)** *[p. 205]*
      Go to 1.j, 1.k, 2.j, 2.k, 2.l
   j. Develop the **System Evolution Description (SV-8)** *[p. 213]*

Go to 1.j, 1.k, 2.k, 2.l
   k. Develop the **Standards Technology Forecast (TV-2)** *[p. 273]*
      Go to 1.j, 1.k, 2.l
   l. Develop the **System Technology Forecast (SV-9)** *[p. 221]*
      Go to 1.j, 1.k

3. **Army Unique Products**

   a. Develop the **OPFAC Equipment Description** *[p. 303]*
      Go to 1.g, 1.j, 1.k, 2.c, 2.f, 2.g, 2.h, 3.b, 3.c
   b. Develop the **Core Systems & Quantities Inventory** *[p. 311]*
      Go to 1.g, 1.j, 1.k, 2.c, 2.f, 2.g, 2.h, 3.c
   c. Develop the **Horseblanket** *[p. 317]*
      Go to 1.g, 1.j, 1.k, 2.c, 2.f, 2.g, 2.h

Section Five: PRODUCT USERS AND USES

CHAPTER THIRTY

PRODUCT USERS & USES

This chapter recaps the "Users and Uses" section of Chapters Two through Twenty-Six. It can be used by an architecture developer to determine the products to be developed for and included in an architecture, based on the projected architecture users and the intended architecture uses.

1. Architecture Product Users:

	OV-1	OV-2	OV-3	OV-4	OV-5	OV-6	OV-7	SV-1	SV-2	SV-3	SV-4	SV-5	SV-6	SV-7	SV-8	SV-9	SV-10	SV-11	TV-1	TV-2	AV-1	AV-2	OPFAC	CSQI	HB
STRATEGIC PLANNER	X	X	X	X	X		X	X							X		X			X	X	X		X	X
OPERATIONS MANAGER	X	X	X	X	X		X	X	X		X	X	X	X	X	X	X		X		X	X	X		X
HUMAN RESOURCE MANAGER	X	X	X	X	X															X	X	X			
RESOURCE MANAGER	X				X				X	X	X	X			X		X		X		X	X	X	X	X
INFORMATION MANAGER	X	X			X	X	X	X	X	X	X	X	X	X	X	X	X	X	X	X	X	X	X		X
QUALITY ASSURANCE MANAGER	X	X	X	X	X	X	X	X					X	X	X	X		X	X		X	X	X		X
FACILITIES MANAGER	X							X	X	X	X		X	X			X			X		X	X		X
SECURITY MANAGER	X	X	X	X	X	X	X	X	X	X	X	X	X	X	X	X	X	X	X	X	X	X	X	X	X
SUPERVISORS	X	X	X	X	X	X	X	X	X	X	X	X	X	X	X	X	X	X	X		X	X	X	X	X
WORKERS	X	X	X	X	X	X	X	X	X	X	X	X	X	X	X	X	X	X	X	X	X	X	X		

357

Product Users & Uses

	OV-1	OV-2	OV-3	OV-4	OV-5	OV-6	OV-7	SV-1	SV-2	SV-3	SV-4	SV-5	SV-6	SV-7	SV-8	SV-9	SV-10	SV-11	TV-1	TV-2	AV-1	AV-2	OPFAC	CSQI	HB
SOFTWARE DEVELOPERS	X	X	X		X	X	X	X	X		X	X	X	X	X	X	X	X	X	X	X	X			
TRAINERS	X			X	X					X	X					X					X	X	X		
RESEARCH AND DEVELOPMENT	X		X	X	X	X	X	X	X	X	X	X	X	X	X	X	X	X	X	X	X	X	X	X	X
POLICY WRITERS	X	X	X	X	X		X	X	X	X	X					X			X		X	X	X		
PUBLIC RELATIONS DEPARTMENT	X				X																X	X			
SALES DEPARTMENT	X				X									X	X						X				
COMBAT DEVELOPER	X	X	X	X	X	X	X	X	X	X	X	X	X	X	X		X	X	X		X	X	X	X	X
CONCEPT DEVELOPER	X	X	X	X	X	X	X	X			X			X	X	X		X			X	X	X		
FORCE DEVELOPER	X	X	X	X	X	X							X		X		X				X	X	X	X	X
MODELING & SIMULATION COMMUNITY	X	X	X	X	X	X	X	X	X	X	X	X	X	X	X	X	X	X	X	X	X	X	X	X	
OPERATIONAL ARCHITECT	X	X	X	X	X	X	X	X	X	X	X	X	X	X	X	X	X	X	X	X	X	X	X	X	
SYSTEM ARCHITECT	X	X	X	X	X	X	X	X	X	X	X	X	X	X	X	X	X	X	X	X	X	X	X	X	X
TECHNICAL ARCHITECT	X		X	X	X	X	X	X	X		X		X		X		X	X	X	X	X	X	X		
PROGRAM, PROJECT, PRODUCT DEVELOPER	X	X	X	X	X	X	X	X	X	X	X	X	X	X	X	X	X	X	X	X	X	X			
SYSTEMS ENGINEER	X	X	X	X	X	X	X	X	X	X	X	X	X	X	X	X	X	X	X	X	X	X	X		
TEST & EVALUATION COMMUNITY	X	X	X	X	X	X	X	X	X	X	X	X	X	X	X	X	X	X	X	X	X	X	X	X	X
TRAINING DEVELOPER	X		X	X	X						X					X					X	X			
MANUFACTURER	X	X	X			X	X	X	X	X	X	X	X	X	X	X	X	X	X	X	X	X	X	X	
WARFIGHTER	X	X	X	X	X	X	X	X	X	X	X	X	X	X	X	X		X	X	X	X	X	X	X	X

2. Architecture Product Uses:

	OV-1	OV-2	OV-3	OV-4	OV-5	OV-6	OV-7	SV-1	SV-2	SV-3	SV-4	SV-5	SV-6	SV-7	SV-8	SV-9	SV-10	SV-11	TV-1	TV-2	AV-1	AV-2	OPFAC	CSQI	HB
Allocation of Communications Assets	X	X	X	X	X			X	X	X	X	X	X	X	X		X				X	X	X	X	X
Baselining of Functionality	X		X	X	X	X	X	X	X		X	X	X			X				X	X	X			
Business Process Reengineering	X	X	X	X	X	X	X	X	X	X	X	X	X	X	X	X	X	X	X	X	X	X	X	X	X
Communications Network Burden Assessment	X	X	X	X	X			X	X	X	X	X	X				X		X	X	X	X	X	X	X
Comparing User's Vision to Developer's Implementation	X	X	X	X	X	X	X	X	X	X	X		X				X	X	X		X	X	X	X	X
Data Modeling	X		X		X	X	X						X				X	X	X	X	X	X			
Database Design	X				X	X	X	X	X				X				X	X	X	X	X	X			
Describing the Architecture and Its Contents														X							X				
Description of Required System Capabilities	X	X	X	X	X	X	X	X	X	X	X	X				X	X	X	X	X	X	X	X	X	
Design of Human-Computer Interface	X		X	X	X	X	X	X	X	X	X		X	X	X		X	X	X	X	X				
Development of Capital Investment Strategies	X	X	X	X	X			X	X	X				X	X		X	X	X	X	X	X			

Product Users & Uses	OV-1	OV-2	OV-3	OV-4	OV-5	OV-6	OV-7	SV-1	SV-2	SV-3	SV-4	SV-5	SV-6	SV-7	SV-8	SV-9	SV-10	SV-11	TV-1	TV-2	AV-1	AV-2	OPFAC	CSQI	HB
Development of Procedures Guides & User's Manuals	X		X	X	X	X	X	X	X		X		X								X	X			
Development of System Software	X	X	X	X	X	X	X	X	X	X	X	X	X	X	X	X	X	X	X	X					
Development of Training Materials	X	X	X	X	X	X	X	X	X		X							X			X	X	X		
Development/ Modification of Operational Concepts	X	X	X	X	X	X		X	X		X										X	X			
Development/ Modification of Standard Messages	X	X			X	X	X											X	X						
Development/ Validation of Models and Simulations	X	X	X	X	X	X	X	X	X	X	X	X	X	X	X		X	X	X	X			X	X	X
Development/ Validation of SOPs	X	X	X	X	X	X	X	X	X	X	X		X				X				X	X			
Development/ Validation of Training Plans	X	X	X	X	X	X		X	X										X						
Development/ Validation of TTPs	X	X	X	X	X	X		X	X	X	X		X				X	X				X			
Functional Allocation	X				X	X					X	X				X					X	X			

360

	OV-1	OV-2	OV-3	OV-4	OV-5	OV-6	OV-7	SV-1	SV-2	SV-3	SV-4	SV-5	SV-6	SV-7	SV-8	SV-9	SV-10	SV-11	TV-1	TV-2	AV-1	AV-2	OPFAC	CSQI	HB
Identification of Functional Information Exchange Requirements	X	X	X		X								X												
Identification of Hardware Requirements	X	X		X	X	X		X			X		X	X									X	X	X
Identification of Information Exchange Requirements	X	X	X	X	X	X	X		X	X	X		X						X				X		
Identification of Operational Issues	X	X	X	X	X	X	X	X	X	X	X	X	X	X	X	X	X	X	X	X					X
Identification of Personnel Requirements	X			X	X									X			X								
Identification/Validation of Operational Needs & Requirements	X	X	X	X	X	X	X	X	X	X	X	X	X	X	X	X	X	X	X	X	X	X			
Organizational Design	X	X	X	X	X	X		X	X		X										X	X	X		
Performance of Cost-Benefit Analysis	X	X	X	X	X	X	X	X	X	X	X	X	X	X	X	X	X	X	X		X	X			
Planning For Organization Exercises	X	X	X	X	X	X	X	X	X	X	X	X	X	X	X	X	X	X					X	X	X
Planning For System Tests	X	X	X	X	X	X	X	X	X	X	X	X	X	X	X	X	X	X	X						

Product Users & Uses

	OV-1	OV-2	OV-3	OV-4	OV-5	OV-6	OV-7	SV-1	SV-2	SV-3	SV-4	SV-5	SV-6	SV-7	SV-8	SV-9	SV-10	SV-11	TV-1	TV-2	AV-1	AV-2	OPFAC	CSQI	HB
Prioritizing Activities For Implementation	X		X		X							X			X										
Providing Roadmap For System Improvement	X	X	X		X	X	X	X	X		X	X	X	X	X	X	X	X	X	X					
Quality Control/Quality Management	X	X	X	X	X	X	X				X			X		X	X	X	X		X	X			
Standardization of Data Elements	X	X	X		X		X						X				X	X							
Standardization of Processes, Activities, and Tasks	X	X	X		X	X	X				X		X					X							
Strategic Business Planning	X	X	X	X	X							X		X	X	X	X		X	X	X	X			
Wargaming Alternatives	X	X	X	X	X	X	X	X	X	X	X	X	X	X	X	X	X	X	X	X	X	X	X	X	X

BIBLIOGRAPHY

1. Command, Control, Communications, Computers, Intelligence, Surveillance and Reconnaissance (C4ISR) Architecture Framework Document Version 2.0, CISA C4ISR Architecture Working Group, 18 December 1997.

2. A Discussion of the Activity Model and Its Role As A Part of the Operational Architecture, Version 1.0, Quantum Research, International, El Paso, TX, 1999.

3. Joint Technical Architecture, Version 4.0 (Draft 1), US Department of Defense, 14 April 2000.

4. IEEE Standard 1320.1-1998, IEEE Standard for Functional Modeling Language—Syntax and Semantics for IDEF0, Institute of Electrical and Electronics Engineers, 25 June 1998.

5. Federal Information Processing Standards Publication (FIPS Pub) 184, Integration Definition For Information Modeling (IDEF1X), National Institute of Standards and Technology, 21 December 1993.

6. Chairman of the Joint Chiefs of Staff Instruction (CJCSI) 6212.01B, Interoperability And Supportability Of National Security Systems, And Information Technology Systems, Chairman of the Joint Chiefs of Staff, 8 May 2000.

GLOSSARY OF KEY TERMS

PART 1: ACRONYMS

A
AM   Activity Model
AV   All View

B
BOIP   Basis Of Issue Plan
BPR   Business/Battlefield Process Reengineering

C
C2   Command and Control
C4   Command, Control, Communications and Computers
C4ISR   Command, Control, Communications, Computers, Intelligence, Surveillance, and Reconnaissance
C4ISR AF   Command, Control, Communications, Computers, Intelligence, Surveillance, and Reconnaissance Architecture Framework
CJCSI   Commander, Joint Chiefs of Staff Instruction
CONOPS   Concept of Operations
CSQI   Core Systems & Quantities Inventory

D
DBMS   Database Management System
DoD   Department of Defense
DOTMPLF   Doctrine, Organization, Training, Materiel, Personnel, Leaders, and Facilities
DRW   Data Requirements Worksheet
DTLOMS   Doctrine, Training, Leader Development, Organizations, Materiel, and Soldiers

F
FEO   For Exposition Only
FM   Frequency Modulation
FOC   Future Operational Capabilities
FoS   Family of Systems

H
HB   Horseblanket

I
ICO   Inputs, Controls, and Outputs

Glossary

ICOM	Inputs, Controls, Outputs, and Mechanisms
ID	Integrated Dictionary
IDEF0	Integrated Definition for Function Modeling
IDEF1X	Integrated Definition for Information Modeling
IEEE	International Association of Electrical and Electronics Engineers
IER	Information Exchange Requirement

J
JTA	Joint Technical Architecture

L
LAN	Local Area Network
LDM	Logical Data Model

M
METL	Mission Essential Task List
MIL STD	Military Standard
MTOE	Modified Table of Organization and Equipment
MTW	Major Theater War

N
NCD	Node Connectivity Description

O
OA	Operational Architecture
OASTD	Operational Activity Sequence & Timing Description
OIEM	Operational Information Exchange Matrix
OPCON	Operational Concept
OPCON	Operational Control
OPFAC	Operational Facility
ORC	Organizational Relationships Chart
OSI	Operator-System Interface
OSI	Overview & Summary Information
OV	Operational View

P
PDM	Physical Data Model

S
SA	System Architecture
SASO	Stability And Security Operations
SID	System Interface Description
SME	Subject Matter Expert
SOP	Standing Operating Procedure
SSCO	Small Scale Contingency Operations
SV	System View

T
TA	Technical Architecture
TACON	Tactical Control
TAMD	Theater Air and Missile Defense
TAP	Technical Architecture Profile
TDA	Table of Distribution and Allowances
THAAD	Theater High Altitude Area Defense
TOE	Table of Organization and Equipment
TTP	Tactics, Techniques, and Procedures
TV	Technical View

U
UDP	User Defined Property
UJTL	Universal Joint Task List

W
WAN	Wide Area Network
WBS	Work Breakdown Structure

PART 2: KEY TERMS

2.a ARCHITECTURE TERMS

ACTIVITY: A function, task, or process that takes place over time and has tangible results.

ACTIVITY MODEL: The Operational Architecture product that provides a graphical and textual description of the activities (functions or processes) performed by/within an organization or system, and the information exchanges associated with the performance of those activities.

ACTIVITY MODEL EXCURSION: A type of Activity Model that changes one or more activities or ICOMs from the original model in order to allow the operational architect or modeler to explore and evaluate alternatives.

ACTIVITY MODEL EXTENSION: A type of Activity Model that takes all or part of the original model and extends or expands its activities and/or ICOMs to provide additional detail.

ACTIVITY MODEL EXTRACT: A type of Activity Model that shows a subset (a "slice") of the original model without changing any aspect of it.

ACTIVITY MODEL VIEW: A special category of Activity Model that presents an alternative view of another existing Activity Model.

ARCHITECTURE VIEW: The three standard architecture views are the ORGANIZATIONAL, the SYSTEM, and the TECHNICAL.

ATTRIBUTE: In an IDEF1X Logical Data Model, an individual element of data about a person, place, thing, event, or concept. Equivalent to a **Column** in a Physical Data Model.

BI-NODAL: The type of Node Connectivity Description or Operational Information Exchange Matrix that depicts the interfaces among and between enterprise nodes by concentrating on two nodes at a time. Each individual diagram shows the connectivity between two, and only two, operational nodes.

COLUMN: In an IDEF1X Physical Data Model, a single element of data about a person, place, thing, event, or concept. Equivalent to an **Attribute** in a Logical Data Model.

COMMON ACTIVITY MODEL: A type of Activity Model that describes those tasks/activities and information exchanges that are common to a number of systems, organizations or functional areas. When it is produced prior to the development of the Activity Models for any specific system, organization or functional area, then it can serve as a template to be used to produce more specific models. When it is produced after the development of specific models, then it can be used to standardize processes and information exchanges across systems, organizations and functional areas.

CONTEXT DIAGRAM: One of four types of IDEF0 Activity Model diagrams. The Context Diagram places the enterprise in context by graphically portraying how the enterprise interacts with its external environment.

CONTROL: One category of information associated with an IDEF0 Activity Model. Controls impose constraints upon or rules that govern the conduct of activities.

CORE SYSTEMS & QUANTITIES INVENTORY: The Army unique architecture product that is a textual list of hardware and software that will be fielded to a single organization.

DATA: Basic facts about real world objects, concepts, or events.

DECOMPOSITION DIAGRAM: One of four types of IDEF0 Activity Model diagrams. The Decomposition Diagram shows how an activity is "decomposed" into the lower level activities of which it is comprised. It also depicts the exchange of information among the lower level activities.

ENTERPRISE: An organization, system, Family of Systems, functional area, or service about which an architecture is developed.

ENTITY: In an IDEF1X Logical Data Model, a person, place, thing, event, or concept about which data is kept. Equivalent to a **Table** in a Physical Data Model.

FAMILY OF SYSTEMS (FOS) ACTIVITY MODEL: A type of Activity Model that is a hybrid between a System model and a Functional Area model. It shows how multiple systems cooperate in the performance of a common function and associates particular activities and information exchanges with individual systems that comprise the FoS.

FOR EXPOSITION ONLY (FEO) DIAGRAM: One of four types of IDEF0 Activity Model diagrams. The FEO diagram can be used to depict a variety of information not captured on the Context, Decomposition, or Node Tree diagrams.

FUNCTIONAL AREA ACTIVITY MODEL: A type of Activity Model that focuses on describing the activities and information exchanges that occur in the performance of a particular function or related group of functions. The Functional Area Activity Model places greater emphasis on defining the activities and information exchanges than on describing the organizations and/or systems that execute those activities or information exchanges.

HORSEBLANKET: The Army unique architecture product that provides a graphical representation of an organization's equipment.

INFORMATION: A group of related facts to support a particular purpose or need.

INPUT: One category of information associated with an IDEF0 Activity Model. Inputs are information or other raw materials that are consumed in the conduct of an activity. Inputs are converted by the activity into outputs.

INTEGRATED DICTIONARY: The architecture product that provides definitions for all the terms, labels, acronyms and abbreviations used in the architecture.

INTEGRATION (or INTEGRATING) ACTIVITY MODEL: A special type of Activity Model that shows how two or more systems, organizations or functional areas may be integrated. It begins with two or more existing Activity Models, and combines them to create a new, integrated Activity Model.

INTERNODAL: The type of System Interface Description that describes the systems used to effect an interface between two or more operational nodes. It may show all the systems available within each interfacing node, or it may only show the specific communications systems that execute the interface.

INTRANODAL: The type of System Interface Description that shows the interfaces between systems within a single operational node (e.g., a single organization or element). It identifies the individual systems that comprise the operational node and depicts the manner in which those systems communicate with each other.

LOGICAL DATA MODEL: The Operational Architecture product that provides a system-independent description of the data elements and data structures required to support the performance of functions described in the Activity Model.

MECHANISM: One category of information associated with an IDEF0 Activity Model. Mechanisms are the persons, systems, or software that perform or are used to perform the activities.

MULTI-NODAL: The type of Node Connectivity Description or Operational Information Exchange Matrix that shoes, on a single diagram, all the operational nodes within the enterprise and the interfaces among and between them, as well as the external operational nodes to which enterprise operational nodes are connected.

NODE CENTRIC: The type of Node Connectivity Description or Operational Information Exchange Matrix that shows all the interfaces associated with a single critical operational node/element.

NODE CONNECTIVITY DESCRIPTION: The Operational Architecture product that is a graphical depiction of those operational elements, organizations and units (i.e., nodes) that are required to exchange information directly with each other, and the types of information they are to exchange.

NODE TREE: One of four types of IDEF0 Activity Model diagrams. The Node Tree shows the hierarchical relationship of activities in the model.

OPCON GRAPHIC: The graphical portion of the Operational Concept Description.

OPERATIONAL ACTIVITY SEQUENCE & TIMING DESCRIPTION: The Operational Architecture that is used to describe the optimal sequencing of activities or to assess time critical activity or information flows.

OPERATIONAL ACTIVITY TO SYSTEM FUNCTION TREACEABILITY MATRIX: The System Architecture product that relates system functions defined in the System Functionality Description to operational activities defined in the Activity Model.

OPERATIONAL CONCEPT DESCRIPTION: The Operational Architecture product that defines, using text and pictures, how available resources and assets will be employed and deployed to accomplish a mission.

OPERATIONAL ELEMENT: A collection of personnel and equipment that perform a function.

OPERATIONAL FACILITY (OPFAC) EQUIPMENT DESCRIPTION: The Army unique architecture product that lists the command, control, communications, and computer (C4) equipment associated with a particular operational element.

OPERATIONAL EVENT/TRACE DESCRIPTION: The type of Operational Activity Sequence & Timing Description that shows the sequencing of individual activities, events, and actions.

OPERATIONAL INFORMATION EXCHANGE MATRIX: The Operational Architecture product that provides a detailed description of the information to be exchanged between operational nodes.

OPERATIONAL RULES MODEL: The type of Operational Activity Sequence & Timing Description that captures the "business rules" associated with elements of the architecture. The rules may prescribe the conditions under which actions or tasks are initiated, performed, continued, resumed, or terminated. Other rules may control or constrain the types or quantities of outputs produced by activities. These rules may take the form of algorithms, mathematical formulae, decision trees, "if/then" statements, Boolean statements, or statements and assertions in plain English.

OPERATIONAL STATE TRANSITION DESCRIPTION: The type of Operational Activity Sequence & Timing Description that describes how enterprise components (i.e., nodes/organizations, and information/data) are modified as a result of the performance of activities and processes.

ORGANIZATIONAL ACTIVITY MODEL: A type of Activity Model that describes the tasks/activities performed by an organization, allocates organization tasks/activities to individuals or subordinate elements, shows how the elements of the organization interact with each other and shows how the organization interacts with its external environment.

ORGANIZATIONAL RELATIONSHIPS CHART: The Operational Architecture product that is a graphical depiction of the operational elements involved in a process and the lines of command, control and coordination among those operational elements.

OUTPUT: One category of information associated with an IDEF0 Activity Model. Outputs are the products that result from the performance of the activity

OVERVIEW & SUMMARY INFORMATION: The architecture product that provides general, descriptive information about the architecture as a whole.

PARTICIPANTS: A listing of individuals, organizations, or communities that should participate in the development of the architecture or architecture product.

PHYSICAL DATA MODEL: The System Architecture product that defines the physical data elements and structures associated with enterprise concepts, missions, tasks, and components.

PURPOSE: The reason(s) for which an architecture or architecture product is/are developed.

RELATIONSHIP (ENTITY): In an IDEF1X Data Model, the association of one entity or table to another. The relationship is stated as a verb phrase.

SCOPE: The depth and breadth of information included in an architecture or architecture product. The scope defines what is and is not addressed in the architecture or product.

STANDARDS TECHNOLOGY FORECAST: The Technical Architecture product that identifies the future or emerging technical standards that are expected to be applied to the enterprise or architecture in the future.

SYSTEM^2 MATRIX: The System Architecture product that defines the relationship(s) between pairs of systems within and external to the enterprise.

SYSTEM ACTIVITY MODEL: A type of Activity Model that describes the internal operations of a system and its interactions with its external environment. A "system" can be defined as a single, self-contained end item that performs one or more primary functions (e.g., a vehicle or a television set), or a collection of components that normally are used together to perform a single function (e.g., a computer, that is composed of a keyboard, a monitor, a central processing unit, one or more disk drives and a printer).

SYSTEMS COMMUNICATION DESCRIPTION: The System Architecture product that identifies the physical characteristics of the interfaces among and between systems.

SYSTEM DATA EXCHANGE MATRIX: The System Architecture product that provides a detailed description of data to be exchanged among and between systems, and of the technical characteristics of the data exchanges.

SYSTEM EVOLUTION DESCRIPTION: The System Architecture product that provides a graphical depiction of how system capabilities change over time.

SYSTEM EVENT/TRACE DESCRIPTION: The type of System Function Sequence & Timing Description that shows the sequencing of individual functions, events, and actions.

System Functionality Description: The System Architecture product that is a graphical and textual depiction of the tasks performed by a system.

SYSTEM FUNCTION SEQUENCE & TIMING DESCRIPTION: The System Architecture product that describes the time sequencing of system functions and processes.

SYSTEM INTERFACE DESCRIPTION: The System Architecture product that graphically portrays the actual or desired interfaces between enterprise systems or system nodes.

SYSTEM PERFORMANCE PARAMETERS MATRIX: The System Architecture product that is a description of a system's level of performance within defined capability areas. It describes both current and future system performance.

SYSTEM RULES MODEL: The type of System Function Sequence & Timing Description that captures the "business rules" associated with elements of the architecture. The rules may prescribe the conditions under which functions, actions, or tasks are initiated, performed, continued, resumed, or terminated. Other rules may control or constrain the types or quantities of outputs produced by functions. These rules may take the form of algorithms, mathematical formulae, decision trees, "if/then" statements, Boolean statements, or statements and assertions in plain English.

SYSTEM STATE TRANSITION DESCRIPTION: The type of System Function Sequence & Timing Description that describes how enterprise components (i.e., nodes/organizations, and information/data) are modified as a result of the performance of activities and processes.

SYSTEMS TECHNOLOGY FORECAST: The System Technology product that identifies emerging technologies that may be applied to the system(s) within an enterprise at some time in the future.

TABLE: In an IDEF1X Physical Data Model, the collection of data about a person, place, thing, event, or concept. Equivalent to an **Entity** in a Logical Data Model.

TECHNICAL ARCHITECTURE PROFILE: The Technical Architecture product that lists those technical standards that are applicable to the architecture and its components.

TECHNICAL STANDARD: Describes how a process is to be performed, how a system is to operate, or how information is to be processed and presented.

TEXTUAL OPERATIONAL CONCEPT: The textual portion of the Operational Concept Description. It abstracts and summarizes all the information contained in the whole architecture and its separate products. In this respect, it may be viewed as an executive summary of the architecture.

VIEWPOINT: The point of view from which the architecture or architecture product is described.

2.b USERS & PARTICIPANTS:

Combat Developer: The military organization(s) responsible for defining required warfighting capabilities to include, doctrine and tactics, organizations, personnel, and materiel/systems.

Concept Developer: The military organization(s) responsible for developing concepts describing how selected combat capabilities (forces and systems) will be employed to perform critical battlefield tasks. Also referred to as **Concept & Doctrine Developer**.

Facilitator: The individual or group of individuals who support the development of architecture products by leading discussion groups and working sessions or conducting interviews with key individuals.

Facilities Manager: The individual or group of individuals responsible for maintaining and managing the use of organization real property (e.g., buildings, grounds, and other fixed and semi-fixed structures).

Force Developer: The military organization/agency responsible for defining organizational structures in terms of required and/or authorized quantities of personnel and equipment.

Human Resource Manager: The individual, group of individuals, or department responsible for initiating, controlling, directing, and terminating personnel actions; maintaining personnel files and records; and managing personnel morale, welfare, and support activities and operations within an organization.

Information Manager: The individual, group of individuals, or organizational element/department responsible for acquiring, developing, maintaining, and distributing organizational information and data. The Information Manager in some organizations also maintains and manages organizational information systems.

Modeling & Simulation Community: The individual or group of individuals who develop, maintain, provide, or use computer models and simulations that represent real world people, systems, organizations, facilities, events, environments, etc.

Operational Architect: The individual, group of individuals, organization, or organizational element responsible for developing and maintaining the operational architecture and individual architecture products.

Operations Manager: The individual responsible for directing and overseeing the actions and day to day operations of an organization or organizational element.

Policy Writers: The individual, group of individuals, or organizational element responsible for developing, publishing, and maintaining formal organization policies in all operational areas.

Program/Project/Product Developer: The military term for the individual (and the associated organization) responsible for managing the development and acquisition of a particular capability, item of equipment, or family of associated equipment items.

Public Relations Department: The individual, group of individuals, or organizational element responsible for all official organization interfaces with external agencies.

Quality Assurance Manager: The individual or group of individuals responsible for monitoring and assessing the efficiency and effectiveness of organization processes and operations, and recommending or directing corrective actions.

Research and Development: The individual, group of individuals, or organizational element that employs the scientific method, conducts surveys and interviews, performs analyses, conducts literature reviews, and performs other similar tasks to develop new products and services or evaluate existing products and services.

Resource Manager: The individual or group of individuals responsible for exercising control over the acquisition, storage, distribution, and utilization of a particular resource or class of resources within an organization.

Sales Department: The individual, group of individuals, or organizational element responsible for selling organization goods and services to external customers. This includes accepting customer orders, processing orders, shipping/delivering products, and receiving payment(s).

Security Manager: The individual or group of individuals responsible for controlling access to organization facilities, property, or information, and for maintaining good order and discipline.

Software Developer: The individual, group of individuals, organization, or organizational element responsible for producing, maintaining, updating, supporting, and delivering software products.

Strategic Planner: The individual or group of individuals responsible for formulating, maintaining and implementing plans that define overarching organizational goals and objectives.

Subject Matter Expert: An individual who has specific knowledge and experience in a particular subject area, and who provides that knowledge and experience to support architecture development.

Supervisors: The individuals who provide guidance and direction to, and establish priorities, goals, and objectives for, one or more subordinate workers.

Systems Architect: The individual, group of individuals, organization, or organizational element responsible for developing and maintaining the system architecture and individual architecture products.

Systems Engineer: The individual, group of individuals, or organization responsible for defining the specific technical performance requirements for a system or family of related systems.

Technical Architect: The individual, group of individuals, organization, or organizational element responsible for developing and maintaining the technical architecture and individual architecture products.

Test & Evaluation Community: The organization(s) and agency(ies) responsible for performing technical and operational tests of new and developmental systems to determine how well they meet published requirements.

Trainer: The individual or group of individuals who provide formal or informal instruction to other individuals (either within or outside the organization) on any subject or task.

Training Developer: The individual, group of individuals, organization, or organizational element responsible for developing training materials and lesson plans.

Warfighter: The individual or individuals assigned to military combat organizations, and the combat organizations themselves.

Workers: All individuals who perform tasks individually or as a part of a group.

2.c USES:

Allocation Of Communication Assets: The association of organization communication systems (e.g., radios, telephones, switches, relays, and antennae) to specific organizations, nodes, or organizational elements.

Baselining of Functionality: The determination and documentation of the core set of critical functions performed, or to be performed, by an individual, a system, a family of related systems, or an organization.

Battlefield/Business Process Reengineering: A process that defines the actions necessary to convert an organization's, system's, family of systems', or functional area's structures and functions from their current state to a more efficient and/or effective future state. Business/battlefield process reengineering includes defining the current state and the desired future state, and comparing the two to identify issues to be resolved and improvement opportunities to be exploited.

Comparing User's Vision To Developer's Implementation: The process of examining how well the system that has been, or is being, developed/built fulfills the vision of the ultimate system user, as that vision is documented in system requirements documents or descriptions.

Data Modeling: The creation of static depictions of enterprise data structures and/or requirements.

Database Design: The process of defining the contents, structure, and function of system, organizational, or functional area databases and data repositories.

Description of Required System Capabilities: The determination and documentation of the capabilities and performance characteristics required of new or existing systems.

Design of Human-Computer Interface: The development of methods and procedures by which operators enter information into and receive information from a computer. Human-computer interface design includes the design of input devices such as keyboards, touch screens, and voice recognition systems as well as the design of system displays, hard copy/printed output, and audible outputs.

Development of Capital Investment Strategies: The process of defining guidelines for the allocation of organizational capital (i.e., funds).

Development of Procedures Guides and User's Manuals: The creation of documents that describe and prescribe how actions, activities, and processes are to be performed (procedures guides) or how systems are to be operated (user's manuals).

Development Of System Software: The design and development of system software modules and products.

Development of Training Materials: The creation of enterprise training plans, training materials, and lesson plans.

Development/Modification of Operational Concepts: The creation or updating of concepts describing how selected combat capabilities (forces and systems) will be employed to perform critical battlefield tasks.

Development/Modification Of Standard Messages: The creation or update of standardized formats for messages used to exchange information among and between organizations.

Development/Validation Of Models & Simulations: The creation of new computer models and simulations that represent real world people, systems, organizations, facilities, events, environments, etc., or the validation of existing models and simulations.

Development/Validation Of SOPs: The development of new standard procedures that define how common core tasks are to be performed, or the validation of existing procedures.

Development/Validation Of Tactics, Techniques & Procedures (TTPs): The development or validation of detailed descriptions of how military warfighting tasks are to be performed.

Development/Validation Of Training Plans: The creation of new plans that describe the tasks to be trained, the conditions under which the tasks are to be trained, and the standards to which the tasks are to be trained, or the validation of existing plans.

Functional Allocation: The association of specific functions with systems, organizations, or organizational elements.

Identification Of Functional Information Requirements: The determination of the information required for the performance of, or produced as the result of, organization or system functions.

Identification of IERs: The determination and documentation of the requirement for the exchange of information among and between nodes, systems, and organizations.

Identification of Operational Issues: The identification and documentation of problems associated with the performance of operational tasks, functions, missions, processes, or information exchanges.

Identification of OPFAC Hardware Requirements: The determination of the computers and communications systems required to be fielded to a military operational facility (OPFAC) for it to perform its warfighting missions and tasks.

Identification of Personnel Requirements: The determination of the numbers of personnel to perform a task or man an organization, and the qualifications, knowledge, skills, and abilities required of those personnel.

Identification/Validation of Operational Needs/Requirements: The development, documentation, or validation of descriptions of system operational performance requirements.

Network Burden Assessment: An analysis and evaluation of the burden to be placed on the communications network by enterprise operations and information exchanges.

Organizational Design: The process of determining the basic structure and functions of an organization.

Performance of Cost/Benefits Analysis: The conduct of analyses that compare the costs associated with the implementation of a proposed action, event, or task to the benefits to be gained from the implementation of that action, event, or task.

Planning For System Tests: The process of developing plans for the conduct of tests to evaluate the performance of new or developmental systems.

Planning For Organization Exercises: The process of developing plans for the conduct of organization training sessions.

Prioritizing Activities For Implementation: The rank ordering of enterprise, system, or organization functions and activities for implementation (i.e., acquisition and fielding) based upon predefined prioritization factors such as the value added; the relative cost of implementation; the expected implementation time; or the number of individuals, systems, and organizations effected by the implementation.

Providing Roadmap For System Improvement: The development of a detailed, step-by-step plan for the modification and upgrade of a fielded system.

Quality Control/Quality Management: The performance of tasks and activities associated with monitoring and assessing the efficiency and effectiveness of organizational processes and structures, and taking appropriate corrective actions.

Standardization of Data Elements: The process of harmonizing and standardizing the names, definitions and structures of data elements used within, among, and between organizations, systems, functional areas, and families of systems.

Standardization of Processes, Activities and Tasks: The process of harmonizing and standardizing the names, definitions, and structures of activities performed within, among, and between organizations, systems, functional areas, and families of systems.

Strategic Business Planning: The process of developing high level organizational strategies, goals, and objectives that get translated into near-, mid-, and long-term actions.

Wargaming Alternatives: The process of examining the relative advantages and disadvantages associated with multiple alternatives for the conduct of a mission, task, or activity.

2.d INFORMATION SOURCES:

Doctrinal Publications: Military documents that describe approved tactics, techniques, and procedures for performing military operations and activities.

Function/Task Lists: Documents that list the functions, missions, tasks, and/or activities performed by or within an organization, system, node, organizational element, enterprise, functional area, or family of systems. The list may also include definitions or descriptions of the functions and tasks.

Future Operational Capabilities (FOCs): A document that describes the capabilities that must be available in future systems or future versions of current systems.

Interface Descriptions: Documents that describe the manner in which two or more systems or organizations exchange information and/or services with each other. The interface description may include the information or services to be exchanged, the exchange media, and the conditions under which the exchanges are executed.

Long Range Plans: Documents that describe the long term goals and objectives for a system, organization, functional area, or family of systems.

Master Plans: Documents that describe near-, mid-, and far-term goals and objectives for an organization, functional area, or family of systems and actions to be taken to achieve those goals and objectives.

Modernization Plans: Documents that describe near-, mid-, and far-term goals and objectives for the modification, upgrade, or improvement of an organization, functional area, or family of systems and actions to be taken to achieve those goals and objectives.

Organization Descriptions: Documents that describe an organization in terms of its personnel, equipment, and facilities; its organizational structures; its missions, goals, and objectives; its activities, tasks, and functions; and its relationships with other organizations.

Operational and Organizational Plans: Military documents that describe the organizational structure and functions of an existing or proposed organization.

Operational Concepts: Documents that describe how selected capabilities (personnel, organizations, forces and systems) will be employed to perform critical missions and tasks. Also referred to as **Concepts & Doctrine.**

Policy and Procedures Guides: Documents that describe and prescribe how actions, activities, and processes are to be performed or how systems are to be operated.

Standards Documents: Documents that describe mandated, approved, acceptable, or emerging service, joint, national, or international technical standards. A technical standard describes how a process is to be performed, how a system is to operate, or how information is to be processed and presented.

Standing Operating Procedures (SOPs): Documents that describe and prescribe the processes and procedures to be used to perform common organizational tasks and functions.

Strategic Plans: Documents that describe high level organizational strategies, goals, and objectives and include near-, mid-, and long-term actions.

Subject Matter Experts: An individual who has specific knowledge and experience in a particular subject area, and who provides that knowledge and experience to support architecture development.

System Descriptions: Documents that describe a system in terms of the functions that it performs, the organizations that use it, and the other systems with which it interfaces.

Vision Statements: A leader's statement of his view of the core values, goals, and of an organization.

2.e TOOLS:

Activity/Process Modeling Tool: A hardware and/or software tool that is used to develop activity models or process models.

Database: The collection of data elements that support a system, organization, functional area, or family of systems, or a listing of those data elements. The data elements may be stored in a single location or in multiple locations.

Data Modeling Tool: A hardware or software tool that is used to develop logical and/or physical data models, data dictionaries, or other data descriptions.

Drawing/Graphics Tool: A hardware or software tool that is used to create drawings and other graphical objects.

Flow Charting Tool: A hardware or software tool that is used to create flow charts.

Network Design Tool: A hardware or software tool that is used to design communications, computer, or other types of multi-nodal networks.

Object Modeling Tool: A hardware or software tool that is used to develop one of many types of Object Models. Object Model types include, but are not limited to, Use Case models and Class Diagrams.

Text Editor: A hardware or software tool that is used to create and edit textual products and information.

APPENDIX: DATA REQUIREMENTS WORKSHEET FORMAT

[The Data Requirements Worksheet serves two purposes: It documents data requirements to guide data modelers in developing the actual Data Model, and it provides a description of the Data Model that can be understood by non Data Modelers.]

Scope: Define the scope of the data subject area to be described in the Data Requirements Worksheet. Identify the bounds of what will and will not be addressed.

Viewpoint: Describe the point of view from which the information in the Data Requirements Worksheet will be described.

Definition: Provide a definition for the data subject area being addressed. Where possible, adopt a previously approved definition. An adopted definition may have to be modified or augmented slightly to conform to the stated scope and viewpoint.

Associated Activity Model Views: List the Activity or Function Model(s) that is/are the source for information requirements to be decomposed to the data element level.

1. Activity/Function Model 1 Name.

2. Activity/Function Model 2 Name.

3. Activity/Function Model 3 Name.

Associated Activity or Function Model Inputs, Controls, and Outputs (ICOs): List the specific Activity/Function Model input(s), control(s), or output(s) that are to be decomposed into data elements. If the ICOs are taken from multiple Activity/Function Models, include the name of the appropriate parent Activity/Function Model following the name of each ICO.

1. ICO 1 Name (Activity/Function Model Name)

2. ICO 2 Name (Activity /Function Model Name)

3. ICO 3 Name (Activity/Function Model Name)

Associated Data Model Views: List existing Data Models from which data elements will be extracted to meet enterprise data requirements

1. Data Model 1 Name

2. Data Model 2 Name

3. Data Model 3 Name

Notes: Document operational rules, constraints, limitations, and assumptions that influence how the data model and its included data elements are constructed. Notes are not applied directly in the construction of individual data elements, but are **considered** during data element development. See **Rules** below.

1. Note 1.

2. Note 2.

3. Note 3.

Rules: Document rules that relate directly to the way that individual data elements are defined or related to each other.

1. Rule 1.

2. Rule 2.

3. Rule 3.

Data Elements: List key data entities and attributes required to meet the data needs identified in the Activity/Function Model(s) as those needs are further refined by the Notes and Rules

1. Data Element (entity or table) 1
   - Attribute/column 1
   - Attribute/column 2

2. Data Element (entity or table) 2
   - Attribute/column 3
   - Attribute/column 4

3. Data Element (entity or table) 3
   - Attribute/column 5
   - Attribute/column 6

Modeling Business Rules: List the verb phrases that describe the formal relationships between pairs of data entities/tables. The business rules may be formulated and documented in the Data Requirements Worksheet prior to their inclusion into the Data Model, or they may be extracted from the Data Model for incorporation into the Data Requirements Worksheet.

Activity/Function Model ICOs to Data Model Entity Crosswalk: Show the relationships between Activity/Function Model ICOs and Data Model entities, tables, attributes, and columns.

1. Activity/Function Model ICO Name
    - Data Model Entity/Table Name
        - Attribute Name
        - Attribute Name
        - Attribute Name
    - Data Model Entity/Table Name
        - Attribute Name
        - Attribute Name
        - Attribute Name

2. Activity/Function Model ICO Name
    - Data Model Entity/Table Name
        - Attribute Name
        - Attribute Name
        - Attribute Name
    - Data Model Entity/Table Name
        - Attribute Name
        - Attribute Name
        - Attribute Name

Algorithms: List rules and formulae that define how the physical values of individual data elements are to be calculated.

1. Algorithm 1.
2. Algorithm 2.

Biography of Charles Babers:

Charles Babers is a graduate of the US Military Academy at West Point. While serving as a commissioned officer, he was responsible for defining and documenting the operational and functional requirements for automated command and control systems for Army air defense and missile defense systems. Since leaving the military, he has developed and or participated in the development of information, operational, system and enterprise architectures for the Army and the Joint Services. He has authored numerous papers and provided formal and informal briefings and training in architecture development techniques to various military and non-military organizations and agencies. He currently provides support to the US Army Air Defense Artillery School at Fort Bliss, Texas; and is considered one of the Army's foremost experts in operational and functional architectures.

www.ingramcontent.com/pod-product-compliance
Lightning Source LLC
Chambersburg PA
CBHW051359070526
44584CB00023B/3215